*Literature
and
Subjection*

Illuminations:
Cultural Formations
of the Americas

*John Beverley and
Sara Castro-Klarén,
Editors*

Horacio Legrás

Literature and Subjection

The Economy
of Writing
and
Marginality
in Latin
America

University
of Pittsburgh
Press

Published by the University of Pittsburgh Press,
Pittsburgh, Pa., 15260
Copyright © 2008, University of Pittsburgh Press
Manufactured in the United States of America
Printed on acid-free paper
10 9 8 7 6 5 4 3 2 1

Library of Congress Cataloging-in-Publication Data
Legras, Horacio.
    Literature and subjection : the economy of writing
and marginality in Latin America / Horacio Legras.
        p. cm. — (Illuminations)
    Includes bibliographical references and index.
    ISBN 13: 978-0-8229-4353-2 (cloth : alk. paper)
    ISBN 10: 0-8229-4353-0 (cloth : alk. paper)
    ISBN 13: 978-0-8229-5999-1 (pbk. : alk. paper)
    ISBN 10: 0-8229-5999-2 (pbk. : alk. paper)
    1. Latin American literature—20th century—History
and criticism. 2. Marginality, Social, in literature.
I. Title. II. Series: Illuminations (Pittsburgh, Pa.)
    PQ7081.L398 2008
    860.9'98—dc22
                                    2008016331

Contents

Literature
and
Subjection

Literature, Subjection, and the Historical Project of Latin American Literature

Beginning roughly at the end of the nineteenth century, Latin American writers launched a project to map the whole convoluted reality of their countries in their literary works. However, Latin American countries were (and still are) notoriously heterogeneous spaces. Soon, then, the literary enterprise was confronted with the task of giving voice to a vast array of people with whom literature shared little in terms of values and cultural makeup. Writers did not recoil from the challenge. Convinced as they were of literature's representational power and its seemingly limitless ethical neutrality, they focused on the best strategies to represent the marginal in its many shapes: the excluded, the downtrodden, the abject, the almost forgotten past. Their effort to reach the outskirts of social representation fostered a modification of the literary form, an enhancement of its capabilities, and a transformation of its principles of composition. There was a moment, however, when it became apparent that the dialogue between the excluded and the literary regime of representation could not continue without a more radical questioning of the literary form itself. This book thus centers on authors (Juan José Saer, Augusto Roa Bastos, Jose María Arguedas, Nellie Campobello) who test the limits of literary representation and thereby interrogate the intrinsic complicity that binds literature to social power. The dynamic by which literature must look to its own arsenal

1

for weapons that may allow it to negate its historical domestication is the one I try to evoke with the title *Literature and Subjection.*

This dynamic, which ties literature to representation and representation to social power, is not the product of independent, contingent, and unrelated personal literary projects, but an affair of literature as a whole. It constitutes a historical project, a project that relies on a conception of literature as a mere form able to lend its dreamlike body to the most variegated materials. In this book, I try to remain faithful to what I perceive as a tension between the supposedly universal reach of the literary word and the singular, sometimes intractable areas of the Latin American experience that literature not only symbolizes but also searches for, that it struggles with or begrudgingly abandons. The combination of a close study of literary formations with an intense attention to the context of their deployment may justify, I hope, the characterization of this book as a cultural study of the literary form. This kind of study is easy to undertake when the researcher is willing to replace the literary experience with a sociological or historical flight of fancy. I have tried to avoid this path. In my view the only way to honor the potentialities of a culturalist approach is to first pose the fundamental question that defines the field of literary studies: What is literature?

The book thus combines two approaches that are often vulgarized as antithetical. I do not follow this path out of a desire to find a "happy medium" between dissentient positions. Rather, the need for a dual approach to literature arises from the conditions that constitute our field. As Antonio Cornejo Polar puts it, any meaningful investigation of Latin America must locate itself at the intersection of historical determinations and theoretical demands (1989, 177). A historical account of literature unable to pose theoretical problems (in this instance, unable to pose the question of Latin American literature as a theoretical problem) is one that will inadvertently inherit and reproduce the limitations already encapsulated within the practice of literature itself. It will remain imperialist and colonialist while pretending to be representative and emancipatory. But a theoretical account of literature that fails to recognize that literature always arises out of a negotiation between literary enunciation and the historical constrictions of what can be said ends up measuring the existent with the yardstick of the nonexistent.[1]

Although this dual perspective puts a notorious strain on the analytical effort, my intention here is to maintain the tension between the two constitutive and essential components of the literary experience: its transcendental aim and its actual form. Attending to only one side of the equation will always result in a certain simplification. Any "transcendental" interrogation of literature remains naive if it fails to address how the primary disposition of the literary leads it to articulate the goal of culture as an apparatus of capture and adaptation.[2] At the same time, no cultural inquiry into the politics or the pragmatics of literature remains valid if it fails to account for the singularity and autonomy of literature.

The intimate relationship between literature and power is by now an academic truism. We are accustomed to approaches that break the aesthetic cordon sanitaire that the nineteenth century wove around the work of art (and that formalist and structuralist emphases later reinforced) and confront the text in its most vital political contexts. So if literature bears the mark of the Kantian identification of art with disinterest, culturally based approaches to society resist this identification and denounce the entanglement of literature with various political or institutional interests. In the field of Latin Americanism, several authors who have delved into the intimacies of state power and literary imagination come readily to mind: Angel Rama, Antonio Cándido, Josefina Ludmer, and David Viñas.[3] The key insight that literature has been historically tied to the evolution of different elites allowed certain authors to question the foundations of canon formation, which in turn facilitated the promotion of new literary names and forms. Finally, a general redefinition of the ways in which power impresses its aims on bodies and populations also helped position literature within a larger cultural landscape.[4]

Yet the risk of such demystification is to imagine that it yields the real structure of the literary experience, that freeing literature from all its mystifying elements (its claim to an immanent value, the aesthetic ground of canon formation, the excess of communication that defines the aesthetic word) will finally render its truth. What escapes those who entertain such an illusion is the simple fact that literature became literature because of these mystifying, ungrounded, and excessive elements, not in spite of them. These elements, in other words, signal the essential center of the literary experience, even if they themselves are not this center.

Here I try to capture the dual being of literature in a simple formula: literature is an institution and, simultaneously, an instituting power. Literary texts exist in a tension that makes literature both a creative power and a set of territorialized practices in which that power is already mediated, silenced, or forgotten. Neither aspect of literature can be said to exist without the other. The "institution of literature," therefore, does not refer here to literature simply as it is conceived by state institutions (pedagogical possibilities, literary prizes, cultural politics, etc.) or by associative institutions such as publishers, national language academies, and academic associations of different sorts. Indeed, in my view, literature's role as an instituting power (one that creates social bonds through enunciation) makes these other institutions possible.

Within the first, institutional perspective, the formation that interests me may be termed the "historical project" of Latin American literature. Briefly, this project entailed the symbolic incorporation of peoples and practices persisting in the margins of society or nation into a sanctioned form of representation. It is more difficult to descry the instituting power of literature. Unlike institutions, instituting power has no history. While its nature is not primary or original, it replicates the inaugural instituting force that manifests itself in and through language. I understand this force along the lines of French philosopher Emmanuel Levinas's differentiation between *said* and *saying* (*le dit* and *le dire*) (1981, 40–42). For Levinas, speaking—independent of what is actually said—is the primary opening of the world. In Levinas's phenomenological phrasing, speaking is an "intuition" of sociality. Speaking always goes beyond its intention because it cannot put forward any meaning without simultaneously building the social frame within which language can make sense. It is with this definition in mind that I refer to literature as the formalization of the instituting power of language. Now, although the instituting function of language has no history, the full extent of its revelation is no doubt a historical event.

...

Institution and *instituting* provide a sort of phenomenological description of the being of the literary. This description, however, is still too broad, because it lacks the defining character of all cultural objects in modernity: historical density. How has the historicity of the literary form—not its contingency, but its being as being-historical—been conceived? Jacques Derrida, in an interview entitled "This Strange Institution Called Literature," begins by circumscribing literature as a "relatively modern form" (1992c, 37).[5] It is not self-evident, he argues, that "Greek or Latin poetry, [and] non-European discursive works . . . strictly speaking belong to literature" (40). This assertion is based on the specific form of institutionalism that literature takes in modernity. As a modern form, Derrida notes, literature "is linked to an authorization to say everything, and doubtless too to the coming about of the modern idea of democracy" (37). While establishing a commonality between literature and democracy runs the risk of presenting literature as nothing but a cultural moment in the evolution of bourgeois political life, if one reads carefully, it is clear that Derrida's argument moves in a completely different direction. It interrupts the matter-of-fact bourgeois identification between "democracy" and the development of the ethos of a Europeanized middle class. In the region of the semiotics of power, however, good news readily turns into bad news, and vice versa. Although, as Derrida explains, "the freedom to say everything is a very powerful political weapon," it is also a weapon, rapidly neutralized "as fiction" (38). The "critical function of literature" (which has been identified as an ideal of political intervention in Latin America and elsewhere for more than two centuries) could thus be undermined by the very thing that grants literature its disruptive force. With literature condemned to be a fictional account of the world, its commitment to criticism may seem hypocritical, and "the writer can just as well be held to be irresponsible" (38). Derrida goes on to rephrase this "irresponsibility" as the highest form of responsibility, since it implies a "duty . . . of refusing to reply for one's thought or writing to constituted powers" (38). Despite the institutional forms that literature must take in order to exist, an unbridgeable distance separates the instituting power of literature from its already naturalized existence in institutions.

It is necessary to bring this apt Derridean description into clearer focus, or at least to bring it more in line with the goals of this study. The historical project of Latin American literature is an equivalent of what Derrida calls the responsibility of literature. But in the case of Latin America, this responsibility appears thoroughly determined by the experience of colonialism, which integrated the continent into the timetable of European modernity. In this context, literature reveals itself to be part of a larger process of intercultural and intersemiotic translation. The representational role that fell to Latin American literature for most of the modern period depends on the simple fact that the representing and the represented instances belong to different orders. For this reason, since the instantiation of national literatures, the translation of the local and the status of the universal have constituted a persistent problem. As Angel Rama suggests in *Transculturación narrativa en América Latina,* this representative character is closely linked to a given work's originality. Unlike Rama, I interpret *originality* to mean a work's proximity to the origin, its meaningful relationship to lived reality. In a postcolonial context, the fissure that separates work from origin is never closed, and its existence is so notorious that it often ends up as the subject of the work. Here lies the explanation for the fact that all the essential concepts of Latin American cultural criticism—transculturation (Ortiz, Rama), heterogeneity (Cornejo Polar), hybridity (Canclini), colonial semiosis (Mignolo), third space (Moreiras), tropological mimesis (González Echevarría), auto-ethnography (Pratt)—underline, with different intonations, the fissured self of Latin American culture as its ineluctable condition of possibility.[6]

This tension between universality and particularity, between literature's translative machinery and the material to be translated, unambiguously calls for a postcolonial perspective in our work on Latin America, notwithstanding all protests against this approach.[7] Either because the vanquished people were able to sustain a cultural-political autonomy through four centuries of imperial or republican darkness, as in the case of the Andes or some areas in Mesoamerica, or even because the national anti-imperialist project reawakened an internal cultural difference (as in *indigenismo, negrismo,* or *nativismo*), the fact is that Latin American literature seems condemned to portray once again this vital disjuncture between modernizing logos and intractable realities. Not only did this postcolonial condition originate in the trauma following the conquest, but it further represents a structural matrix. This matrix speaks of an ever-unfinished dialectic between knowledge and reality, of an almost existential crisis—to use an unfashionable but necessary expression—in the relationship between Latin American populations and their ways of inhabiting the world. Later I will discuss how some of the most meaningful acts of symbolic decolonization have emerged linked to the question of production as the poietic appropriative event of cultural life. For now, suffice to say that in its most basic dimension, literature betrays its postcolonial character any time that it understands itself as translation—any time that it registers the uncomfortable resistance of a cultural Real in the stories it tells.[8]

While every literature is a translative device, and while it may be objected that the difference between Latin American and European literature is one of degree rather than kind, I would argue, like Hegel, that differences of degree become differences of nature. In fact, the German philosopher offers an instructive way to clarify our predicament. Hegel, although writing in a country that represented the rearward of capitalist modernization, nonetheless attempted an endeavor that was quite free from the constraints of coloniality.[9] He strove, first in *The Science of Logic* (1812–16) and later in the *Encyclopedia* (1817), to show that the conceptual order of thinking and the real order of the world not only coincided but were actually the same thing. His logic, as subsequent commentators noticed, was simultaneously an ontology (C. Taylor 1998). Literature has long been Latin America's most explicative ontology. It is, moreover, an ontology that constitutes the world according to a set of rules that precedes its involvement with the facticity of events or the brute materiality of life. Perhaps for this reason, whenever Latin American literature has tried to portray the identity between thinking and being, it has been denounced as an agent of violence and domination.[10]

Is not all this an exaggeration of the importance and reach of the literary word? After all, Julio Ramos has shown that at the end of the nineteenth century, literature appears as little more than an outcast from the domain of serious discourses. Further, Roberto González Echevarría has convincingly argued that the authority of the literary word depends, in the case of Latin America, on the authorizing presence of a master discourse (law in the nineteenth century, anthropology in the twentieth) that validates literature's claims (1990). This relative dependence of literature upon law or ethnography is, although real, inessential. The *coming after* of literature does not compromise its grounding role. Its word is always inaugural. Asserting the foundational value of literature does not mean ignoring all its ideological uses, all the petty appropriations of the discourse of origins. Ontologies too grow discredited and fade. Here lies the charm of the literary: unlike most ontologies, literature has resisted historical criticism and managed to become the undisputable space for intercultural translation. It has become, in other words, a hegemonic form of universality. This is why I am reluctant to classify literature as a "white mythology" and prefer instead to advance some queries that will guide the interrogation of literature in the chapters to come: What if literature is marked not in its content, ideology, or morality, but in its very form, by the presence of elements belonging to a regional—mostly European, mostly bourgeois—design? What if this form—especially since it is always historically incarnated—reveals itself to be content? And finally, what if a notion of literature as the ideology of the total commensurability of experience, the transparent translation of any location, has survived all the attacks on the universal that we have seen in the development of structuralism, post-structuralism, postcoloniality, and postmodernity? These critical and theoretical breaks have done very little to "dislodge," as Neil Larsen puts it, the basic categories of the aesthetic with which "most of us were effectively indoctrinated" (1995, 105).

To illustrate my point, let me refer to Mario Vargas Llosa's novel *The Storyteller* (*El hablador,* 1987). This novel is told from the perspective of a narrator who acts as Vargas Llosa's alter ego: an intelligent, sensible, skeptical, and defiant intellectual. Some chapters, however, immerse the reader in the world of the Machiguenga Indians, by way of a narrator who tells a Machiguenga story *as if he were a Machiguenga speaking to a Machiguenga audience.* In these chapters, the reader is pulled by twin, almost contradictory currents. On the one hand, he/she has access to an indigenous worldview, or rather, to its translation, but a translation that strives to be, point by point, identical to its original. On the other hand, the reader seeks to restore a logical narrative to the story because he/she perceives the structure as a deviation from a norm of narration. In following this antinomy, the reader retreats from any real possibility of questioning the standard literary form, which, now sovereign, acts as a transcendental schema ordering the coordinates of the ethical encounter. Another culture is thus read and reduced through an appeal to literature as the primary form of a dominant universality.

Not by chance, *The Storyteller* is one of the Latin American books most persistently included in the canonical lists of world literature programs. The expression *world literature* itself suggests a democratic expansion of the actual universality of the literary—an expansion based on the ideology of literature that I have been questioning, which holds that literature incarnates the last and only lingua franca available to us. Far from constituting a truly democratic step, this assumption turns the concept of world literature into a platitude. The quasi-adjective *world* adds no diversity, but leaves the concept stranded in a certain state of unworldliness. World literature, a valid and valuable enterprise in other respects, cannot deliver the critical promise evoked by its name, because a dismantling of the dominant universality inherent in the conception of literature cannot be achieved by adding names to the membership list of a club that has long recognized a most exclusive membership. Dismantling is, above all, a task of determination and destruction.

And yet translation remains a concern for the peripheral writer, the kernel of his/her intellectual function. But what is to be translated, and how? Faced with the seemingly insurmountable problems of cross-cultural translation, the conscientious translator soon reaches an apparent paradox: a successful translation is always a failed one. For this reason, all ideologies of translation have undergone an epochal change when confronted with the historical and political process of global decolonization.[11] Today, translation can no longer be a process of giving the alterity of meaning a secure space of being and a true language because the conditions for this universality have been shattered. Translation is always, in the last instance, a translation of difference. The project of translating difference speaks directly to a final possibility of cross-cultural translation that I have not yet mentioned, although it is the very matter of this book: a resistance to translation strong enough to make the translative machine break down. This breaking-down also figures the collapse of hegemonic universality. And if the most resilient form of this universality is the literary form, this breaking-down entails, as many of this book's analyses will suggest, the failure of literature itself. I don't impose this language of failure on literature from the outside. Literature—not the individual texts, but their transtextual solidarity, the institution of literature—fails according to its own standards, its own historical project. This takes me to the next point.

The Historical Project of Latin American Literature

The universalization of literature that offered a rationale for cataloging any product of the imagination as "literature" is a relatively recent development. In the case of Latin America, it was not until the first decades of the twentieth century that the emergence of representative national-popular states fostered the need to map all the vast and disparate products of the imagination and incorporate them into a broad concept of national literature (with subdivisions like "folklore," "traditional folk tales," "oral literature," "urban narrative," etc.). The institutionalization achieved by popular forms and materials entailed recognition as much as co-optation. If these forms were incorporated into a larger and prestigious framework (that of literary expression), they entered into this arrangement in a subordinated position where their former plasticity is lost, insofar as the cultural apparatus that brought them recognition favors the perpetuation of certain traits deemed idiosyncratic to their poetic disposition.

In this process, literature is simply playing along with larger sociopolitical forces. The process of incorporating peripheral voices into the store of "national" expression coincided with a vast redefinition of the notion and function of culture, a redefinition that, while severing the idea of culture from that of civilization, led to the popularization of the so-called anthropological notion of culture as referring to the totality of a society's material and spiritual life. This shift granted an enormous purchase to anthropological discourses in the process of the imaginary constitution of modern Latin America. Its giants include figures like Manuel Gamio in Mexico, Gilberto Freyre in Brazil, and of course Fernando Ortiz in Cuba—who coined the most influential term in the history of Latin American cultural criticism: *transculturation.* My intention is to grapple with the work Ortiz crafted several decades before he became an advocate of transculturation in order to show that the representational drive that characterizes the deployment of the literary institution in modern Latin America is part of a larger process that involves enlisting cultural productions in the calculations of modern governmentality.

In 1906, Ortiz published *Los negros brujos*. This "ethnographic" book on Cuba's black population answered a continental demand that intellectuals reach out to the constitutive others of every national formation. Ortiz here speaks from an autonomous discourse, that of ethnography, but nonetheless remains hesitant about the proper boundaries between his obligations to the state and his commitment to scientific work. Ortiz conceives of anthropology as an autonomous science, free of moral prejudices and able to build its own set of rules for the evaluation of social reality. Likewise, the Cuban state is here no longer identified as the enforcer of a moral set of rules, but rather as a neutral apparatus for the articulation of social means and needs. But even in this case, the line dividing the ethnographer from the state functionary remains fragile. For example, Ortiz the ethnographer, having embarked on a study of Afro-Cuban religion (Ortiz's word is *fetishism*), does not hesitate to call for the persecution of black sorcery and the confiscation of "idols, images, necklaces, fetishes, altars . . . from the sorcerer's temples" (1973, 246).[12] Ortiz advises the police to remove the idols from the temples and destroy them, thus employing state force to supplement one of the goals of his book. But a few sentences later, as if resenting the scientific autonomy he has sold so cheaply, Ortiz changes his mind: "The most characteristic [of these objects] should be spared and sent to one of our museums. . . . It is important to preserve these kinds of objects for the sake of scientific knowledge" (246).

Despite its hesitations, Ortiz's text already displays the cultural conditions that would soon make the life of the people indistinguishable from the life of the nation. The deep identification of researcher with material is one of the standards of the emerging configuration. One can hardly fail to mention that this passionate inquisitor of black sorcery would end up practicing the rituals he condemns in this early work, while also promoting the identification between black popular culture and national culture in Cuba. The underside of this identification between *popular* and *national* is that once culture becomes national expression, its operations appear increasingly mediated, facilitated, and monitored by state institutions, be they repressive (the police) or ideological (the museum).

Ortiz's double convocation of the repressive power of the state and the seductive exemplarity of culture foreshadows the evolution in Latin America toward the national-popular state form. This shift was, in a sense, the same one that Antonio Gramsci mapped for the physiognomy of the state in Europe. For Gramsci, the development of the modern state in the twentieth century required that the state be redefined as "not only the apparatus of government, but also the private apparatus of 'hegemony' or civil society" (254). In the new conception of the state (Gramsci's ethical state), culture becomes so entangled with state policies that even the most private endeavors can be understood as aiding the consolidation of modern state form. When, many years later, Louis Althusser defined the task of ideological state apparatuses as the reproduction of the social conditions of production, he had Gramsci's intervention in mind. Now no society can reproduce itself without taking some form of pride in its own constitution. Literature was a valuable tool for constructing the desirability of the present in the process of the rationalized reproduction of the social in various modernizing Latin American countries. New hermeneutics evolved with the sole goal of singing the praise of that which existed, although they could also revert to criticizing, a movement exemplified by two early Latin American international best sellers, *Doña Bárbara* and *El mundo es ancho y ajeno*. Of course, the structure of supplementarity between culture and governmentality was not exclusive to Latin America. In Europe and the United States, too, literature served to negotiate the agonistic tensions that marked capitalist development (Lloyd and Thomas 1998). But while in the metropolis social enfranchisement was achieved mainly through the promotion of market relationships, and citizens' incorporation through the juridical sphere of rights, in Latin America—where these routes were deficient, blocked, or nonexistent—aesthetics acquired paramount importance, not only supplementing other forms of enfranchisement but attempting to replace them because of their shortcomings.

At the beginning of the twentieth century, the concept of national literature was consolidated through the creation of different departments in major Latin American universities. The establishment of this conceptual framework amounted to an ethnicization of literature based on the differential value of the Spanish language, immediately marginalizing vigorous oral, popular, and sometimes even indigenous traditions. This ethnicization further entailed the notion that literature was a repository of national virtues and a site of revelation of the national character. Cornejo Polar points to the importance of Alberto Sánchez, who single-handedly created a modern concept of Peruvian literature by claiming the hitherto uncharted region of colonial expression as an organic part of this tradition (1989, 117–18). Similar enterprises were widespread in Latin America at the time. In 1910, Ricardo Rojas published *Historia de la literatura argentina,* which expanded the horizon of the national to encompass not only the remote colonial past but also forms of writing that took the concept of the literary beyond a merely belletrist ideology, such as historical documents and essays. This movement took on continental proportions, to the point that we may say, despite the years that sometimes separate them, that Sánchez in Peru, Rojas in Argentina, Alfonso Reyes in Mexico, and Franz Tamayo in Bolivia constitute essentially the same intellectual figure (the paradigmatic case may be the supranational Pedro Henriquez Ureña). In his memoirs, José Vasconcelos scorns this new breed of intellectuals, which he sees represented in his old friends from the Ateneo—noisy proponents of a new aesthetics who managed to build their careers without ever writing, much less publishing, any of the revered creative books insinuated in the bohemian nights of pre-Revolutionary Mexico (1964, 234). Vasconcelos's accusation is unfair, and not just because he should have directed the same reproach at himself. It is unfair because, as he knew quite well, in the origin of the historical project, critical reflection precedes artistic production. By the second decade of the twentieth century, however, creative writers were catching up with turn-of-the-century "critical intellectuals" as they began to produce literary texts that were consonant with the historical project essayists had initiated some years earlier.

A common desire to incorporate residual and peripheral subjects and communities traverses such otherwise dissimilar movements as *criollismo* (in Venezuela, Mexico, Argentina, Chile, and Uruguay), *indigenismo* (in the Andes, Brazil, and Central America), and *negrismo* (in Central America and the Caribbean). The search for the nation's essence became the subject of many literary works, prompting the reader to receive them as sociological works rather than as works of imagination. *Doña Bárbara* (1929), by Rómulo Gallegos, symbolically retakes the plains of Venezuela from barbarism by educating the region's unruly inhabitants (Marisela) and inauthentic visitors (Santos Luzardo); Arguedas's *Yawar Fiesta* (1941) reminds the authorities that indigenous traditions are to be respected in all their unwieldy idiosyncrasy; Ricardo Güiraldes's *Don Segundo Sombra* (1929) claims the nomadic existence of the gaucho for the national community; Carpentier's *Ecué-Yamba-O* (1933) replaces the false identity provided by modernity with the bongo "antidote for Wall Street"; and Martín Luis Guzmán's *The Eagle and the Serpent* (1929) strives, despite the author's aversion to violence, to uncover the essence of Mexico in those revolutionary men "used to the weight of the rifle" (1965, 87). The conceptual culmination of this movement uniting the hermeneutical authority of the nation with literature as an active transculturative machine came in 1949, with the publication of *Hombres de maíz*, by Miguel Angel Asturias.[13]

All these examples bear witness to a single, continentally unified function of literary formation (sometimes operating alongside or competing with other cultural forms such as magazines, newspapers, *folletines*, theater, popular songs, carnivals, and parades). Since the late nineteenth century, the institution labeled "Latin American literature" has been entrusted with mediating between an emerging nation-state and a disenfranchised population. From its intermediary position, literature has strived to make the nation-state conscious of its own vast heterogeneity. Simultaneously, it has tried to make heterogeneous populations aware of their national destiny. These attempts at modernization often present themselves robed with the garments of tradition. But narratives invoking indigenous legends or ancestral lore were not governed by nostalgia. Rather, they addressed the problem of how to fit even the most traditional (and sometimes seemingly backward) forms of national culture into the emerging notion of a national popular state.[14] In calling attention to the functionality that literature suddenly acquired, I am far from suggesting that it falsified its nature to serve as a sort of propaganda for the process of state formation. Literature did not betray its essence in putting itself at the service of this process. The autonomy of the literary work secured for it a privileged relationship to the modern question of subjection.

Subjection

Subjection means, of course, becoming a subject. There are two dominant and to some extent antithetical accounts of how subjection comes into being in modernity, one stressing the role of ideology, the other maintaining that subjection is the material effect of routines and practices. Both approaches reject the dominant liberal narrative that sees the subject as the product of a gradual education through which the values of conscience and agency are interiorized.[15] In already classical studies, Jürgen Habermas and Ian Watt have both observed that the first expansion of the novel took this liberal subject as its default hero (Habermas 1993; Watt 1957). Structuralist and post-structuralist theorists—particularly Michel Foucault and Louis Althusser—harshly criticized this approach and provided a different account of the formation of the subject, one in which the subject's constitution depends on bureaucratic and regulating apparatuses (prisons, hospitals, ideological state apparatuses). Between these two positions, the all-too-optimistic assertion of the freedom fostered by liberalism and the all-too-pessimistic affirmation of structural serfdom, it is possible to distinguish a third, more nuanced approach. In the work of Jacques Lacan, the subject becomes a subject by entering into the symbolic order, which is alienating and preexisting. In the Lacanian model, the subject chooses— although in a complex and convoluted logic of "choosing"—to embrace the symbolic and give up plenitude. By choosing after the fact the lot that in any case will befall him or her, the subject retains a slight but important margin of self-foundation. Foucault's later work followed a similar path as Foucault began to theorize the possibility that forms of power can be rearticulated into manifestations of resistance. I will use the word *subjection* in reference to this constitutive ambiguity, by which, as Judith Butler puts it, "the subjection of desire require[s] and institute[s] the desire for subjection" (1997, 19). Subjection becomes visible in our increasing inability to determine the exact limits between our desires and the realm of social impositions.[16] These questions will be the focus of chapter 4, but for now, I wish to stress the fact that literature, which Roland Barthes credited as the formal presentation of subjectivity in modernity, is the cultural practice that codifies—perhaps like no other—the possibilities and predicaments of this epochal transition from open coercion to the incorporation of the law as a desire of the subject.

· · ·

The double edge proper to subjection finds a neat exemplification in the notion of transculturation, championed by Angel Rama, among others. As is well-known, Angel Rama borrowed this concept from Fernando Ortiz and went on to make it the most influential paradigm for the study of Latin America, to the point at which it was even understood as the region's proper historical modality of existence. According to this narrative, when Christopher Columbus set foot in the New World, he triggered a dynamic of cultural contact that has been part of Latin American history all along.[17] Today, it is obvious that a good deal of the currency obtained by transculturation stems from the ease with which it describes the subjective changes necessary to adapt Latin American populations to the most general conditions of capitalist modernization. In Alberto Moreiras's account, Fernando Ortiz's initial "loosely anthropological sense" of the term readily gave way, in Angel Rama's work, to an idea of transculturation as the incarnation of "cultural plasticity," a regulative machine for the constant adaptation of backward practices and populations to the demands of a centrally driven modernization (Moreiras 2001, 186). It is true that Rama may have viewed transculturation as simply providing an apt description of the path of modernization in Latin America, but as Moreiras warns, transculturation "does not simply refer to a social relation but rather is 'itself a social relation'" (2001, 186). From being merely descriptive and critical, transculturation became prescriptive and administrative. Increasingly throughout the twentieth century, transculturation appeared as the specific cultural discourse that the ideology of modernization acquired in Latin America. In this sense, the project of transculturation far exceeded the realm of literature. It became a project of epic proportions, a continental cultural machine for reading the relationship between center and periphery. It prompted the constant adaptation of Latin American populations to an ever-increasing flow of social information and commodities emanating from the modernized world; and it simultaneously offered Latin American states invested in integration into the global economy a narrative capable of negotiating the impact of this integration upon the native population.[18]

Although most accounts of transculturation pay attention merely to its synchronic aspect, the power of transculturation is only fully revealed in its diachronic dimension. From a syntagmatic point of view, this power resides in the concept's ability to override the seemingly unavoidable sense of contradiction in everyday life in favor of an integrated sense of national community. But this power is always dependent on the possibility of paradigmatically accommodating the historical multiplicity of past times, subsuming them into the time of the nation. In the ideology of transculturation, the nation takes the form of an "underlying necessity" imparting a unified narrative to a disparate multiplicity of interests and events. The nation-state gathers and recalls all these past events and emotions (whether grievances of the Creoles, the subordination arising from the colonial relation, or the people's common belonging to traditional forms of culture) and becomes, to use a Hegelian expression popularized by Slavoj Žižek, a posited presupposition. The nation appears to be always already there, as an undeveloped, embryonic form of the contemporary nation, guaranteeing the identity of the present and the past by its very transhistorical subsistence. There is thus a specifically historical dimension of the *trans* of transculturation, a dimension that produces identities out of disjointed temporalities.

To illustrate this point, we can refer to Alberto Flores Galindo's *Buscando un inca,* in which the Peruvian historian and sociologist discusses the slow sedimentation of the idea of a unique indigenous (Andean) people unified under a political utopia that would end colonial suffering through the return of the Inca rulers (*la utopía andina*). Nationalist historiography in modern Peru appropriates this long sedimentation, producing a concept of Peruvian or Andean "indigenousness" out of a disparate variety of cultures and peoples, as proof of a national spirit active throughout the centuries. Flores Galindo, in contrast, painstakingly points out that, despite all appearances, the building of an Andean utopia was a dynamic process that may have been marked more by dissent, internal warfare, and overlapping alliances than by any unified protonationalist idea of race, political allegiance, or regional belonging. As Flores Galindo notes, any protonationalist and hegemonically oriented indigenous revolt, like the one commanded by Tupac Amaru around 1780, failed precisely because of the extremely disaggregated character of those involved in the uprising (1988, 103–70).[19]

Like any true form of subjection, the process of transculturation cannot be exhausted by the meaning it acquired in the hands of the different Latin American elites. Everywhere the people left their imprint on the historical process of Latin American societies. No criticism of transculturation can disregard the fact that the establishment of hegemonic states in Latin America was a positive and democratic step that opened venues for the action of subaltern and oppressed peoples. As John Kraniauskas remarks, "Narrative transculturation . . . figures a process of contradictory cultural democratization and integration, the widening of the hegemony's cultural parameters under the impact of the expanded reproduction of capital and the ideology of development" (2000, 115). Transculturation, in other words, is not just the historical presentation of a tamed domination; it also rests on elements of emancipation without which it would be unable to validate its operations.

In spite of its historical role in the constitution of a Latin American identity, the once-celebrated idea of transculturation has today come under fire.[20] Some of the reasons for this sudden shift in fortune have to do with the very place of enunciation for professionals involved in the hermeneutics of culture. The crisis of the nation-state's sovereignty, which granted a space of action to intellectuals throughout Latin America for almost two centuries, has left hermeneutical activity in search of a new critical vantage point: transculturation can no longer be said to afford such a critical position. Yet it would be inaccurate to assert the partial dismissal of transculturation as a phenomenon fueled by the present conditions of our knowledge; the fractures in the process of transculturation were always too glaring to be ignored. Literature's own relationship to the historical project is ambivalent. If we look for the counterproof to the teleological narrative of the nation-state, we will find it, many times, in the same literary texts that champion the ideal of transculturation. Santos Luzardo cannot educate Doña Bárbara, and she flees the plain; Alejo Carpentier regrets his inability to capture the voice and the essence of the Haitian migrants in *Ecue-Yamba-O;* any time Guzmán gets hold of the "indefinable essence of Mexico," this essence slips away beneath adjectives like "formless" and "inhuman"; Don Segundo Sombra simply withdraws with no intention of returning; and Arguedas finds that the demand for recognition by the Indians of Puquio is incommensurable with the prose of recognition that the Peruvian state is willing to grant.

Recognition

Recognition is of interest to us for one fundamental reason: José María Arguedas makes it the center of his rebuke of dominant society in the Andes, and in translating this refutation into his texts, he effectively closes the historical project of Latin American literature. The caliber of Arguedas's accomplishment in his thematization of recognition as the center of political subjection can be appreciated in terms of the deep naturalization that has veiled the nature of recognition in most contemporary scholarship.

In a recent book, Paul Ricoeur wonders why there is no important philosophical work that bears the title *Recognition* (Ricoeur 2005, 23).[21] The fact that *recognition* cruises our supposedly hypervigilant gaze without question already constitutes an interesting enigma. If anything, recognition is almost unanimously greeted as the hard-won right of our late democratic times. From political theory to ethnography, and from literature to philosophy, every discourse seems to bend before the mighty prerogatives of a word that combines the rights of the particular with the irrefutability of an ethical apology. There is certain agreement that in being recognized, our freedom and individuality shine forth, unbound of all the chains that history, violence, and culture weaved around us.

Recognition is, in other words, part of the critical interest that the issue of ethics has attracted recently across the humanities. The ethical underpinnings of the term are eloquently argued in *Time and the Other,* a work on critical ethnography by the Dutch anthropologist Johannes Fabian. Classical anthropology, Fabian contends, operates through what he calls a denial of coevalness, inviting us to think that the time of the other and the time of the ethnographer (which is also our time) do not coincide. Leaving the other to exist in a differential time, essentially removed from the time of the researcher, amounts to disavowing the other's presence, and for that reason, Fabian concludes, cognition is obtained in classical ethnography through the denial of recognition (1983, 37–69). For Fabian, the only valid knowledge of the other is the one obtained through acknowledging the singularity and validity of the other's points of view and beliefs. The importance of Fabian's claim lies, above all, in the way it inverts the authoritative relationship between science and subject, introducing an as yet unresolved (and probably irresolvable) crisis in the rules of validity and truth for the "sciences of man."

Perhaps no other contemporary intellectual did as much to promote the rights of recognition as the Canadian philosopher Charles Taylor. Like Fabian's criticism of the denial of coevalness, Charles Taylor's critique of the social contract rests on ethical claims about the nature of the social link. As Taylor asserts in "The Politics of Recognition," "Due recognition is not just a courtesy we owe people. It is a vital human need" (1994, 25). His politics of recognition dresses itself in the garments of the absolutely singular and, firmly planted in this ethic, speaks fundamentally of an "equality before the other," which is implicitly opposed to the devalued liberal notion of "equality before the law." Equality before the law continues to be, of course, an active force in politics and society, but only as negativity. Most of the actual positive contents that affect social and cultural behavior are based on an idea of rights, anchored in the lived experience of human beings. At this point, it is appropriate to recall that both the attack on transculturation and its defense make similar claims about the recognition of differences. Transculturation is said to have performed this act of recognition through the sublation of difference into the transcultural product. Critics of transculturation—even subtle ones, such as Cornejo Polar—charge transculturation with obliviousness to the singularity of cultural experiences, which are erased rather than salvaged in the process of transcultural incorporation.

Most approaches to the concept of recognition unproblematically adopt the dubious liberal trope of "natural rights," with its implication that individuals preexist and transcend the society that has created them. Culture, language, and action thus become elements that these subjects possess, rather than some of the many means that they use and submit to in the construction of their social experience.

In spite of all its current prestige, the promotion of recognition has an ironic and untimely ring to it. Far from being a new development, the present recognition of recognition simply brings to the foreground one ideological kernel of the expansion of modern capitalism. Recognition always turns out to be recognition of a property. (As Hegel unwillingly suggested, there is nothing to be recognized in the juridical figure of a real slave.) As a matter of fact, property appears as almost indistinguishable from recognition in the history of modern liberalism, in whose narrative every expansion of the democratic liberal ethos was accompanied by an expansion of property/recognition. From a historical perspective, then, the present reign of recognition, which makes of the concept an uncontestable universal right, perhaps needs to be weighted with regard to the current unprecedented general expansion of the notion of property (intellectual rights, virtual rights, trademarks), as every inch of the planet is subjected to the juridico-political relationship of late capitalism.

In Latin America, the original scene of capitalist recognition takes place at the end of the nineteenth century, when the continent is integrated into the world market. Only at this point are local elites forced to recognize the most coveted property: the labor force. However, as we know quite well, modernization in Latin America is never a straightforward process. Resistance to modernization arises from the modernizing elites themselves, for whom modernization almost always takes the form of an irresolvable tension between a welcomed economic modernization and abhorred processes of social change. The question of gender is perhaps the point at which this contradiction is most egregious. As a rule, late nineteenth-century capitalist modernization incorporated an important contingent of women as labor force, while simultaneously condemning and even criminalizing the spatial and social mobility of proletarian women in the public space. Likewise, the need to recognize the labor force often took perverse forms, such as the racialization of the working class and the use of an extensive discourse of eugenics that barely distinguished between the working person and the socially excluded who constituted the capitalist army of reserve labor living in almost infrahuman conditions. Even in the most dynamic economies of the time, such as oligarchic Argentina or Porfirian Mexico, recognition and ownership of the labor force were pitted against each other in spite of this pair's essential unity.

That recognition always recognizes a property means, among other things, that it is a system that presupposes both an economy and all the ungenerosity that comes along with it. Although recognition seems to advocate the cause of the underdog, which to some extent it does, we must confront the fact that recognition is above all a strategy through which power reasserts itself in the minute details of the everyday. The recognition granted by the state (or by literature as a state apparatus) is never a gift, but a loan that is finally collected in kind. In this economy of reflexion and return, the state provides recognition in exchange for recognition. The recognizing activity of the state depends on the fact that the subjects receiving its favor must first recognize the state as the recognizing instance. In this structure, one cannot win legitimacy without giving up historical initiative, and one cannot claim autarky without consenting to sanction from above. Every recognition granted by the state further empowers the state's own imaginary constitution. In the end, the state's recognizing activity is an exercise in self-recognition. This structure does not pose major problems when the cultural makeup of the nation is relatively uniform, but it is destined to progress via waves of violence and suppression in those regions, like Latin America, where the heterogeneity of society cannot be easily reconciled with the centripetal impulses of nation-state formation. In such heterogeneous contexts, the false morality of recognition becomes even more blatant. Finally, recognition's link to the contractual notion of sovereignty is obvious: recognition serves as the visible and pristine counterpart of this enigmatic, abstract process, through which the people is said to transfer its sovereignty to the state's sphere of action.

Recognition binds capital and culture through their common reference to property. It also binds literature and labor force in the crystallization of the historical project (the three great *novelas de la tierra*—*Doña Bárbara*, *La Vorágine*, and *Don Segundo Sombra*—are all about the adjudication of resources and the labor force). Although this binding is an appropriation, it is not a lie. There is a common ground to art and labor that we express through the notion of work. Like labor, art and literature are primary ways of inhabiting the world. This is why we keep going back to them, expecting to find in them the disclosure of a productive dimension that, bringing us full circle in the system of our determinations, will provide a genuine possibility for overcoming the postcolonial heritage that keeps logic and ontology separate in our experience of the world.

Foundling
Selves,
Foundational
Others

Juan José
Saer's *The*
Witness

Like philosophy for Plato, the narration of the New World begins with a
sense of wonder: the wonder of new lands, new animals, new people, and
above all a new sky. With the discovery of America, it is said, modernity
comes into being, and the Middle Ages end. A traditional view images
the Middle Ages as a period during which human beings stood crucified
between the small piece of land where they were born (and where they
would, in all probability, die) and the heaven toward which both their
thoughts and their soul were directed. Modernity, on the other hand, introduces along with the motif of the traveler the constant experience of
the transient.

    The Witness, a novel published by Juan José Saer in 1983, re-creates this
dawn of the world; its point of departure is a real historical occurrence—the
ten-year captivity of a young Spaniard among an indigenous tribe of South
America in the first half of the sixteenth century. A new and complex spatiality frames the whole book, from its opening ("What I remember most
about these empty shores is the vastness of the sky" [1990, 9]) to its close
("What came after that . . . was the sound of seas and cities, the beating of
human hearts, whose current, like an age-old river that washes away the
useless paraphernalia of the visible, deposited me in this white room, to
write, hesitantly, by the light of some almost spent candles, of a chance encounter that was both among yet with stars" [167]). This life of wandering

and discovery gives way to a completely new understanding of the existent: "the world is infinite" (136). The new sense of the world triggers a new sense of the self, one of an unprecedented depth: "my memories are also infinite" (137).

Despite the presence of so many wonders, the colonizers rarely granted themselves the experience of being overwhelmed.[1] This relative lack of genuine surprise in the face of the unknown is even more telling in relation to the usual conviction that the discovery of America presided over the earliest self-understanding of modernity. Even philosophy, the discourse responsible for the representation of a new worldview, seems to have lingered in a certain intellectualism in the face of the sensuous. It was not until Martin Heidegger, writes Emmanuel Levinas, that the intellectual orientation was shaken to its core. Until then modernity had tried to build "[a] reason freed from temporal contingencies, a soul co-eternal with the Ideas . . . a reason that has forgotten itself or is unaware of itself, a reason that is naive" (1996, 2). All this does not negate the fact that a new experience of space, even space qua experience, presided over the foundation of the modern world. But we should not subscribe too hastily to the view that the colonization of the Americas was the one decisive fact in the formation of a modern worldview that would soon be imposed on the whole globe. The experience that shook the medieval conception of space to its roots was, rather, the new physics inaugurated by the Copernican revolution, which destroyed an image of the cosmos that had for centuries assured every real (and even unreal) being a secure place in a well-contained field of existence. Saer's novel situates itself in this time when the skies became infinite, the stars dazzling, and the attributes of humankind, to use a word often repeated in the book, problematic.

The protagonist of the novel is a young member of Juan Díaz de Solis's expedition to the River Plate, who, after all his fellow crew members are killed and eaten by the Indians, lives with his captors for ten years.[2] One day, without any explanation, the Indians return him to another Spanish party exploring the Paraná River. As he leaves the region where he grew up, the witness sees the river fill with the corpses of the Indians killed by the new Spanish expedition, and as the ships cross the Atlantic back to Spain, he sinks into melancholy. Once in Spain, he is protected and tutored by an educated priest who teaches him how to read and write. Upon Father Quesada's death, the hero leaves the convent to tour Europe with a theater company, enacting his own story as a captive with great success. With the money earned in this enterprise, he secures a place in a coastal town, where he devotes the rest of his life to writing the book that we are now reading.

The whole book, the narrator says, is an attempt to repay the Indians for the incalculable gift of having opened him up to a new and unique life.[3] He wants to bring to life the faces of those who made him a human being.[4] He will tell the Indians' story in terms of what really makes it unique. And what makes the Indians' story unique is that they regard themselves as "the true men" (los hombres verdaderos) and deem unreal all other tribes and groups with whom they come into contact. The unreality of their neighbors (and of the first Spanish expedition) does not prevent the Indians from fighting, hunting, and eating them in an orgiastic cannibalistic feast that Saer recounts in minute detail. The dubious nature the Indians assign to other men parallels the doubt they cast on the world as a whole. As the narrator tells it, the best index of this "deep distrust of reality" is the fact that in their aboriginal language the verb "to be" is absent. The Indians say not, "it is a tree," but "it seems a tree" (Saer 1990, 130).

A blend of travel narrative, bildungsroman, and existential adventure, *The Witness* fuels in its readers a thirst for revelation. The imprecise promise of the disclosure of an unfathomable reality—the promise that constitutes the book's fundamental gesture—marks the book almost from its opening lines. Simultaneously, however, the narrator lets us know that the lesson in uncertainty ciphered at the heart of the Indians' language (which cannot proclaim the existence of the tree but must content itself with its appearance) is the real stuff of his narration, because the Indians have even succeeded in poisoning his perspective.[5] For him too the world and the language that he uses to refer to it will become dubious and strange, to the point that the only story told in these pages is the story of the impossibility of reporting the Indians' world. Such a failure is all the more noticeable because the hero was not altogether unprepared for the overwhelming experience of desolation that he endured in the New World. He was already familiar with deprivation: he lacked a mother and father, the novel says, and at the time of the adventure could neither read nor write. He had already faced the new, oblivious to the cosmic flight of the old gods.

The Witness, it may be clear by now, is a book about books, which did not fail to elicit the interest of a theoretically sophisticated readership.[6] It revisits the fundamental problems brought to Latin American literature by discourses such as *indigenismo, testimonio,* heterogeneous literatures, and postcolonial studies. In all these discourses, the concept of otherness holds a prominent position, and none of them is free of the fantasy of hearing the other of the West speaking in the text of literature. *The Witness* dismisses this aspiration as a contradiction in terms. The writer may want to speak of the other *as other*, but the other is by definition that which cannot be grasped without being turned into a figure of the same. An accomplished act of witnessing, one in which the narrator could reveal the nature of those to whom he bears witness, would constitute an even more painful shortcoming, because witnessing requires precisely the recognition of alterity, not its subsumption into an alien narrative or epistemological framework. Otherness cannot be subsumed in a (re)presentational discourse and still be *other*. There seems to be no way out of this paradox, given that the whole project of intersubjectivity runs on the subtleties of imaginary identifications. *The Witness* does not stop at this formal impossibility. If the enterprise is a mirage, the novel seems to say, the desire that impels it is real: we cannot dismiss it with an untroubled gesture. Whose desire is at stake here? The answer is obvious: literature's desire and literature as desire. But if, as Hegel said, the truth of desire lies in the other, literature (or in this case the novel that represents literature) is responsible not only for its own desire but also for what we may name the other's call. There is no literature without that call. In saying this, I am not positing literature as a mystical, sublime project beyond historical determinations. On the contrary, I speak of literature as a historical constituent of modernity. Literature asserts itself *historically* in a desiring structure of alterity. In the interplay of calls, a world takes shape. This call is beyond knowledge, or, to advance the language of our demonstration, it is more fundamental than any knowledge.

The Wanderer without a Shadow

Philosophy and literature took the destruction of the medieval worldview seriously. Both proceed, in their modern incarnation, from the rift opened up in the European consciousness by the exhaustion of old forms of learning when faced with an infinite universe that now seemed to take an eternity to fathom. The European imagination filled with descriptions of distant lands, the crossing of dangerous oceans, and meetings with new people. This process triggered the search for new languages and styles. Forms like the picaresque and the road novel emerged. And in all these literary forms, including their monumental accomplishments (*El Lazarrillo de Tormes, Garagantua et Pantagruel, Don Quijote*), the question of "commerce with the world" remains constant and central.

At the beginning, imagination experienced the new configuration of the world as a simple expansion, an addition that could be mastered through effort and perseverance. Soon, however, the consciousness arose that the infinitization of the world (which gave way to our universe) demanded a deep and total transformation of the relationship between thinking and reality.[7] René Descartes systematized these determinations in the realm of philosophy, and it is perhaps not coincidental that Cartesianism may provide, even if indirectly, the fundamental tools for a reading of Saer's enigmatic novel. The Cartesian themes of certainty, memory, and subject are the same ones that torture first the Indians in their relationship to the outer world and later the witness in his relationship with his memories. But the "solutions" Saer's novel offers to these questions are quite different from, even opposite, the ones advanced by the French philosopher. We know that the Cartesian subject is the reconstitution point of a whole world shattered by the presupposition of the evil genius. This subject is strictly correlated with the world, and it is by virtue of this correlation that the subject can become the foundation of the whole world. But this subject is condemned to find the traces of its own image everywhere because it is completely invested in yielding an undoubtedly certain figure: the ego of the inquirer. And the question of ego reveals a startling difference between the witness and the Cartesian narrator. The *I* that appears no less than a dozen times in the first paragraph of Descartes's *Meditations* delineates a figure of mastery and authority. Even the argument of the all-powerful evil genius is unable to shake his voice's calm and secure pace. The witness, on the other hand, abandons himself to the evidence: "the fragile hand of this old man struggles to make real with his quill the images that memory autonomously sends him, who knows how or whence" (Saer 1990, 59). It is hard to imagine Descartes using such a disempowered and melancholic tone. In Descartes, there is no autonomy of memory, much less automatism. Perhaps, however, there are automata: the others that Descartes sees through his window but whose humanity remains uncertain for him.[8] In *The Witness*, on the other hand, the automatism of memory comes from a sending that has the lost Indians (by no means confused with automata) as its origin and agent.

Although slightly at odds with the rules of academic engagement, the comparison of a fictional character with a founding philosophical figure is sustained by a series of striking similarities. Almost contemporaries, Descartes and the witness are both travelers whose voyages furnish the obscure kernels out of which their narrations grow. One in Holland, the other in Spain, both have settled down to write after wandering the world for exactly the same span of time, ten years. Both can say that they have lived among people "extravagant and ridiculous to our apprehension," even if these words belong only to Descartes (1996, 4). Most important, both have lived in perpetual exile without finding a place that can, properly speaking, be called home. *Home* and *outside* are the essential tropes of what, in the colonial experience, may still belong to the nature of the encounter. Those who travel, said Rousseau in a remarkable note in his *Second Discourse*, come to a better understanding of the value of home, although it is doubtful that they ever reach a knowledge of the outside.[9] In his books, Descartes is always at home, writing. As we know, for him writing has an intrinsic relationship with the subject of return. Ceasing his rambles through Europe was a precondition for giving his ideas the fixity and rigor of a system. Hegel, as always, was able to encapsulate this crucial movement of the real in a powerful poetic image: with Descartes, he writes in his *Philosophy of History*, "we are at home and, like the sailor after a long voyage, we can at last shout 'land ho'" (1956, 131). The return home ended in the assertion of a philosophy of return that in the language of philosophy is called *reflection*. This operation is far from constituting an instance of solipsism. Interest and not disinterest, actual gains of power instead of imaginary losses of mastery, are at stake. The thinker thinking on the verge of the fabulous expansion of the West even seems exaggeratedly optimistic about the virtues of his method, one, he says, that will "make of us, European men, masters and possessors of the earth" (Descartes, qtd. in C. Taylor 1992, 161). The philosopher returns to his home as the adventurous traveler returns to his point of departure, either defeated or loaded with treasures. In any case, an imperial logic of accumulation already reigns in this worldview, for which the whole extension of the existent has become an object of availability and appropriation. It is not difficult to hear in the word *return* the racket of ships, gold, and violence that forms the iconography of the colonial expansion and, along with all the noises of empire, the more subtle murmur of the self coming back to itself in the philosophy of reflection. But it is different for the witness. Already exposed to what in the novel he repeatedly calls "an outside," the narrator cannot go back to a language, just as he cannot retrace his steps to any sense of home.[10]

Mastery over the world is acquired through a certain economy by which the materiality of experience has to submit to the formative potency of the I, as the rivers and mountains of the New World submitted to the nominative rage of the colonizers. Still, what is left of Descartes the wanderer strives to preserve the redolence of the world in the isolation of writing. In the *Meditations,* we read of "this piece of wax. It has been taken quite recently from the honeycomb; it has not yet lost all the honey flavor. It retains some of the scent of the flowers from which it was collected" (Descartes 1996, 67). Rarely does Descartes leave his reader without an accurate sense of the environment that surrounds his thoughts: "I remained for a whole day by myself in a small stove-heated room" (34); "I am sitting next to the fire, wearing my winter dressing gown" (60). But we already know that when subjected to radical doubt, this description is condemned to skepticism. There is an apparent contradiction at work in the relationship between Cartesian philosophy and Cartesian world-experience, a contradiction we may summarize as follows: at the very moment that the universe expands into an infinite realm, at the core of the European worlding of the world, the philosopher who is most involved in the determination of this process retreats to the monastic space of the chamber. Things multiply around Descartes, and he copes with this proliferation by secluding himself and meditating on the existence or nonexistence of the whole world. But the contradiction is only apparent. What we witness is instead the first far-reaching systematization of the epistemic consequences of the emergence of the modern notion of world through a solution that mirrors the most general strategy of the science of the time. Struggling with the question of how taxonomy, the medieval strategy for coping with the variety of experience, could accommodate infinity, the astronomy of Kepler and Galileo *reduced* the whole complexity of the skies to a mathematical model. Likewise, Descartes reduces the perceived world to an intentional mechanism.

No such reduction is possible for the witness—in the first place because his discourse is a discourse on memory. A discourse of certitude ignores time. In Descartes, memory itself, although the only guarantee of the existence of a transcendental subject, is also an undesirable instance of nonpresence. A discourse of witnessing, on the other hand, is necessarily based on a problematic relationship to a remembered reality. So while memory as discursivity—as the play of retentions and protentions—remains for Descartes in the innermost circle of the cogito's certainties, for the witness the very opposite is true. The materiality of the event, the possibility of reproducing it in discourse, constitutes the unsolvable problem of the narration. He is not able to write because he is not able to forget, and his memory fails him because of the very intensity of remembering. Memory is what menaces all imaginary consistency in the name of a deeper remembrance:

> Each flicker of the candle flame makes my shadow tremble on the white walls. The window is open to the silent dawn in which the only sound is the scratching of my quill and, now and again, the creaking of my seat or my cramped legs stirring beneath the table. The pages I slowly cover with writing and which I add to those already written, produce a very particular rustling whisper that echoes round the empty room. . . . Even if the periodically surfacing memories manage to make a crack in that thickness, once what has filtered through has been deposited there like parched dry lava, the heavy persistence of the present closes ranks and the paper becomes once more dumb and smooth, as if untouched by images from other worlds. It is those fleeting, ghostly worlds, no more palpable than the air I breathe, that must have been my life. And yet there are times when

the images spring up inside me with such force that the thick wall crumbles and I move between two worlds. (Saer 1990, 59)

Memory is, so to speak, encrypted in the narrator's body. It is a scar that cannot be translated into meaning. What is actually remembered becomes mere debris on the page. This impossibility of putting memories down on paper, this impossibility of witnessing that constitutes the core of the narration, could be thought of as a shortcoming, as something that undermines the narrator's authority and reliability. But such a conclusion would only prove how accustomed and subservient we are to the whole constellation of the modern subject as a "subject conscious of" and to the effects derived from that structure. This is a constellation of thinking that comes from Descartes or that we imagine as coming from Descartes.[11] But if there is more than frustration to this text, what kind of intervention may one expect from a disempowered and melancholy witness? There must be such intervention, because we know that few fictional texts in the Latin American tradition convey such a deep commotion of well-rooted convictions as *The Witness* does. Saer's novel is no doubt an impressively authoritative text, and its authority, as we know, comes from materials and standpoints absolutely different from—even opposite to—the venerable tradition that begins with the discovery of the cogito as the solid foundation of modern metaphysics.

Natural Reason and the Metaphysics of Light

Since Descartes, as I noted above, the universal has been obtained not by an additive system, but by the opposite: the reduction of the whole to a small set of invariants. But one reduction has remained, for essential reasons, hidden: by the beginning of the seventeenth century, the world—the very object of desire of colonial expansion—had become light.[12] When Michel Foucault referred to the Cartesian project as a "mathesis of light," he may have had in mind a book that Descartes prepared for publication around 1630 under the title *The World; or, Treatise on Light*. Galileo's trial in Rome convinced Descartes to withhold the book, which was published posthumously.[13] *The Witness*, an account of the world, cannot fail to also be an interrogation of light.

In Descartes, light is the universal medium, and as such (as medium and as universality), it acquires unprecedented import. There are good reasons for this importance. "Light is intrusive," writes Hans Blumenberg; "it forcibly acquires the irrevocability of Spirit's consent. . . . It is the gift which makes no demands, the illumination capable of conquering without force" (1993, 35). Blumenberg hits the mark when he couples light with force. The observation doubtless partakes of an old tradition that goes back to the theme of the Platonic cave. As Blumenberg recalls, the light/force pair is explicitly thematized in Descartes, who presents his confrontation with the Scholastic philosopher as a war between light and darkness in which he obtains victory for his own point of view by forcing the Scholastic thinker out of the cave. Light conquers without force—or, better, light hides force. As Levinas would later come to argue, our past contains the forgotten violence of light.[14] One transition should not be missed. Descartes's disenchantment of the world started with a convocation of "the light of nature" (shorthand for what would be later called "reason"). Although, according to Descartes, innatist laws are still readable in the human soul, Descartes's philosophy—in a countermove to his initial strategy of reclusion—represents a movement toward the exteriorization (and consequent verifiability) of the law. The light of nature makes the secret design of God "readable" in the general layout of the universe. The world has its prose, and although it may be written in mathematical language, it constantly bespeaks a teleological organization. As Charles Taylor summarizes the spirit of the time in *Sources of the Self,* "no one can understand this order while being indifferent to it or failing to recognize its normative force. Indifference is a sign that one has not understood" (1992, 161). The whole system of metaphors tying "nature" to "light" and "reading" (the book of nature, the writing of God, etc.—all metaphors, as Ernst Curtius points, of a medieval provenance) is the constitutive step in the process of universalization through reason (Curtius 1953). So although the metaphors are old, they point to a new relation between subject and world. Light as the fundamental stepping-stone of knowledge is inseparable from the subject as the guarantor and origin of all illumination. In Descartes's *Optics,* the mind receives meaningless bits of data and categorizes them into reliable representations. In other, more speculative books, this centrality is generalized into a metaphysical argument. It is not only that the whole deployment of a new theory of truth as *adequatio* relies on optical metaphors (*clear* and *distinct* ideas whose value becomes *evident* by the *light* of nature); the main point is that this system predicated upon the world finds verification only in the solitude of a confined and culturally specific egoicity. From now on the world has to confirm a reduced ipseity. It has to become its mirror.

It is the passage from nature to subject, from "crisis" as separation to reason as a call for unity, that the master stroke was designed to conceal, because the light of nature is not primitive or natural. It was created to supplement the light extinguished by the Copernican loosening of the metaphysical contract that for centuries had held the earth and its sun together. For Nietzsche, this event signals the death of God. In *The Gay Science*, he tells the parable of the madman "who lit a lantern in the bright morning hours" and ran to the marketplace crying, "I seek God! I seek God" (1974, 181). The madman frames his discourse in unequivocal Copernican words: "What were we doing when we unchained this earth from its sun? Whither is it moving now? Whither are we moving? Away from all suns?" (181). The illumination of the light of nature follows and supplements this moment of endless darkness, a moment in which, as the madman concludes, "night comes on, darker and darker" (181).

Nothing is revealed by light. Rather, light is straight evidence. If this is so clear, what do we make of the scene in which the narrator reports the death of Father Quesada? "He must," the narrator recounts, "have lain dying beneath the open sky, with his face turned toward the same intense, enigmatic [indecifrable] light that his intelligence had confronted all the days of his life" (Saer 1990, 108). How can light be undecipherable? Why is light in *The Witness* thematized as such? This is not an isolated example; the reader frequently encounters such passages: "Though the high sun lit up everything, it still somehow failed to make the world before us seem any more immediate or present" (24); "We revolved dazed and lost in the white light" (109). If, as Blumenberg writes, Plato accomplished (through light) "the *naturalness* of the connection between Being and truth" (1993, 33), what does this insufficiency of light signal? Can light ever lose its naturalness? The madman of *The Gay Science* shares this mistrust of light. He points toward a logic of supplementarity and proliferation that is in itself a refutation of the presumed autonomy of natural light/natural reason. He rambles and asks, "Shall we not have to light lanterns in the morning?" (Nietzsche 1974, 134). *The Witness* echoes this strategy. In the novel's multiple scenes of writing, light is always present, but it is never, strictly speaking, natural light, daylight. The very naturalness of light is problematized by the narrator's obsessive references to lamps or candles any time writing is mentioned, even in passing: "I see my hand . . . leaving a black trail in the lamplight" (35); "Each flicker of the candle flame makes my shadow tremble on the white walls" (59); "Even now, sixty years later, writing by candlelight on this summer night" (82); "It left me in a room with the dying light of the candle" (155, translation modified). What does this coupling of nature and *tekné* mean? Furthermore, what does it mean that Descartes never writes? His scenes of writing are in fact scenes of *speech*. The philosopher, present *à soi*, speaks; the witness, uncertain even of himself, writes. A whole series begins to order itself. On one side we have *light, presence, truth, origin* (the writing of nature as the writing of God), *home, certainty, solitude*—all themes gathered around the metaphysics of presence.[15] On the other side we have *absence, uncertainty, abandonment, errancy,* and *remembrance beyond memory.*

The Prose of the World

The World; or, Treatise on Light, the book that Descartes never published in his lifetime, is already, at the level of its title, a vast epistemological and tropological intervention. On its epistemological side, the book proclaims the supremacy of representation, provided that one possesses the correct tools to measure its accuracy. Its tropological side announces the opening of the world to an unobstructed visibility even as it hides its constructed nature under a rhetoric of transparency. The paradoxical outcome is that this illumination leads to an occlusion of the world. It can only recognize the unfolding of its *programma* because there is already a program at work at this particular historical juncture, a program that (following the characterization of Levinas) I will call the imperial ego. The imperial character of the ego emerges, according to Levinas, through a reflective relationship to reality by which both ego and world are constituted (Levinas 1981, 110). In

Dermont Moran's words, Levinas "sees the history of Western metaphysics as a grand project of totalization, of reducing everything to the sphere of the ego." Levinas indicts the whole history of Western philosophy, starting with Parmenides and the Eleatic tradition, for this identification of being with thought, "wherein being is reduced to whatever is thought-of, or represented in thought. This absorption of being into thought concludes with the highest kind of being: being understood as self-consciousness" (Moran 2001, 241). The absorption of all reality and its correlative reduction to knowledge proposes that only one standpoint—one that has become neutral and unspecific through a process of "objectivation"—is the valid measure of the world. "For the Western philosophical tradition," Levinas writes in his programmatic essay "Substitution," "all spirituality is consciousness, the thematic exposition of Being, that is to say, knowledge" (1996, 80). And insofar as knowledge seeks to reduce all exteriority to the limits of its own being, it becomes inextricable from violence. Thus, "the logos that informs prime matter in calling it to order is an accusation or a category" (1996, 87). It is a logos that has replaced the primacy of a true relationship to reality and the other for the sake of creating an objective world—a world where the direct object can abide. This ego engenders a discourse that "cannot leave anything outside, has no outside" (Levinas 1996, 5).

The search for this outside of the workings of an imperialist logos marked the whole development of Levinas's philosophy. Levinas identified this outside alternatively with traditions peripheral to the dominant narrative of Western philosophy (e.g., Judaism) or with the possibilities afforded by the phenomenological method itself, which in his case uncovers not the powerful figure of a constitutive transcendental ego but the uncanny face of a world-granting coconstitutive other. While the phenomenological reduction is customarily understood as the search for a ground zero of human constitution, it is important to understand that what Levinas postulates as this ground zero is already society—although primordial or unformulated. The material world that looms so large in Levinas's actual phenomenological descriptions of habitation is always already sublated into the dialogue of I and other.

The world whose density so dazzles the Indians and their captive in Saer's novel remains problematic in this philosophy, a philosophy that wants to celebrate facticity but simultaneously needs to guard its argument from the temptation of atheism. The eulogy of facticity partakes in an outright rejection of materialism in Levinas's thinking. The project of recovering the world's brute materiality, which can also be set in opposition to the imperial ego, thus demands that we move beyond Levinas, and we find such a critical possibility in Maurice Merleau-Ponty's version of the phenomenological intervention. For Merleau-Ponty, too, reduction is a critical tool that allows a vantage point from which to criticize the reification of the worlds of culture and nature. Despite its accomplishments, modern culture represents a retreat from the abundance of experience that early modernity had so laboriously wrested from the Platonic and theological tradition of the Middle Ages. In a passage from *The Visible and the Invisible,* in which the name of Descartes reverberates, Merleau-Ponty denounces the economy of fear and dogmatism that presides over the modern retreat into idealism: "As passive beings we feel ourselves caught up in a mass of Being that escapes us, or even maneuvered by an evil agent, and we oppose to this adversity the desire for an absolute evidence, delivered from all facticity" (1968, 109). From this unfortunate beginning, philosophy, which should discover the world, inaugurated a movement away from the sensual, a movement that sought to exhaust the world in a representational structure. Philosophy fell into the trap of viewing the world with an eagle's gaze. From this position, Merleau-Ponty goes on to elaborate an abyssal ontology, one in which "the effective, present, ultimate and primary being . . . offer themselves . . . only to someone who wishes not to have them but to see them, not to hold them as with forceps, or to immobilize them as under the objective of a microscope, but to let them be and to witness their continued being—to someone who therefore limits himself to giving them the hollow, the free space they ask for in return, the resonance they require, who follows their own movement, who is therefore not a nothingness the full being would come to stop up, but a question consonant with the porous being which it questions and from which it obtains not an *answer,* but a confirmation of its astonishment" (101–2).

Merleau-Ponty named the mutual constitution of subject and world "wonder." The imperial standpoint, the standpoint that does not let the world be, establishes on the other hand what Levinas called "a present without fissure or surprise" (1996, 5). Wonder points to a dimension of excess that is the real register of the event at the level of the subject. The imperial standpoint, on the other hand, seeks to strip experience of its element of wonder and surprise and reduce it to familiar categories of the same. The intertwining of event and language is the constitutive knot of *The Witness*. The first event, the ur-event of this tale of conquest and encounter, is no doubt the landing on the new continent. The first moments in America stage the battle between event and imperial ego in a striking way: "When we arrived we scattered like stampeding animals. Some just ran aimlessly off in all directions; others ran round tracing a tight circle on the sand while others again jumped up and down on the spot. One group lit a huge bonfire, its flames pale in the midday sun, and stood transfixed by it. Behind them, inland, at the foot of a small hill, several men were chasing birds that looked like chickens with multicolored plumage. Some men climbed trees, others scratched around in the earth" (Saer 1990, 15). The description defies all the received iconography that accompanies the literary and visual genre "landing in America for the first time." Here we see no banners or crosses or ceremonial kneeling down to claim the territory for the queen or the king. As soon as they land, the crew members scatter "like stampeding animals," and their very *humanity* dissipates. The intentional structure of the ego gives way to a "lived" form of the relationship between body and space (some run "aimlessly," others run in circles, while still others jump "up and down on the spot"). There is no trace here of an ego seeking to tame the novelty of the world through its own categories. The description resembles Levinas's refutation of the Heideggerian ontology, the French philosopher saying that the world is not a place for knowledge or a system of tools, but a context for enjoyment. Progressively, however, wonder and surprise give way to an iron logic through which the world becomes a predicate of the self. In Saer's novel, the suggestion of an imperial ego appears linked to the figure of the captain. For the captain, the landing in America is first and foremost an overwhelming experience of reality: "The captain had completely laid aside his authoritarian manner, adopting instead our wonder and caution, though with no show of humility" (23). It is this sense of overwhelming wonder that the captain immediately attempts to cancel with his discourse, a discourse that, not by chance, begins defining the new in terms of absence and that Saer with magnificent irony cuts off, literally, at its source: "Finally, looking at us with that same expression of mingled belief and distrust, he began: 'This is a land without . . .' at the same time raising his arm and shaking his fist, trying perhaps with that gesture to reinforce the truth of the statement he was about to deliver: 'this is a land without . . .' those were the captain's precise words when an arrow shot out from the undergrowth that rose up behind him and pierced his throat, so suddenly and unexpectedly that he remained standing there with his eyes still open, frozen for a few moments with his arm raised in that affirmatory gesture, before falling to the ground" (25–26).

With this cutting interruption of the first European words uttered about this region of America, several motifs unravel. Something of the order of the act occurs. A profound change comes with the death of the captain, and later of almost the whole company. First, the agency of the "encounter" is literally reversed. Not only is the discourse on America canceled, but from this point on it is the Indians who "encounter" the only survivor of the expedition. Second, since in the long run the result of the encounter is the unavoidable restitution of agency to a European enunciation (the witness will tell his/their story in Spanish), there begins here a complex dialectic for which terms like *metissage* or *hybridity* are thoroughly inappropriate. Finally, the figurative dimension of the narrative, literally read, also adds some elements to the hermeneutic of the passage: it is in the interrupted ontological discourse of the captain that the voice of the witness will finally emerge.

The Aporetics of Witnessing

Witnessing comes after the silence of a master discourse. An arrow has cleared the space of its intervention. But the silence that comes with the demise of the master discourse is not enough to provide the witness with the space in which his voice can unfold. The perspective of his words will remain uncertain, a fact already announced in the (mis)translation of the title of the novel. The original Spanish title, *El entenado*, literally means "adoptive son." The word *entenado* is not commonly used in Spanish; it even fails to appear in a number of dictionaries. Like the meaning of many words referring to kinship, that of *entenado* is attached to a historical universe of relationships. When this universe disappears, the meaning of the word is loosened. *Entenado* is already a sign of untimeliness. The difficulty of translating this title mirrors uncertainty about the level of the witness's inclusion or detachment in the indigenous community, which he is simultaneously within and outside.

Few elements register the ambivalent enunciative position of the hero better than his sparse and hesitant references to the Indian language. Although he has spent ten years among the Indians and learned their language to the point where he has forgotten the sounds of his own maternal idiom, the hero reports just one noun of all the chaotic language the Indians taught him: *def-ghi*—the name the Indians give him on the first day of his captivity.[16] When the novel was first published in the early 1980s, there were some attempts to unveil the meaning of this word. Some suggested the possibility of linking the name to the structure of the Tupí-Guaraní languages; others ventured into no less improbable philological ruminations. Meanwhile, as the narrator slowly realizes, *def-ghi* is not a name but an injunction. The word conceals a secret hope, a pressing command. That is why the Indians spared his life while killing all the other Spaniards. As he sees the other captives disappear, he slowly realizes his own function: "They wanted me to reflect like water the image they gave of themselves, to repeat their gestures and words, to represent them in their absence. . . . The Indians wanted there to be a witness to and a survivor of their passage through this material mirage; they wanted someone to tell their story to the world" (Saer 1990, 144).

We can realize the complexity of this process through its very formulation: to witness is to duplicate like water the image of something that comes from afar, to reflect the reflection of a culture that is unable to cling to the driftwood of speculation and, as a consequence, is suspicious of any representation. Furthermore, the philosophy of reflection has been coopted in advance by a structure that ties representation to knowledge and knowledge to power. The process of witnessing would thus require a narrator divested of cultural prejudices and assumptions, a narrator able to identify and confront the complex net of preventions that imperial reason has woven around him. How can the witness become this narrator? In the novel, the solution is quite simple: he becomes a member of this culture. He is born again in a new motherland. After his rebirth, the first trouble the narrator faces is the ambivalence of his own gaze. Ten years among the Indians have made him familiar with their practices and customs, but a certain level of exteriority must be preserved if he is going to realize his role as *def-ghi*. This transition has a phantasmatic quality and places the narrator in an eccentric position with respect to both his culture of origin and his culture of adoption. Belonging is forbidden to him; orphanhood is the condition of any testimony.

Yet despite all these transformations, the witness remains estranged from the life of the community. We will miss the novel's point if we ascribe this failure and frustration to a certain lack, to a fate that could have been evaded or deceived. In the book we are told about other *def-ghis*. One in particular impresses the narrator. This *def-ghi* comes one afternoon and remains in the tribe for a couple of months. During that time, he shows nothing but contempt for the Indians: "He understood. He knew the score not only as regards his own role, which he performed with a kind of prolix fervor, but also as regards mine" (Saer 1990, 84). But this knowledge builds a wall between him and the tribe: he is unable to perform his task because he knows the *nature* of the task. The witness, on the other hand, remains forever uncertain about the nature of the hope the Indians have placed in him, and this uncertainty is the last guarantee of his faithfulness to their call. For him, reality, even a beloved reality, is unspeakable; but this failure does not originate in the inexhaustibility of the world *in itself* nor in the insufficiency of language as a tool. It is the other's point of view—the other's gaze, even—that ruins the possibility of reporting him, describing her. The day the Indians decide to send the witness back to the Spaniards, the whole tribe escorts him to the beach, screaming and gesticulating, competing for his attention so that, as the narrator says, "I would then recognize and hold them in my memory for longer than the others and keep their image fresher in my mind" (93). He recalls the beach, the sun, and the morning, but he cannot, properly speaking, remember them, and even if he could, the narrator concludes, he would never be sure that the images through which he remembers them are the same images through which "they wished to be remembered" (93).

In *The Witness*, any time the ethical relation is manifestly in default, the whole world seems to crumble under the weight of inauthenticity.[17] For this reason, a full-fledged Levinassean reading of *The Witness* seems an obvious approach, and one can only wonder why such a reading has not been already undertaken. Levinas's point was precisely the upsetting of ontology by ethics as the primordial relation between world and being. Clearly, the same equation holds in Saer's novel, where any word upon the self, the world, or experience is mediated by a demand from the Indians that the narrator is never able to comprehend.

On the Ambivalence of the Word *Call*

For Levinas, there is no opening before language, and there is no language that is not addressed to someone. This anteriority of language announces the anteriority of the ethical relationship. The witness lives already immersed in this anteriority. Before endowing him with the responsibility of being a witness, the Indians spoke to him. They did not just give him a name; they gave him a name that bears the structure of a call. *Call* and *name* are not equivalent terms. Indeed, the two words signal wholly different destinies concerning the relationship to power.

In "Is Ontology Fundamental?" Levinas redresses his argument for the primacy of the ethical over the ontological through an analysis of the word *call* when applied to other human beings. One calls things, lending them names. But in calling another person, one simultaneously summons that person. This link between naming and convocation is the source and force of the injunction that the Indians cipher in the word-call *def-ghi*.

Levinas begins by recognizing the seminal importance of Heidegger's philosophy. The renewal of ontology in contemporary thinking resides in the acknowledgment of the factual situation of the knower within the situation of knowledge. Ontology is fundamental only if it inquires into the being of the questioner itself.[18] But according to Levinas, "The philosophy of existence immediately effaces itself before ontology" (1996, 4). "Existence," Levinas explains, "is interpreted as comprehension," to the point that our concrete existence must accommodate itself to the language of ontology. Levinas anticipates the reader's objection, the question of how "the *rela-*

tion with *being* [can] be, from the outset, anything other than its *comprehension* as being" (6). This description, contends Levinas, does not apply to our relationship to the other. While this relationship consists in wanting to comprehend the other, "this relation overflows comprehension" (6). While ontology understands being in terms of concepts, the understanding of the other can never be reduced to a concept: "The other is not an object of comprehension first and an interlocutor second. The two relations are intertwined. In other words, the comprehension of the other is inseparable from his invocation" (6).

Levinas gives a particular turn to the hermeneutic ground that, since Husserl, has governed phenomenology and existentialism. If we always already arrive into a world that is pregnant with meaning, it is a matter of upholding this view and its consequences. Speech precedes language as the very instrument of positing the world. The other, furthermore, appears only in conversation. Speaking, concludes Levinas, is an "intuition of sociality" (1996, 7); sociality itself is originally established in speaking. The intuition of sociality is simultaneously the intuition of a shared world of meaning. Something is accomplished even if the "content" is in default. For Maurice Blanchot, who follows Levinas in this respect, something is accomplished *because* content is in default. In *The Writing of the Disaster,* Blanchot contends, "Writing (or Telling, as distinct from anything written or told) precedes every phenomenon, every manifestation or show: all appearing" (1986, 11). Ontology is not really fundamental (it lacks a foundation) if it is oblivious to the fact that language and discourse (and then, derivatively, the world) are *owed to the other.* The formulation in which Levinas comes to terms with the inescapable dissymmetry governing human sociality appears with exceptional condensation and economy. "The relation with the other . . . is not therefore ontology. This tie to the other. . . which does not reduce itself to the representation of the other . . . but rather to his invocation, where invocation is not preceded by comprehension, we call *religion.* The essence of discourse is prayer" (1996, 8).

By identifying the essential character of discourse with prayer, Levinas seeks to stress not only the connection between the two but also their disjunction. I find this call for separation most important. All too frequently, excessive sympathy turns into unacknowledged imperialism. The extended conviction among the colonizers in the nineteenth century that they were helping a backward world is not as grotesque a delusion as it now seems. It is with this possibility in mind that *The Witness* teaches a lesson on restraint. This novel does not seek to occupy the other's place. It does not see in the other a vantage point from which to escape logocentrism, Eurocentrism, and so on. In short, it does not believe in an outside to this configuration that makes the matrix of our culture a perpetual movement toward its limits. Could this imperialism of going beyond, trespassing upon frontier after frontier, pertain to the definition of literature itself? That is probable. But it is necessary to learn the other side of this lesson as well. Saer, as I will argue later about other writers, may go beyond literature, beyond its historical configuration, but only by keeping himself in its shadow, by operating inside literature's paradoxical temporality. In the same vein, our goal of transcending the imperialism of our own gaze will be better reached by traveling toward its real center than toward its imaginary border.

For all these reasons, the structure of the call is not alien to literature. In fact, it is central to its constitution. This is what I mean when I describe "literature's desire" and affirm that this desire is inherent to its responsibility. Unlike science or history, literature holds responsibility that does not arise in the strictures of the concept or the urgencies of nomination. This responsibility is strictly attached to the work of instituting, to the unfathomable materiality of the sign, to its secret. The revelation at stake in *The Witness*—and its style is not extraneous here—is fundamentally the revelation of language: the revelation of language's otherness. Michel Foucault said of Don Quixote that he was, "as a sign, a long, thin graphism, a letter that has just escaped from the open pages of a book" (1971, 46). Saer's hero, not so different, is not an interruption but a confirmation of the order of language, and this order of language is the formal condition as well as the content of the injunction: a b c *d e f—g h i . . .*

The Other and the World

To recapitulate, a reader may approach *The Witness* expecting a revelation. The book, however, replies with a discourse of uncertainty, a condemnation of representation, and a questioning of ontology as having a univocal, dogmatic relationship to reality or acting as an authoritative subject of remembrance and expression. I have tried to extract a whole set of notions that, while criticizing the language and structure of traditional and positivistic forms of witnessing, do not disdain the enterprise as negative or nostalgic. I have referred to the region of primordial ethics—the only region where the word *other* can have a satisfactory denotation today—as a region of primal concern for the novel. I have also stressed that the question of otherness, a question that recurs in the cultural understanding of Latin America, should be considered alongside the historical development of a philosophy of reflection, a philosophy that has been instrumental in grounding the universalization of European cultural patterns, simultaneously endowing them with an intrinsic superiority. This is not the same as saying that the philosophy of reflection per se carries colonizing consequences.[19]

Important as it is, the collusion of idealism and coloniality (the trick that allows the European man to be master and possessor of the earth) is only half of the story. The other half concerns the fact that *historically* the colonial deployment of the imperial ego thematizes a relationship to the world as the object of colonial desire. For that reason, a criticism of the colonial relation cannot bypass the original epistemological violence incarnated in acts of naming and operations of knowledge, to proceed without further ado to an encounter with the universality of a community of ethically bounded beings, as if the very subjectivity of the peripheral subjects to be elevated to the universal were not marked by the inaugural colonial gesture of objectification and epistemological domination. This move forces us to relativize—not to disdain or entirely jettison—the Levinassean inflection exhibited earlier in this chapter. In stating this point, I am not just advancing my own position but following Saer's novel to the letter.

In *The Witness*, the question of otherness is never *simply* a question of a powerful subject conceiving another, disempowered one. The encounter between same and other occurs in the world, and this world is neither a background nor an alterity already subsumed in the movement of a language. The world as a reserve of meaning, as space of contestation for the operations of the imperial ego, is of paramount importance for an anticolonialist politics, and this strategy is confirmed by almost every prominent thinker of decolonization, from Waman Poma de Ayala to Frantz Fanon. Its

significance is so marked that even when the memory of an alternate evaluation of the world is not actually present, it has to be nonetheless presupposed by the anticolonial discourse. For instance, Stuart Hall's discussion
of the colonial identity of the Caribbean, in a text like "Cultural Identity
and Cinematic Representation," is organized around three presences that
define the coordinates of the colonial legacy: first, an African presence,
which is of course diasporic; second, a European heritage embodied in the
language which and against which Hall speaks; third, a properly American presence. Now, since there is no population "native" to Jamaica, Hall
"reads" this presence not in an indigenous substratum but rather in locality
itself, and he calls it "ground, place, territory" (1989, 78).

This need to attend simultaneously to the colonial foreclosure of the
ethical moment and the ontological assault on the lived world differenti-
ates the postcolonial thinking of witnessing from the standard European
approach to the same subject.[20] In a colonial situation, the aporetics of witnessing is doubled, because it entails not only the impossibility of substi-
tuting oneself for the other but also the acute awareness of the limitations
of one's own language in translating the other's world; or, better yet, given
that the witness is as a rule a member of the dominant society, the act of
witnessing confronts the witness with the scars of the ontological colonization of the world inside his or her own discourse. This triadic conception
articulates the colonial subject not only to the privileged subject of history
but also to the colonial location of their encounter. If we miss this equation
between subject and world, we also miss the fundamental movement of *The
Witness,* insofar as the only way to overcome subjectivism is to incorporate
the world as a meaningful framework of experience. The world is the third
term that, in destroying the specular trap, liberates this structure from the
endless repetition of its epistemic failure.

From Witness to *Entenado*

The world inscribes itself in the narrative of *The Witness* under two modalities: the absolute certainty of the sky and the equally irrefutable experience
that opens itself through the cannibalistic feast. Back in Spain, haunted by
the memories of the Indians and still puzzled by their relentless distrust of

reality, the narrator abruptly says, "It took me a long time to realize that the reason they were burdened with all these cares was that they ate human flesh" (Saer 1990, 137). In this sentence, the cognitive problem directed at the world (the Indians' burden: the improbable character of the outside world) springs from an ethical problem (the fact that the Indians eat other human beings). The narrator does not substantiate his revelation immediately. For a few pages, he holds back his explanation of the connection between ontological uncertainty and cannibalism. Then this narrator, comfortably located in the sixteenth century, offers a Freudian solution to the whole question of cannibalism. Eating other human beings, he concludes, is not a pleasurable experience for the Indians. To some extent, they do so against their will. While eating human flesh, they taste not the exterior or the unknowable but, rather, "an ancient experience beyond memory" (138). The Indians know, the narrator insists, that since the exterior is false and unreal, they are not actually eating anything. Thus a barely veiled reference to the Freudian compulsion to repetition explains the enigma of cannibalism: "If it is true, as some people say, that we always try to repeat our early experiences and in some way succeed in so doing, the anxiety the Indians felt must have had its origins deep in the past, in the bitter aftertaste their desire still left them with even though the object of that desire had changed" (139).

The first object of this desire is far more palpable and true than the fallacious exteriority they confront every day: it is they themselves. For at this point, the novel introduces a second surprising revelation: "That must have happened before they began eating the flesh of those who were not true men, those from outside. Before, in the dark years when they floundered with the others, they used to eat each other" (Saer 1990, 139). To an important extent, the Indians fail in their attempt to regain a grip on the real because the object of their desire is not an object at all, but the repetition of a lost identity. In developing the dialectic that forces the Indians to seek in the other the memory of their own flesh, the text falls from open Freudianism into orthodox Lacanianism. Devoid of representations, the Indians have been able to achieve the impossible: to resist the alienation into representation without succumbing to the psychotic stage that would follow from its repulsion. Eating themselves, the narrator explains, the Indians have "experienced the reality of the void" (139). But as Lacanian wisdom goes, any gain in the symbolic is paid for with a loss in the Real. When the Indians finally constitute themselves as an identity by turning on the others and eating them, they lose any contact with the real of reality, and everything turns away from them as simulacra. For the Indians, the whole universe is plunged into a shadow of doubt because on the one hand, they cannot return to their primitive experience of communion (literally speaking), but on the other hand, the system of representations that compensates for the loss of that reality is perceived as dubious and insufficient.

Is not this speculation about belonging and detachment, self-certainty and representation, a highly suggestive metaphor for the relationship of witnessing itself? If so, the only meaning of witnessing is located in the type of failure that it incarnates. The faces and world of the other are irretrievably lost, and this loss is what lends the act of witnessing its value. Here as in other areas of the novel, however, the reader must learn to turn frustration and defeat into productive gain. From the Indians the narrator learns, even if indirectly, that there is an outside to the workings of an imperial ego. Like them, the narrator, who goes unnamed, must avoid making his words an accusation of the world. As I pointed out earlier, the original Spanish title of the novel, *El entenado,* means "stepson" or "adopted child." *Entenado* and *witness* are woven together in the question of inheritance and, through inheritance, in the issues of testament and survival.[21] The protagonist of Saer's novel does not have to bear witness to the Indians' "culture," only to the fact that he is alive and they are dead. Yet he cannot be completely alive if the world of the Indians has perished. (It is in this light that the many enigmatic references to the fact that the Indians sustained the reality of the world should be read: when they die, there is no more reality, although the living continue to live.) What the *entenado* inherits from the Indians is precisely this outlook that he turns on the Indians themselves; but in remaining faithful to their fundamental insight, he fails—from a traditional standpoint—to be their witness.[22] In inheriting the Indians' perception of the world, the narrator accomplishes what Merleau-Ponty perceived as the goal of any meaningful philosophy: "True philosophy consists in relearning to look at the world" (1962, xvi). The center of a true philosophy remains for Merleau-Ponty what he calls the "living body," a concept that he expands in the daunting hypothesis of reversibility between world and subject.[23] The living body marks the center of a holistic structure that refuses to let itself be understood in terms of a definitive separation from the world.[24] If the reflective subject wants to close in on itself "by incorporating every other and assimilating all difference, the living body ... remains open to what is other than, and different from itself" (M. Taylor 1987, 69). The sailors who stamped like animals in their first contact with the new land may figure the nostalgia that the disciplined body feels for its ancestor: the living body. In *The Witness,* the world of the Indians seems to be in a state of transition between an awareness of the flesh and the exigencies of representation. Through the act of cannibalism, the Indians seek evidence of the endurance of the world in the unmediated experience of themselves. But this search for unmediated experience gives way to a vicarious experience that is, paradoxically, an experience of representation. They turn toward the flesh of the world but do not recognize the memories of self-appropriation in its taste.

The narrator, in his obstinate fidelity to the Indians' teaching, attempts the opposite voyage, from representation to the real. But of the real he gets only the scar—in any case, enough material to give to the word *witnessing* the exact coordinates of its true meaning.

Night Falls upon the Discourse of Light

There was a time when, while meditating on the paradox of a responsible discourse toward the other, Jacques Derrida entertained the idea that not-responding could be a sign of respect. Such a conclusion, however, would be—as Derrida soon came to realize—a misrepresentation of the essence of language and its function in the institution of a sociality on whose horizon the other appears. The paradoxical structure that presides over the question of the other always implies, beforehand, the problematic of an "answer." After dismissing silence as a proper relationship to the other, Derrida proposed the figure of the "oblique" to think the "proper" or "almost proper" ethical relationship: a humble gaze, a gaze that will not attain a definition or comprehension of the other. Later he abandoned that characterization as still trapped in the language of the line and the plain—trapped in a language, that is, in which the other will come after the world (see Derrida 1992b). But perhaps we may still avail ourselves of the oblique if its geometrical language restitutes for us the world, not in its abstractness, nor in its always interested essentiality, but in the infiniteness of its experience, which also figures the impossibility of separating the world from the living body that experiences it. This constellation of problems gives the final scene of the eclipse its place in the novel. This is a disconcerting moment. The reader gets the impression that much is at stake here, without being able to assert the precise character of the investment. However, because the eclipse plays with the extremes of being and appearance, for the narrator the eclipse confirms the Indians' worldview: "In a place which was being transformed before their very eyes into blackest night, the vanishing moon, which custom had convinced us was imperishable, was confirming by its gradual extinction the ancient belief that, whether the Indians were conscious of it or not, manifested itself in their very thought and action. What was happening now, they had known about since the very beginning of time" (Saer 1990, 165). The eclipse is a different version of the proverbial phenomenological riddle expressed in the persistence of sayings such as "the sun rises." For us the sun rises, and will keep rising, perhaps forever, even if we know that strictly speaking the sun does not "rise." We have to live in a world where our most trusted perceptions could be rebuked. The same logic, completely inverted, holds here. For the Indians, the error of perception is a confirmation of a deeper truth: the contingency of the world.

Husserl, who always took seriously the idea that the subject looks at the world from a specific standpoint, toward the end of his life wrote an essay whose title alone reveals the tense relationship of the phenomenological project to established science: "Subversion of Copernican Teaching: The Earth, as Primal Ark, Does Not Move" (1934).[25] Isn't this what the earth is for the Indians—a primal ark? It is in the context of realizing the primordial character of embodied knowledge that the witness finally comes to what we may call, properly speaking, a revelation. Unlike the Indians, who were perhaps terrified by the eclipse, the narrator knows what it was. One can measure the extent of his transformation by his reaction to this knowledge. "Coming as I did from the ports," the narrator says, "where so many men depend on the sky for survival, I knew this was an eclipse" (Saer 1990, 166). In this paragraph, the narrator still residually incarnates a position akin to the one held by an imperial ego: the cancellation of wonder. He knows about the phenomenon beforehand and finds in this anticipation a function of consolation and a feeling of safety. However, almost immediately he adds that this knowledge is just a hallway toward a deeper truth: "But knowing is not enough. True knowledge is recognizing that we know only that which condescends to reveal itself to us" (166–67). What or who "condescends to reveal itself to us"? Does this sentence refer to the world or to the other? In either case, one speaks about the sky as one would speak about the other. Is this just chance? Communication—as Levinas writes—overflows comprehension. This overflowing is presented in *The Witness* through the metaphoricity of celestial bodies. The moment of deepest comprehension comes along with the eclipse, that is, the cancellation of light. To reiterate a point I made earlier, this whole novel is framed by references to the sky, which marks its opening and its closing. The experience of the cosmos is itself an experience of infinity in which meaning necessarily exceeds comprehension. Levinas certainly had this sense of the sky in mind when he took the Cartesian notion of "infinity" to define the character of the social relationship. For that reason, the encounter with the other is also an encounter with the most high. Though this repetition could be a matter of chance, the same sky works as the oblique place of inscription of the moral law in Kant's practical reason.

But it could be argued that all this is just banal confusion over similar words. After all, Levinas's "infinity" and "most high" are intended as philosophical concepts, well beyond any seeing, well beyond any sky. Kant's inscription about the moral law of the soul reflecting the perfection of the stars is just a marginal (although final) comment, a poetic moment within the serious business called philosophy. Fiction must not be confused with reality or with the discourses whose business it is to address reality. Yet no otherness, not even the one that presents itself as the most high, can be recognized, much less respected, outside a language of appearance, beyond its quality of phenomena.[26] The most high must remain fairly close by. As for Kant, doesn't the moral imperative, the moment of command, have the structure of fiction (*als ob* / "as if")? And isn't it through metaphors, as Levinas notes, that we go "beyond the given" and enter a region quite different "from pure receptivity" (1996, 33)? It is with these motifs of the "high," "fiction," "chance," and the "oblique" in mind that I read the last paragraph of the book: "What came after that, what I call 'years' or 'my life,' was the sound of seas and cities, the beating of human hearts, whose current, like an age-old river that washes away the useless paraphernalia of the visible, deposited me in this white room, to write, hesitantly, by the light of some almost spent candles, of a chance encounter that was both among yet with the stars" (Saer 1990, 167). This passage talks about a defamiliarized world, about a facticity that does not relapse, as is so usual, into banality. It talks, overwhelmingly, about an encounter with the other and about the devastating effects of this encounter. Life is no longer life; speech has become an insistent murmuring. Yet the other is not mentioned even once in the paragraph. It is not encountered *as such*. It is merely alluded to in that "also" (*también*) that makes of the ellipsis the figure of the human. Perhaps there is no road to the other that does not pass through the stars. Such is the only actual encounter in the novel: *a chance encounter that was both among yet with the stars,* an encounter that, through metaphor or obliqueness, was taken away to somewhere else, and one that manages after all to constitute the whole horizon of the story. *Horizon* means both origin and end. *I write them in the name of those who are no longer with us,* the narrator says; I write in their place. The other is absent, the narration untimely. In this untimeliness, however, discourse achieves its essence as prayer.

In *The Writing of the Disaster*, Maurice Blanchot discusses the performative dimension of language in relationship to its "content":

> Among certain "primitive" peoples (those whose society knows no State), the chief must prove his dominion over words: silence is forbidden to him. Yet it is not required that anyone listen to him. Indeed, no one pays attention to the chief's word . . . and he, in fact, says nothing. . . . The discourse of the chief is empty precisely because he is separated from power. The chief must move in the element of the word, which is to say, at the opposite pole from violence. The chief's obligation to speak—that constant flow of empty speech (not empty, but traditional, sheer transmission) which he owes to the tribe—is the infinite debt which effectively rules out speaking man's ever becoming a man of power. (1986, 9)

Blanchot is careful to attribute this structure of a purely performative use of speech to stateless societies. In these societies, the process of subjection that has become "natural" to us is still incipient or perhaps absent. The chief "says nothing." His silence indicates his separation from power. The whole situation is understood in a Levinassean key that opposes speaking to war. In *Otherwise than Being*, Levinas confronts two dimensions of language: *said* and *saying*. Language qua *said* "can be conceived as a system of nouns identifying entities, and then as a system of signs doubling the beings, designating substances . . . in sum, designating" (1981, 51). Designation serves the imperial ego's "rigorous book-keeping" of existence. Nothing escapes the calculations of the essence, and everything returns to it in an economy that recognizes no loss. The *saying*, on the other hand, is pure generosity, which cannot be stored up in the expectation of a profit or return. It precedes the economic dimension of life and is the nonthematized opening to the other and to the world, through which speaking constitutes an intuition of sociality. How does this economy of *said* and *saying* play itself out in the horizon of the complex net of protocols that Walter Mignolo calls "colonial semiosis" (see "Colonial Semiosis," in Mignolo 1995)?[1]

A foundational story may provide the opportunity to place this structural Levinassean principle into some sort of historical perspective. In chapter 4 of his *Comentarios reales,* the Inca Garcilaso de la Vega relates the convoluted origin of the word *Peru.* In a scene that has the virtue of redressing all the motives pertaining to the colonial relation (event, wonder, cognition, recognition), Garcilaso tells the story of a group of conquistadores who, while exploring the coast of Peru, spot an Indian ashore. The Indian is fascinated by the Spanish vessel: "He was lost in amazement and stood astonished and bewildered, wondering what the thing he beheld on the sea before him could be" (1966, 15). His absorption facilitates the task of his captors, who decide to bring him on board the ship for further interrogation. Once the Indian is on the ship, the Spaniards "asked him by signs and words what land it was and what it was called. The Indian understood that they were asking him something from the gestures and grimaces they were making with hands and faces, as if they were addressing a dumb man, but he did not understand what they were asking, so he told them what he thought they wanted to know" (16). In line with the cognitive drive that characterizes the imperial enterprise, the Spaniards ask for the name of the land. The Indian, however, supplies a different answer. He replies "by giving his own name, saying, 'Berú' and adding another, 'pelú.'" Garcilaso explains, "He meant: 'if you're asking my name, I'm called *Berú,* and if you're asking where I was, I was in the river.'" The Christians, Garcilaso concludes, "understood what they wanted to understand" (16), and by an arbitrary corruption and conflation of the two words, they arrived at the name *Perú.*

As Garcilaso is quick to suggest, the Spaniards completely disregard the claim on recognition implied in the Indian's answer and assume that he has guessed their question and is providing the required information. Both

parties are equally misinformed about the subject of the exchange, yet sociality, as Levinas would put it, is actually established. But we cannot say
unproblematically that this intuition of sociality has left power behind.[2] It
is their desire to comprehend and compute the new land that makes the
Spaniards oblivious to the claim on recognition they receive from the Indian and drives them to understand his answer in purely cognitive terms.
Garcilaso's story tells us that language, even in this inaugural instance, in
which it breaks the ground of an encounter, is immediately encrypted into
the unevenness of the colonial relationship.

This small allegory of disavowal brings to mind Johannes Fabian's characterization of the ethnographic moment as based on a denial of coevalness.[3] For Fabian, "denial of coevalness" names a general structure of temporary displacement that "creates" the other in ethnographic thinking. The
differential time of the colonial event must be replicated in the structure
of discourse itself, because language is not alien to its construction but
consubstantial with it. The displacement that Fabian registers at the methodological level of the ethnographic exchange appears always already lin-
guistically codified in the colonial context. Roberto González Echevarría
notices, apropos of the Inca Garcilaso, that "writing in the Middle Ages and
the Renaissance . . . was not conceived as an activity whereby a naked consciousness, faced with a fresh empirical or spiritual phenomenon, expresses
its reaction *ex nihilo*. Writing was then an activity that took place within
a grid of strict rules and formulae which comprised what could loosely be
called rhetoric" (1990, 44). In this rhetoric, which the Andean mestizo Espinosa Medrano so lucidly termed a "logic," the relation of power-subjection
was patrimonial, meaning that a chain of personal allegiances tied even the
last subject to the king. One should not be deceived by the presence of heavy
bureaucracy. As Cornejo Polar observes, "The fact that the [colonial chron-
icles] almost unanimously appeal to the King, or to other instances of pen-
insular power, is a courtesan gesture, but also, more profoundly, it is a sign
of a system of communication that prevails in the chronicler's statements"
(2004, 106). The paradoxical effect was that the tone of the chronicles, even
within the bureaucratic machine, was that of a personal communication.
This structure explains the personal and testimonial inflection of so many
Creole and indigenous "memorandums." Outstanding among these is the

"Nueva Corónica" of Waman Poma de Ayala, in which Waman Poma addresses himself to the king.[4] In Spanish, the formula *dirigirse a* (to address) precedes written communications. (Waman Poma does not use this form, but the vocative is certainly present at the beginning of the letter.) *Dirigirse a* contains both a sense of direction and a sense of a message to be delivered. In *addressing* other people, the speaker reveals the dimension of facticity that overdetermines his or her communication and inscribes in the letter the singularity of his or her situation. The subject who addresses an other is constituted not in the abstract and reassuring universality of language, but in the vulnerability and opening of speech. But as the anecdotal origin of the word *Peru* teaches us, language as a field of exchange is even less open in a colonial situation than in others. Inside colonial semiosis, any exchange is subjected to the possibility of silence—no answer, no return. As a matter of fact, nobody read or answered Waman Poma's address—or almost nobody.[5] To reply would have meant to cross so many barriers, to fight so many denials of coevalness, that in the end it would have required the undoing of the specific protocol of subalternization encrypted in the colonial bureaucracy.

I do not confuse, as if disregarding Blanchot's warning, *saying* and the *said* or *writing* and the *written*. Rather, the question I want to advance is, what are the conditions for undoing the power relationship inscribed in language? Levinas points to the possibility of a desubstantivization of the said. If through the said, an imperial logos comes to replace a prereflective openness, it cannot do so without bearing the scar of a saying that is the very condition of possibility of its own existence. Waman Poma's manuscript, after all, was finally found and read: Richard Pietschmann found it in 1908 at the Royal Library in Copenhagen, and the French Americanist Paul Rivet published it almost thirty years later. But by the time it was found, the "ideality" of the work had changed. It was no longer a letter or a memorial. It was now, first and foremost, a piece of *literature,* coming from an age when literature itself was at its dawn. The change in ideality was not the work of aging, yet time did play its part: time separated Waman Poma's words from power.

A noticeable paradox appears right at the beginning of this story. Literature defines itself through distance from a constitutive power. Yet the nonrelationship of literature to power results not from a disengagement with the brutalness of reality but, quite the opposite, from a deeper engagement with the history of subjection. What we read today as literature are those colonial writings that were engendered by a desire to set the record straight. Without that desire, we would not have Waman Poma, Garcilaso de la Vega, Alva Ixtlilxochitl, or the wealth of mestizo and indigenous writings composing the archive of the encounter between the people of the New World and the ancient technique of writing. What we discover in these texts that we read, against every textual justification, as literature is that the deployment of the imperial ego does not exhaust the meaning of the colonial encounter. The epochal project of the interest of the essence is accompanied by a messianic dimension of justice. It is this messianic dimension that grounds our claim that these texts represent the past of Latin American literature.

On the other hand, the acritical extension of the concept of literature to any form of textuality is a process fraught with risks. The powerful concept of literature itself is to be blamed for this shortcoming. The prevalent ideology of the literary, based on its universal institutionalization, has the effect of hiding the nature of the literary. This ideology is operative whenever we claim that a pre-Cortesian song that came to us through the collecting action of Spanish friars, or a text that we artfully translated from codices or from an ancient wall, is in fact a piece of *literature*. In such cases, we boil literature down to a mere form and claim for it a universal validity, a virtually unlimited space of circulation.[6] In these instances, literature is envisioned as an enormously flexible tool for the translation of difference into a familiar language. At first, it may seem that this conception of literature as an intrinsically transculturative device sees in the literary form a sort of Noah's Ark that can contain and preserve undamaged all sort of messages and cultural peculiarities. The truth is, however, that the real assumption at work is the opposite: whatever message is able to transcend time and location is immediately endowed with a restrictive set of attributes. When we read in a literary fashion (and how many other fashions do we know of?), the act of reading does not take the form of a leap over an uncharted territory of otherness; it is, rather, an activity governed by a rule through which the reader finds in the text those categories already familiar to his or her own hermeneutical activity. The reasoning is insidious: literature is the properly *modern* Western form of uncontestable universality, and whatever particular wants to stake a claim to the universal can do so only by submitting beforehand to this appropriative grammar. All cultural objects become cultural objects *for us,* and their meaning is understood to be immanent to our intellectual disposition. In this sense, literature's attributes are not merely formal or culturally unspecific. Rather, they mirror a system of values and beliefs that we can sum up in two words: Western humanism.

The empowering of literature through its monumentalization undermines its real strength: its ability to manifest the dimension of the saying. How then to restore to writing the rights of instituting that the prevalent ideology of the written—as work of art or as document—has tended historically to eclipse? And how to do so in a context, such as colonial times, in which, strictly speaking, literature did not yet exist? The obvious strategy would be to locate an event that, although unable to maintain its autonomy, nonetheless points to this form of universalization that we have come to identify with the literary operation. I find such an event in the unintended expansion of alphabetic writing among indigenous people, which began already in the midyears of sixteenth-century Mesoamerica. I call the introduction of alphabetic literacy an event because it dramatically altered the system of cultural heritage (e.g., how communal knowledge was preserved and transmitted) and rearranged the rules of subjective production for a vast array of Indian communities. Central to my discussion is an exploration of how this epochal divide fractured historical memory and called into question the identity of the actors involved in the practice of writing and the identity of all the people their writings were said to represent. The relative popularization of writing added another shock of transformation to the rules of formation of personal and communal identity. It is not just that the introduction of the alphabetic script produced most of the knowledge that we possess about the vanquished people, but also that the very concept of "people" is closely tied to this formative event. In this sense, the introduction of alphabetic writing marks the beginning of an inaugural force of instituting to which we are still, like the chief of Blanchot's tribe, somewhat indebted.

Indigenous Literatures?

Gordon Brotherston has advanced perhaps the most extensive and cohesive argument for a sort of "natural" continuation (the sense of which is discussed later in this chapter) between our modern notion of literature and the many pre- and post-Columbian indigenous expressions codified in an enormous variety of "texts" that reached us through oral transmission, glyphs, chronicles, and inscriptions on monuments. In his essay "La visión americana de la conquista," Brotherston claims to seek to "delineate a concept of [pre- and post-Columbian] American indigenous literature able to correspond to the ubiquitous and all-powerful discourse brought to the continent by the conquistadors" (1993, 66). A similar assimilation of indigenous expressions to literature is also a trait of Brotherston's earlier book *Images of the New World.* There Brotherston describes "the literatures of the New World" as "texts in which the Indians . . . speak for themselves. As in most other literatures, many older traditional texts were originally oral compositions" (1979, 15). Later, this conception was amplified and widely documented in Brotherston's accomplished *Book of the Fourth World* (1992) and *Painted Books from Mexico* (1995). *Book of the Fourth World* classifies texts as diverse as "Watunna, Popol vuh, Dine bahane, Runa yndio and Auvy rapyta" as literature (1992, 39). If we pause and consider some of these examples, such as *Auvy rapyta,* some problems become immediately noticeable. León Cadogan, who compiled the series of texts representing ancient Guaraní lore and cosmology, never applied the label of *literature* to this corpus, but the editor of the latest edition, the Jesuit Bartolomeu Meliá, does so repeatedly (Meliá 2002, 9). As Cadogan's introduction to the volume makes clear, these texts represent a sacred corpus whose knowledge was meant to remain inside the boundaries of the community—that is, well beyond the universality that we ascribe to literature. On the other hand, the translation of the Guaraní text into Spanish—a process minutely discussed by Cadogan in his notes to the Guaraní version—at times takes on a "literary" modality that attests to the dominance of the literary register in the transtextual operation of interpreting alien cultures.

The critical attitude that perceives indigenous scripts and oral memories as pieces of literature reveals a truly democratic and progressive ethos in the researcher. But the democratic eagerness to reverse colonialism by asserting that the Indians *already possessed writing, already possessed literature,* promotes an interpretive schema that runs the risk of ignoring the specificities of cultural production. The position of the progressive researcher does not lack theoretical sophistication and critical insight. Few cultural analysts can be said to be more sensitive to the traps of a colonizing epistemology than Gordon Brotherston or Miguél León Portilla, two outstanding scholars who repeatedly identify indigenous expression with literary expression. Brotherston attempts to guard his field of studies from the temptations of unduly expanding Eurocentric categories, but the need to identify pre-Columbian expression with modern literature overrides this consideration. León Portilla explicitly warns about the risks of imposing alien categories on Nahua materials and, in *The Aztec Image of Self and Society,* declares his unease with translating the Nahuatl terms *Ihtoloca* (tradition) and *Xiuhamatl* (annals) into Spanish or English. However, this philological hesitation, interestingly, is absent when what is at stake is the application of the concept of *literature* to the indigenous productions (León Portilla 1992, 39). The image of literature as a merely translative device runs deep in this scholarship. The following quote, taken from *La filosofía Nahuatl estudiada en sus fuentes,* cannot but leave us wondering about the real limits of our ability to self-police our linguistic tools: "True Nahua poetry manifests a unique path of knowledge that is the result of an authentic interior experience. In other words, it is the result of an intuition. Poetry becomes then a veiled expression that, armed with the wings of metaphor and symbol, allows man to express that mystery he has just been able to perceive" (León Portilla 1966, 143–44).

The defense of an all-encompassing (universal) humanism goes on even at the risk of flagrant contradictions in the argument. If coherence in contradiction always reveals the force of a desire, what desire is here at stake? And how is this desire connected to the emancipatory impulse, to the democratic eagerness that grounds, historically and existentially, the activity of these scholars? The main epistemological service that the extension of the concept of literature to indigenous productions makes is the positing of a will, a subject, or at any rate an identity in the text that is incorporated, via literaturization, into the general flow of universal transmissibility. This is the reason that "voice" appears as the fundamental category that organizes the entry of alternative forms of worlding into the body of literature. León Portilla writes (somewhat surprisingly) that the *transvase* of codices into the alphabetic script "silenced orality" (1996, 14). But how can the alphabetic script, phonemic in its structure, silence an orality that was hardly present in a hieroglyphic tradition? Even the Maya script—the one that, according to León Portilla, approached "writing proper"—did not possess many means to reproduce orality (León Portilla 1996, 121).[7] Except, of course, that we think that the voice at stake here is not the mundane voice recorded in the text, the one that emerges in its deictic structure, but rather a transcendental element inseparable from the cultural identity conveyed by the text. In this case, *voice* or *word* is a sign that refers to an element able to transcend the trauma of death and desolation that breaks in two the historical time of preconquest and postconquest indigenous identity. This "voice" is less a mundane attribute than the element that comes to figure the essence of an indigenous expression as *spirit*. The problem with this equation between voice and identity is not that voice is not a proper subject of inquiry. On the contrary, few concepts are more vital to an understanding of Latin American literature and its tradition. The trouble is that, insofar as the concept of voice appears identified and exhausted in an ideal indigenous identity, the result is a voice without the voice. *Voice* appears in these texts as a transcendental concept, and like any transcendental, it carries with it a certain skepticism about the rights of the actual.

The metaphysics of the voice combines with the pervasive dominance of literature in transcultural translation to lead to a rather surprising assertion: that not only the ancient tales of the indigenous people but also the pictographic productions of Mesoamerican cultures—the famous pre- and post-Cortesian codices stored today in different museums around the world—are to be considered forerunners of our contemporary idea of Latin American literature. The obvious incommensurability between the literary form and the different pre-Columbian traditions of record keeping does not trouble this equation. This incommensurability refers to the fact that the retransmission of indigenous lore through pictograms and other forms implied processes such as memorization, alternative genres, schooling in particular competences, and interpretation through the existence of a special caste of "intellectuals" devoted to the lore's transmission (all elements that enter into literature only indirectly and in a veiled form, as with all cultural products in the age of commodities). As James Lockhart observes, the Nahua tradition of record keeping was not formal in nature, but instead "part of a larger communication system from which we cannot separate it without great loss of insight" (1992, 378).

Recent scholarship has been persistent in revisiting some problematic assumptions about the defining characteristics of a writing system, and above all its relationship to voice and speech. In the Western tradition, which is dominated by phonetic script, writing is always understood as the transposition of speech. Writing is conceived of, in Elizabeth Hill Boone's words, as "visible speech," and this presupposition is transposed rather acritically to the study of other scripts—such as the one prevalent in Mesoamerica before the arrival of the Spaniards, which attests to an altogether different relationship among culture, inscription, and subjectivity (see Hill Boone 1994).[8] For Hill Boone, the main obstacles to an accurate comprehension of the role of writing in the early colonial world are in fact our many "ethnocentric" preconceptions about the relationships among the different components involved in the act of communication through writing. Conceiving the codices as literature (and not just as writing) further expands the risks of ethnocentric misreading. My concern, however, is not philological in nature: I am above all preoccupied with the relationship between text and subjectivity. In this sense, it seems fair to say that the subjectifying effects of the cryptograms appear to be incommensurable with the ones that we find in the literary text, dominated as the latter is by a subjectivist ideology that makes consciousness and the self the building blocks of the literary form.

Conceiving of indigenous productions as literature was a good solution in the face of political necessity. But a political gain in one quarter can readily become a deficit in another. Fixing our eyes on the essential continuity of a culture entails a certain blindness. Such a blindness may lead to a concealment of the ways in which a culture not only persists in the face of genocide but also finds in new and unthought articulations the means of its reinvention. One such instance of reinvention—an instance that is, moreover, critical for the genealogy in whose name the colonial literature of Latin

America becomes literature at all—is the expansion of alphabetic writing in the early sixteenth century.[9] This expansion of literacy implied a confrontation and negotiation with colonial power, and the force sustaining that confrontation was a permanent object of desire for the institutional development of the literary canon. The Promethean act of stealing writing is an event constantly reduced by a culturalist ideology that favors a metaphysical sense of identity above the realities of change and survival. Writing, we are told, is a technique like any other, just a means for conveying an essentially unchangeable meaning via a surface that is always exterior to that meaning. In opposition to this belief, I argue that because of a conjunction of fortuitous and structural factors (i.e., because of a historical causality), the adoption of alphabetic writing among many indigenous communities marks a deep breach in the severe logic of colonial rule. Its meaning does not exhaust itself in the function of carrying over an endangered lore into our days. If this had been writing's only function in the colonial past, this past would perhaps never have reached us in the present.

Writing as Power

In *Pre-Columbian Literatures of Mexico,* León Portilla offers an unambiguous idea of the promise that literature brings to the terrain of cultural hermeneutics: "There is probably no more eloquent picture of the inner and outer life of any culture than its literary production. In the case of ancient cultures, if a literary legacy remains, it serves as key to a deeper understanding of the past" (1969, 3). Reading in such a heavily hermeneutic way has the inconvenience of making too much of the message while inviting us to lose sight of the dense materiality, symbolic import, and ceremonial weight that surrounded the act of writing in the centuries before the popularization of the press. In the colonial past, writing was an event, and so was reading. But writing was above all, as Angel Rama reminds us in *The Lettered City,* an event of power.

Specific attention to the strictures writing brought into the organization of the colonial world has largely been the province of historians and ethnographers, all professionals less prone to share (but by no means free of) the tendency to make any form of indigenous expression a variant of art or literature. A case in point is Joanne Rappaport's reflection on the inextricable relationship between literacy and colonialism in the Andes. While she acknowledges that "alphabetic literacy exerted a considerable influence in the reconstruction of a native Andean world view," Rappaport adds that "the written word was also instrumental in erasing the past as indigenous people had remembered it" (1994, 271). Rappaport points to a double effect of phoneticism. On the one hand, literacy disrupts old forms of organizing the transmission of cultural information; on the other, it is instrumental in the creation of previously unknown forms of political subjection. As Rappaport observes, it is a historical fact that the implementation of literacy among the native elites was supplemented by the systematic destruction of indigenous forms of record keeping and communication. However, rather curiously, the colonizers spared the *quipu* for a while. Rappaport cites Tom Cummins on the strange survival of the Andean *quipu* well into the sixteenth century. For Cummins, Rappaport notes, "the incommensurability between the form of the *quipu* and European forms of memory meant that the *quipu* was not immediately the object of early campaigns of destruction as were the 'books' of Mexico that were burned.... It is only after the threat posed by the Taqui Onkoy movement in the 1560's and the subsequent concern with Andean memory as addressed in the Third Lima Church Council (1582) that the *quipu* came under the destructive power of Spanish surveillance" (1994, 194). Although Cummins correctly points to the conqueror's zeal to destroy indigenous forms of memory, his reflection on the incommensurability between the *quipu* and the alphabetic form of writing brings to mind a similar incommensurability between the *quipu* and the many Mesoamerican pictographic forms, an incommensurability that may help to explain the somewhat divergent destiny of the traditions.

As is well-known, the encounter between the European book and the local population followed a different path in the Andes and among the Maya and other Mesoamerican cultures.[10] As famously recounted first by Francisco de Jerez and later by Waman Poma de Ayala, the Inca ruler Atahualpa was baffled by the object "book" when he was presented with one at Cajamarca.[11] On the other hand, in Mesoamerica, as Pedro Martir de Anglería recounts in *Décadas del nuevo mundo*, indigenous people were not particularly impressed by the fact that Europeans had books, since they themselves possessed similar objects. James Lockhart points out that one of the best indications of the familiarity of Mesoamerican culture with the form "book" is that the introduction of the Spanish alphabet did not imply the usual phenomenon of linguistic borrowing to name the "new" concept. The indigenous words for paper (*amatl*) and ink (*tlilli*) remained "in use in post-conquest Nahuatl and were applied to the Spanish variants, precluding the adoption of the relevant Spanish vocabulary" (Lockhart 1992, 2).

This preexistence of an indigenous tradition of writing explains to some extent the important dynamism that characterized the deployment of alphabetic literacy in Mesoamerica in the early years of the sixteenth century. After mounting the new imperial state on the facilities provided by the vanquished empires, Spaniards retrained indigenous *tlacuilos* as colonial scribes. The idea was to provide the colonial bureaucracy with minor functionaries, while simultaneously using literacy as a caste privilege that might facilitate the political goal of containing the indigenous noble class.[12] But writing was popularized beyond the frontiers of the noble class, and a body of alphabetic texts in Nahuatl, whose grammatical norm differed from that taught at the colonial schools attended by the surviving Mesoamerican nobility, had irrupted at different points of the Mexican geography by the first decades of the sixteenth century.[13] By 1570 or even earlier, writes Lockhart, "the smallest *altepetl* had a new-style notary or two attached to *cabildo* and church, and in the larger centers there was a whole corps of such figures," as well as a number of laymen "able to write in Roman letters" (1992, 330). As a matter of fact, already by the middle of the sixteenth century, some documents had appeared that "give the impression of having been written not by the professional or near professional notaries, church employees, and *altepetl* officials who were responsible for annals, songs, plays, and mundane documentation, but by amateurs" (Lockhart 1992, 413).

The relative popularization of alphabetic writing in sixteenth-century Mesoamerica (especially in the center of Mexico) and the uses that many indigenous people made of the new technique illustrate Joanne Rappaport's observation that writing is an ambiguous and unreliable medium of cultural domination. As Rappaport observes, although writing was a tool for the colonial administration of the Americas, the practice of writing by indigenous actors also cemented "native authority" in a way that was particularly troublesome for the Spaniards, since "they themselves recognized the tremendous force of authority that the written word wielded within their own system" (1994, 278). In the case of Mesoamerica, the appropriation of the alphabetic script is even linked to the reemergence of a cryptographic tradition. As the phonetic script extended its influence, an important body of texts emerged that combined the new script with the traditional glyphs and logographic elements proper of the preconquest tradition. It appears that far from subsuming indigenous forms of record keeping, as seemed to be the case in the Andes, alphabetic writing revived and legitimized the old cryptograms. Lockhart comments on the Codex Osuna, a petition and complaint received from the *cabildo* of Tenochtlan by Spanish authorities in 1565 that required "extensive supplementary oral communication to convey the overall message" (1992, 346). ("Codex Osuna" was not itself a primordial title, although its content did concern a land dispute.) This revival seems to suggest that their incommensurability with alphabetic writing, which helped to preserve the *quipu* in the first decades of colonial rule, may actually have accelerated their later disappearance. There is no doubt that, as Cummins points out, writing—even writing in Nahuatl and postconquest cryptographic writing—deepened the colonial grip over indigenous communities. The prestige of many "caciques" and the very survival of the "Republic of Indians" hinged on their capacity to comply with the taxation imposed by the Spaniards and to comprehend the complex Spanish legal system, both goals implying proficiency in the use of written language and its communicative protocols. But on the other hand, it is equally true that alphabetic writing introduced a form of domination that is not reducible to a clean distinction between colonizer and colonized. The symbolic economy of colonialism itself is disturbed by this event. The expansion of literacy took place (at least at its beginning) among indigenous intellectuals familiar with aboriginal forms of inscription, forms characterized as being highly mediated, ritualistic in nature, and involving a clear correspondence between writing and a particular region of the cultural being of society. Alphabetic writing introduced an upheaval that transformed the world (becoming an object of communication as a whole) and the subject (now exposed to writing as a form of self-affection, the continuity between *my* speech and *my* writing), even while it cleared a horizon of meaning under the figure of an unfathomable reader.

Perhaps the single most important consequence of the extragovernmental expansion of writing lies in the promotion of the figure of the reader. Of course, all texts and all forms of inscription imply the reader. But the peculiarities attached to alphabetic literacy draw a figure of the reader that is particularly salient for the constitution of a new political subjectivity. Many colonial texts are traversed by the conviction that alphabetic writing opens a realm of transcendence for its authors. It is in relationship to this realm that we see the regular, predictable emergence of an addressee that is no longer the colonial state. It is not only that, as Rappaport puts it, "alphabetic literacy exerted a considerable influence in the reconstruction of native . . . world view and historical memory"; if one pays attention to the anonymous author that Rappaport invokes as an example of the problematic of literacy in the Andes, it also becomes plain that alphabetic writing brings about changes that affect, in the last instance, the concept of "life" itself: "If the ancestors of the people called Indians had known writing in earlier times, then the *lives* they *lived* would not have faded from view until now" (Rappaport 1994, 271; my emphasis).

It may be objected that existential transcendence through writing or oral composition was already a feature of the Mesoamerican world well before the conquest. Angel María Garibay, in his *Historia de la literatura Náhuatl,* quotes a song that proclaims, "I am a poet, my songs will live on earth / through songs, my servants will remember me" (1971, 96). But this song, like many that have been collected from Maya and Aztec sources, is bound to the particular, to a prefixed path of expansion, a foreseeable orbit that the message, like a celestial object, is doomed to complete. We can contrast this song to a will quoted by Enrique Florescano that was written by a barely schooled mestizo: "I write this my will [testamento] and title [título], which contains the truth before God. And I write this *relación* which should never be erased. I, Alonso Pérez, for you, my sons and my grandsons, so that from now till the end of time this relation will not be lost" (2002, 22). Although the message has an explicit addressee, it also opens to a futurity that the author naively holds valid till the end of time. It is precisely the receding space ciphered in the expression "end of time" that claims our attention. We are inscribed in it and, actually, already subsumed in its infinitizing movement.

The Classical Genres of the Colonial Transition: Annals and Primordial Titles

The "popularization" of alphabetic literacy further split the traumatic identity of the indigenous people who survived the cataclysm of conquest. On the one hand, writing served to perpetuate some traditional forms of coding memory and experience; on the other, it began to function mainly as an instrument in the adaptation of indigenous people to the symbolic and legal world of the colonizers. A practical consequence of this coexistence of aims is that the memory of the indigenous past is not free of the contaminating effect of the alien code, while at the same time the structures of colonial subjection that the new coding sought to impose (the specific form of subjection attached to writing as a protocol of power) are not free of the many interferences brought about by the sublation of the colonized cultural past in the dominant language of the time. These exchanges did not take place in a historical vacuum but were themselves "coded" and negotiated in the space of well-established genres.[14] The issue of genres is crucial because not only does it introduce the question of a vast and complex ethnography of writing, but it also comes to weigh on the issue of the disappearance or survival of cryptographic forms of record keeping. James Lockhart observes that the use of pictographic expression in the postconquest era was far more likely in those cases in which there existed preconquest forms that corresponded to the Spanish forms in which the cryptogram would now be embroidered (e.g., tributes, cadastral registers). Especially noticeable is the fact that cryptographic writing is largely absent in the case of new forms that seem to have thematic affinities with preconquest genres but that are actually tied to the emergence of new social relations, as in the case of wills.

Among all the indigenous genres, annals are unanimously considered the most prestigious form of Nahuatl expression in the preconquest tradition and represent a properly historical genre. Nahua culture was careful to record different events under specific years, counted according to the indigenous calendar. As a norm, the year would provide both the heading and the principle unifying a particular cluster of information. The year-chapter, Lockhart explains, includes "a miscellany of distinct topics having in common only the fact of having occurred in the same year" (1992, 377). Perhaps it was the great prestige enjoyed by this form that endowed it with an afterlife in the writings of indigenous and mestizo authors who flourished in the first 150 years of colonial Mexico. As Lockhart points out, a colonial chronicler like Domingo Chimalpahin follows the "organizational norm" of the annals "to the letter" (1992, 387).

Domingo Chimalpahin authored the *Relaciones,* an impressive historical account of the Nahuas, based on his consultation of ancient books (*amoxitl*), that stretched from 1063 to 1520—until just a few years before the onset of the terrible Spanish persecution and destruction of indigenous forms of record keeping that would last until 1540. He also wrote, in a different style, a more vivid account of the life of Mexico City under colonial rule, under the title *Diaro.* (Chimalpahin did not provide titles for these pieces, a practice common to Spaniards but alien to the indigenous tradition.) In the *Diaro,* as in the *Relaciones* (eight in number), each discrete entry is arranged either by year or by specific date. However, Chimalpahin's text cannot be conceived as representing some kind of pure endurance of indigenous traits; rather, it is a vast attempt to translate the whole history of a region from the language and logic of the codices to alphabetic Nahuatl. In light of the immediate development of the indigenous and mestizo chronicle, it is difficult not to see the *Relaciones* as an act of mourning, a last gasp of the vanishing breath of the pre-Columbian spirit. Although the encroachment of Spanish elements (like the use of the Western calendar) is already visible in the *Relaciones,* the tradition of the annals enters into a sharp decline from this point. Fernando Alvarado Tezozómoc, a personal friend of Chimalpahin, wrote the *Crónica Mexicáyotl* in Nahuatl around 1609 and, immediately after, penned the *Crónica Mexicana* in Spanish. In the latter, only the superficial organizational elements of the annals are present. The text reproduces the Spaniards' secularized notion of time; Mesoamerican time, on the other hand, is highly ritualistic: quite often preconquest indigenous authors superimposed great events in the history of the state and its leading figures upon the cycle of events related in mythological tales.[15] In this sense, a text like Muñoz Camargo's *Historia de Tlaxcala* belongs almost completely to the historical imagination of the Spanish canon. Its scattered indigenous elements are mostly cosmetic and unable to connect the narration with the previous vitality of the indigenous cosmogony.

Chimalpahin is a special figure in this canon. Like Garcilaso, he incarnates the figure of the informed translator of the indigenous past, to which Chimalpahin adds both the philological edge of fluency in Spanish and Nahuatl and the ability to read the old cryptograms. It is perhaps meaningful that the double system of Chimalpahin's allegiances wells up in his use of the calendar—which, as noted earlier, acts as the centerpiece of pre-Columbian conception, to which all narration was directly or indirectly subjected. At many points Chimalpahin gives the opening date in both the Nahuatl and the Christian calendars: "7 Calli, 1577" (1965, 25). The *Segunda relación* even dates the birth and death of Christ as 4 Calli and 10 Calli. The ideological world presented here is also hybrid. Although Chimalpahin writes mostly as an acculturated mestizo, he does not deprive himself of the right to speak for his people; although he wrote the *Diaro* in Nahuatl, he uses and quotes Spanish sources, literally transposing them into the indigenous language, using a grafting procedure quite common among early mestizo chroniclers.[16] Thus, the *Diaro* resembles the Bakhtinian definition of the novel as an all-encompassing container able to harbor the most diverse discourses, although it "lacks," to some extent, the unifying function of the author who conjugates, in the case of the novel, such variety into a single worldview.

But perhaps the most notorious element of Chimalpahin's text is the acute sense of actuality that, not coincidentally, emerges tied to the possibilities afforded by the deictic system of the alphabetical script. The annals were meant to preserve a past whose history was, in the case of Mesoamerica, closely knitted with that of the nobility. (Chimalpahin wrote his *Relaciones* at the request of a noble claiming land tenure in the Chalco-Amaquemecan region.) However, this text that is to some extent without author bears a subjective mark that can even claim to be the spokesperson for a whole community. The historical situation of the annals in Chimalpahin's time resembles the notion of history that Michel Foucault saw as prevalent in the West roughly from the emergence of Roman hegemony to the end of the sixteenth century. In "Society Must Be Defended," Foucault quotes Petrarch's complaint, "Is there nothing more to history than the praise of Rome?" (2003, 74), to characterize the limitations of this form of historical awareness. For Foucault, the end of history as endless praise of Rome only comes about through a counterhistory that slowly develops through the sixteenth and seventeenth centuries. History as the eternal praise of Rome is always "the history of sovereignty" (Foucault 2003, 68). The history that comes to replace the history of the sovereign is the history of nationalist race struggle. This counterdiscourse enumerates "not so much victories, as the defeats to which we have to submit during our long wait for the promised land and the fulfillment of the old promises that will of course reestablish both the rights of old and the glory that has been lost" (Foucault 2003, 71). The Mesoamerican annals were also created for the praise of monarchs, but something akin to a counterhistory emerges in Chimalpahin's and other chroniclers' conviction that the annals should make room for criticism of the mighty. It is significant that this criticism should appear as an exercise of a form of history whose deictic system clearly tells us that the voice and presence of the narrator are at stake: "Eighty-four years have gone by since, in the year 7 Calli, 1525, Señor Don Hernando Cuahutemoctizn died. They hung him from a Ceiba, along with Don Pedro Tetlepanquetzaztin, *tlatohuani* of Tlacopan. They were condemned by a false accusation, and the person who sentenced them to death was the Marquis Hernando Cortés" (1965, 167).

The articulation of the rights of the indigenous communities and the inscription of their political will are, however, missions accomplished not through the prestigious annals but through a much more humble textual production, so humble that even today it has scarcely attracted the attention of scholars and commentators.

The Primordial Titles

The primordial titles represent a genre directly tied to the popularization of alphabetic writing and one that exploits to its furthest limits the political possibilities opened by literacy. As a matter of fact, it is to these titles that we owe what Serge Gruzinski calls the "passion for writing" that seems to have swept central Mexico in the sixteenth and seventeenth centuries. The different authors who have written about the titles suggest that the vitality of this form traverses almost three hundred years of colonial history, finding perhaps its pinnacle in the seventeenth century.[17] The properness of the term *title* for this corpus is often disputed. There is also disagreement about which texts this characterization includes.

The primordial titles present similar features, despite their vast geographical extension and the diverse historical conditions under which they were composed. The Mexican historian Enrique Florescano describes the titles as "documents that try to legitimate the (indigenous) rights over land through its detailed description" (2002, 185).[18] James Lockhart sees them as documents "cast at least partly in the first person" in which "an elder speaks to the young and future generations with essential information on the *alte-petl* and advice on how to preserve it" (1992, 415). Finally, Serge Gruzinski describes the titles as "anonymous documents" recording "the borders of a territory [and] urging the local Indians to defend them with determination" (1993, 98).

Although "discovered" in the nineteenth century, the titles have only recently attracted the attention of scholars of the colonial period. The earlier lack of interest was perhaps a result of the way in which these texts differ from the Western notion of "document." As Florescano observes, the social condition for the emergence of the titles lies in the pressure exerted on indigenous communities by the Spanish legal system to substantiate indigenous claims to land possession. Confronted by this pressure, the newly formed "pueblos" turned "to their paintings and maps as the basis for their juridical claims" (Florescano 2002, 206). As I noted earlier, the primordial titles are linked to the reawakening of the old cryptographic tradition, as many titles borrow their organizational schema from the ancient scrolls. Sometimes communities resorted to paintings that were made for purposes other than litigation and that, as a consequence, paid little attention to specific landmarks or limits, but Mesoamerican people considered these paintings suitable for further improvement. Maps were made more precise or simply redrawn. Drawings were added to even the most ancient *lienzos*.

Florescano refers to the *Códice Colombino*, which was presented in court in 1717, as "showing the addition of numerous glosses that were in no way related to the original document" (2002, 207). Unadulterated authenticity, then, was not a defining textual criterion for the communities, and forgery was not unusual. Florescano makes the point that many titles purport to be older than they really are (2002, 194), and Lockhart observes that the popularity and utility of the titles were so vast that they made profitable the establishment of "a factory or studio for false titles, where towns in need could have a document made to order, complete with pictures in a pseudo-sixteenth-century style, indigenous-style paper, and a final smoking to give the appearance of age" (1992, 414).

Although land titles and similar texts appeared in the Mexican geography for a span of almost three centuries, it was only after 1650 that the titles became widespread. After the great epidemics of the mid-sixteenth century, there was strong pressure to regroup the remnants of indigenous groups in individualized pueblos. This process, indeed, had begun much earlier. From 1530 on, in the context of the political confrontation between the Iglesia Indiana and the Spanish authorities in America, colonial authorities encouraged the creation of the Republic of Indians, self-governed communities that would gather different indigenous people within a single pueblo. But the pueblos that led the titles to flourish had a much looser connection to the indigenous past than did the primitive Republic of Indians. These new communal arrangements, having been formed by contingents of indigenous populations decimated by the plagues that had wiped out entire regions of Mexico, may well have been characterized by a sense of bare survival. The new groupings of people of different ethnic, cultural, and linguistic backgrounds were based on a system of territorial allegiances that was relatively alien to the indigenous tradition of ethnic identification. These conditions, then, strongly affected the composition of the titles, which are simultaneously an assertion of the present strength of the community and a usually failed attempt to ground this strength in a common history and tradition that is more guessed than known. "Toward the second half of the eighteenth century," Enrique Florescano writes in *Memoria Mexicana*, "the vast majority of Indian people living in the pueb-

los had already lost the sense of belonging to a larger ethnic community"
(1994, 362). As a consequence, by the end of the eighteenth century, the
vast majority of pueblos also "lacked any articulated tale able to link the
present to the indigenous past" (Florescano 2002, 363).

In this context, the titles came to play an important role in the construction of a social and political identity that was still Indian, although bearing all the marks of an intense confrontation with the strictures of colonial
power. Its fundamental gesture, then, was one not only of rememoration but
also of the pragmatic construction of an indigenous identity. In the context
of a massive lack of connection with the past, the emergence of the primordial titles represent, despite their monotone and repetitive character, a major creative act. As a rule, the titles attempt to ground the community in a
past that, although populated by historical figures, is clearly mythical. The
fact that the authors of the titles seem to ignore that the pueblos they seek
to defend did not exist at the outset of the Spanish colonization (their foundation is usually referred as immemorial) reveals the deep historical fracture that presides over the production of these texts. This fracture, with
its historical references that are transformed into quasi-mythical figures of
authority, makes it difficult to accept, as recently argued by Paula López
Caballero, that the titles are a result of the collection of an oral lore (2003,
9–81). It seems, rather, that the titles depend on a strategic calculation that
orders the selection of references, the modalities of textual authority, and
the system of historical appellation.

One's view of the titles' origin (ethnic continuity through oral tradition
or sheer act of self-invention) affects the role one attributes to them. I am
interested in underlining the pragmatic and extratextual dimension of
these texts. In other words, I am interested not so much in what the titles
say (they are boring documents for the literary critic) but in what they *do*
through that saying. It seems to me that a primary, notable aspect of the
titles lies in the multiple instances of representation opened by their existence. The message directed to the colonial authorities is always, simultaneously, a message addressed to the community for which the titles acted as
an instance of self-knowledge and self-identification. The titles represented
the communities not only to the colonial state but also to the communities themselves. Lockhart remarks that the titles were "prepared by local

figures primarily for a local audience," and they often include not only general information on the *altepetl* but also "versions of the first foundation of the town, the coming of the Spaniards, and the establishment of Christianity" (1991, 44). Simultaneously, their communicative arrangement points beyond the colonial circulation of messages, producing a third "reader" that, despite its anonymity, manages to affect the textual being of these documents.

It is above all the third reader, neither community nor state, merely formal and absent, that summons our attention. This addressee is inscribed in the formal properties of written alphabetic language. Its figure belongs to a vaguer community of interpreters, whose location outside the strictures of colonial legality is evident in the fact that many titles were written not in the original language of the *altepetl* but in Nahuatl, which thus comes to be understood as a vehicular language. At this point, it is apposite to recall Gruzinski's distinction between two ways of exerting memory in postconquest Mesoamerica. One, which reenacts the sense of history as eternal praise of Rome, is the memory of the noble class, a memory attached to a lost world and inexhaustible mourning. The other is the memory of the pueblos, the memory conveyed by the primordial titles, a memory that thrived in the construction of culture as a tool for social survival. With the titles appears not only a new articulation of the communities as subject of history but a renovated form of memory for this subject itself. Like the chronicle of the chronicler, which uses the present to pass judgment on an injured past, the textual being of the titles cannot be exhausted by their dimension of record keeping, or more plainly, of "keeping." They further possess a foundational value that, in the cultural and linguistic terms of interest here, is also an instituting value. What, then, do they institute? The community, of course, but insofar as this institution occurs in the dimension of the letter, it is a community bound only by the letter itself.

The letter stakes out a territory, but this territory exceeds the geographical boundaries of the pueblo. Unlike the pre-Columbian relationship between writing and community, here the former is not the representative of the latter, but a principle of organization. "Whoever you are," reads one of the titles quoted by Serge Gruzinski, "if you know how to read and write, you will discern the reasons of the elders that are inscribed here" (1993,

100). The voice of the elders concerns whatever reader in whatever time. But in the same movement, a whole system of hermeneutical authority—whether indigenous or colonial—is dismissed. The use of the conditional ("if you know how to read and write") marks on the one hand a departure from a sacralized form of reading, while on the other hand, it *performs* a form of universality negated at the level of the colonial protocols of discursive exchange. Like every construction of a social identity, this step implies the formation of a new political consciousness, one that, while active at regional levels, was also able to transcend the local and point to an encounter with colonial rule in its totality, no matter how deficient its mapping of the social might have been. Commenting on this subjectifying role of the primordial titles, Lockhart goes so far as to label them a form of "popular culture." For Lockhart, although the titles helped to preserve invaluable elements of the preconquest heritage of pictographic writings, there is also an important sense in which they constitute a first and primordial *American* expression.[19] Whether or not one regards the titles as an American expression or the first spark of popular culture, it is clear that their importance in the web of colonial textuality lies not in what they meant for the colonial authorities but in what they meant for the communities. This meaning is not hermeneutical in nature, but practical. In other words, it is a meaning fixed less in the semantic attributes of the composition than in the performative, pragmatic dimension of their existence.

This performative dimension holds a complex relation to the past cultural identity of the pueblos. The production of the titles, not just their reading, introduces new communicative protocols. They made possible the emergence of a new set of indigenous intellectuals no longer subject to the traditional forms of social reproduction, but rather "created" by the forms of address made possible by the introduction of alphabetic writing in the vernacular. Behind this writing, one can half glimpse the presence of many go-betweens, inhabitants of the pueblo used to dealing commercially with the Spanish bourgeoisie. This new way of speaking also created a new way of listening and a new horizon of understanding that affected even textual composition. The difference with the indigenous tradition ciphered in the codices is both historical and structural. The subjective constitution of a political identity through the universalizing effects of the letter was not a process available in the pre-Columbian world of cryptographic expression.[20] It is true that the word *tonalámatl,* as the book recording the laws regulating the relationship between men and gods was called, means "papers that concern everyone" (from *tonali,* "that which concerns everyone," and *amatl,* "paper"). However, such works concerned everyone not because everyone was called by them, but only because everyone was counted (in a cosmogonic arrangement) in their pages. The very system of writing varied according to social demands or genre specifications, to the point that Lockhart even calls for a cautious use of the expression "writing" in our approach to the codices. This larger communicative system operated primordially at the level of reading as a form of social control of the meaning of the originals. Universality was given only relatively, only to be taken immediately away. The *calmecac,* the wise men in charge of preserving the codices, were indistinguishably called "the owners of the books of painting" and "the knowers of hidden things" (Gruzinski 1993, 9).[21]

The primordial titles engaged the colonial administration on the very terrain of the colonial protocols of communication. They did so by exploiting the virtues of writing beyond the constrictions of the formal rules of colonial semiosis, a semiosis that established very clearly who could speak (write) to whom and in what capacity. In that sense, the titles' mere existence attests to a politico-epistemological achievement of enormous proportions.[22] Despite the ingenuity of these operations, the titles attest above all to the struggle of subalternized people to validate their claims in a hegemonic language. The conditions of their composition could not but load them with contradictions. Lockhart quotes at length a title produced in 1699 by indigenous officials from Soyatzingo. This title displays little regard for historical accuracy (Cortés and Viceroy Luis Velasco are amalgamated into a single person and referred to as Cortés don Luis de Velázco Marqués), and the protocols of Spanish communication are followed only loosely. As Lockhart observes, such confusion reveals a certain remoteness of the authors from the cultural world of the conquistadores, a problem that certainly would never have confronted chroniclers such as Tezozómoc, Chimalpahin, and Garcilaso.

The system of possibilities that the titles exploited is inscribed in language and in the alphabetic script, but nothing guarantees that this potentiality will actualize itself in the world. There were other destinies for the written word in the colonial period. One of them was its totemic reduction to mere object, a view that is powerfully rendered in Rosario Castellanos's *Oficio de tinieblas,* a novel in which an indigenous tribe rambles through the wilderness preserving and holding sacred a bunch of papers they cannot read or understand and that are, moreover, the opposite of a promise of deliverance. The lettered tradition has also one-sidedly insisted on the inability of the indigenous popular strata of the colonial and postcolonial periods to entertain a "true" relationship with the written word. General Arroyo's discovery of the primordial titles in Carlos Fuentes's *Old Gringo* and the intellectual gringo's later dismissal of the papers as "meaningless" are among many examples of such reduction of the commerce between writing and the popular to the dimension of imaginary, deceitful, and quasi-magical interaction. In *La voz y su huella,* Martin Lienhard writes that different indigenous authors "seem to conceive of the written as possessing an immanent efficacy, independent of the political apparatus that guarantees this efficacy" (1991, 11). But isn't this fetishism of the written also characteristic of the colonizer's worldview? For the colonizers, too, the written word was a thing, an object to be cherished and revered, as Angel Rama illustrates in several passages of *Lettered City.* Finally, symbolized forms of identification are ideological and political weapons as powerful as any other kind. In a certain sense, the titles' expediency cannot be separated from this reification of communication and from the pragmatic dimension of creating that gave them a meaning that was not easily absorbed by the colonial rules of semiotic exchange.

A final comment is due on the uncanny fact that the kingdom of the letter as the arrival of modernity seems to be in my account an indigenous rather than a European event. What happens in the realm of colonial rule in regard to this unstoppable rise of the logic of the letter? The crown and the colonial authorities felt themselves threatened by this development, and it is at least ironic that the moment of the communities' intense use of the technology of writing to ground their claims and build their cultural identity should coincide with the eclipse of the Spanish chronicle. As the colonial state expanded its grip over the American territory, the crown became less and less tolerant of nonauthorized versions of the colonial societies and their people. The eventual creation of the position of *crónista y cosmógrafo de Indias* promoted a caste of scribes obsessed with pleasing the political authorities and policing the philological accuracy of a mountain of documents that would remain unpublished for centuries.

Letter and Enunciation

Because pre-Columbian record keeping was not conceived as holding a direct representational relationship with spoken language, the paradoxical path taken by Nahua alphabetic writing in relationship to the reproduction of orality is all the more noticeable. Lockhart and other authors find in Nahua texts an insistence on reproducing the oral component that is relatively absent in most comparable European texts. Further, "the primary original purpose of alphabetic writing in the Nahua system of communication was to reproduce the oral component, and though things would change with time, this orality would always adhere to Nahua alphabetic documents" (Lockhart 1992, 335). Regarding the primordial titles of central Mexico, Paula López Caballero underlines the vitality of their oral component: "What is outstanding about the primordial titles is the importance granted to oral forms. Their narrations are as a rule articulated following the traits of an oral discourse" (2003, 34).

This marked presence of the reproduction of orality has never been satisfactorily explained. Miguél León Portilla ventures an explanation, describing the Nahuatl text as "performing" the act of reading the old cryptograms. In his translation of Alvarado Tezozómoc's *Crónica Mexicayotl* into Spanish, León Portilla understands Tezozómoc's text as a performative "translation" of the old lore contained in pictograms. In León Portilla's rendering, Alvarado Tezozómoc presents his quest with these words: "He aqui, empieza aqui, se vera aqui, esta pintada aqui, la muy buena, muy notable palabra" (1996, 7). A particular problem that confronts us at this point is that the other existing translation of the *Crónica Mexicáyotl* offers a different gloss, one in which what is "painted" is not a word.[23] It is well beyond my expertise to discuss the philological value of León Portilla's or any other translator's work. Besides, as I noted earlier, the "voice" at stake in León Portilla has, paradoxically, little relationship to the actual occurrence of a voice and represents, rather, a transcendental principle of identity. I am interested in the effect that the letter has on the titles, not only in terms of *voice*—which is a concept never reducible to the actual, historical utterance—but more fundamentally in terms of *enunciation*. The single most important effect of the introduction of a dimension of enunciation is the temporalization of the present, the preemptive creation of a space of futurity. This opening of the future of the titles and other colonial texts surfaces above all in the deictic markers that expose the unguarded dimension of the address as essential to its textual being. Domingo Chimalpahin, referring to the sources of his account, hails his reader with these words: "Y tu, quienquiera que seas, tu lector, que leerás este libro de pinturas de la antigua relación oral de la ciudad de Tzacualtitlan Tenanco" (You, whoever you are, reader who will read this book of the paintings of the old tale about the city of Tzacu-altitlan Tenanco) (qtd. in León Portilla 1996, 57). Sometimes the figure of a communal reader is explicitly evoked by the titles: "Here we, Don Nicolas Tlacamazatzin and Don [Miguel] Zitlaliztac, make this deposition. . . . We want to clarify and to write down [poner por memoria] what belongs to the community [naturales] so at any time in the future they will know and defend what belongs to them" (qtd. in López Caballero 2003, 37).

The intuition of sociality performed by the titles and other similar texts is inseparable from the fact that they are *written* texts; that is, it is inseparable from the fact that in them transpires a dimension of the letter. The letter expands the cultural and political horizon of colonial semiosis not because it serves the preservation of memory or a more efficient transmission of information (which, indeed, like other forms, it does), but because it is the first *formal* suggestion of a universal dimension of communication no longer subject to the constrictions of the existent. The new practice of alphabetic writing produced a vast rearrangement in this tradition of communal preservation and the reconstruction of identities. This change in the order of subjectivation is not unlike the one that Michel Foucault registers for Europe in *The Order of Things*. Foucault explains that the condition for the emergence of our modern concept of the letter was "the end of the old interplay between resemblance and sign" (1973, 46), a general weakening of the centuries-old tradition of authorized mimesis. From the sixteenth century on, the letter clears a space for itself that makes it independent of the transcendental voice, reluctant to be captured by any concept. I am tempted to suggest, evoking a provocative Lacanian hypothesis developed by Jean-Claude Milner (1995), that this new dimension of the letter is the appearance of the letter *as such*. For Lacan, Milner explains, the modern empire of the letter (modernity defined here by the primordial role of the letter in relation to subjectivity) reveals the nonsubstantial character of the subject, the constant slide of its being toward nullity, the zero that lies at its center. This zero, the number rediscovered by Renaissance mathematicians but not unknown to the Aztecs, signals for both ethics and mathematics the dawn of a new politics and the emergence of a new ontology (un)firmly grounded in the enormous power of negativity that the letter brings to bear upon the world.[24]

In the Order of Inheritance

One knows that an event is really an event when one discovers oneself living in the wake of its effects. Here I am calling attention to the event of the creation of a new community of meaning arising out of the universalizing effects of alphabetic writing.

This is one of the two halves that constituted the fissured self of Latin American literature; the other half is the subject of the next chapter. This enunciation opens a futurity that interpellates us as the guarantors of time in its historical form. By reading these texts and claiming them for our archive, we constitute ourselves as their addressee. But what we inherit, primordially, is not the said but the saying. We only inherit the said with the condition of the promise of reawakening its saying. These texts still speak to us not through some philological trick, but through a more profound (even if imprecise) conviction about an essential continuity between the colonial past and the postcolonial present. It is not unusual for Latin American literature to reflect upon this complex structure of inheritance, and many of its fundamental texts spring from this desire to capture a lost saying. Miguel Angel Asturias passionately pursued that goal in *Hombres de maíz*, a book so exceptional that it hardly fits in the category of the literary.

The act of inheritance does not come about because we, with the relative freedom that our destiny may accommodate, choose to be the destination of these words. The process of cultural inheritance is also factual in nature—factual and convoluted, in the case of a colonial text like the *Historia de la nación chichimeca*. The book itself is, like many other colonial manuscripts, lost. It was written by Fernando de Alva Ixtlilxochitl, a seventeenth-century mestizo historian (the son of a Spanish man and a mestizo woman) whose genealogical tree went back to Nezahualcoyotl, Lord of Tezcoco. The lost manuscript once belonged to Carlos de Siguenza y Góngora, who received it as a present from Juan de Alva, son of Fernando. The manuscript that passed to the library of the Colegio Máximo de San Pedro y San Pablo—where Lorenzo Boturini and Francisco Javier Clavijero read it—disappeared toward the middle of the eighteenth century. A further complication arises when we consider that, according to Boturini, the book held at the Colegio Máximo was not the original but already a copy.[25] The avatars of Ixtlilxochitl's manuscript thus move between a Borgesian predicament of lost manuscripts that someday will be used as a base to engender the precursors of the present and the Lacanian admonition that a letter, even a lost one, always reaches its destination. It is through the adventures of inherited and lost manuscripts that a certain phantasmatic presence of the literary begins finally to coalesce. A thin line runs from the universalizing effects whose first outbreak comes around the primordial titles and the corpus of texts that we have come to identify as "colonial literature." One can say that to some extent, most colonial productions are for us "primordial titles" that no longer possess the illusion of staking out and defending a particular territory because this territory has become—through the virtual process of universalization opened by the letter and the working of memory and forgetting—a symbolic, historical, and cultural kingdom.

Literature as Presentation of the Subject

> As a form of power, subjection is paradoxical. To be dominated by a power external to oneself is a familiar and agonizing form power takes. To find, however, that what "one" is, one's very formation as a subject, is in some sense dependent upon that very power is quite another.
>
> Judith Butler, *The Psychic Life of Power*

A fundamental mutation in the question of agency takes place between two movements, in a space that we can label the Enlightenment/post-Enlightenment divide. Literature is one of the cultural sites that embodies the consequences of this mutation. As Peter Bürger notes, there is a point at which the activity of the philosophes needs to slide from philosophical inquiry into aesthetic production to carry out the project of the autonomy of reason (1992, 8–11). Through this movement, aesthetics in general and the literary domain in particular become the site of absolute freedom in modern societies, that is, a site where any encroachment, limitation, or intervention on expression is felt as a diminishing of these expressions' very being (literature at the service of a partisan or state project is no longer literature, etc.). However, we should be wary of this consecration of a discursive autonomy that comes of age at exactly the same historical moment in which, according to Michel Foucault, all discourses are increasingly harnessed to the centripetal forces of power formation. If the literary form is said to clear a space for the emergence and inscription of an expression or voice, how can this figure of what is most human survive, untouched, a transformation that we understand as a slippage from individual to subject? The age of literature as absolute autonomy is also the age in which the subjection of the

83

individual seems to figure the unsurpassable horizon of all emancipatory discourse.

This problematic is explored at great length by Judith Butler in *The Psychic Life of Power*. Through an extended discussion of Hegel's master/slave dialectic, Nietzsche's building of reactive forces, Foucault's excess of power, and Freud's reversal of the drives upon themselves, Butler seeks to account for the fact that through modernity "one inhabits the figure of autonomy only by becoming subjected to a power" (1997, 83). Subjection is not only accepted but also willed, because it promises the individual protection from annihilation: "Subjection exploits the desire for existence, where existence is always conferred from elsewhere; it marks a primary vulnerability to the Other in order to be" (Butler 1997, 21). At this point, Butler is ready to tackle the tripartite goal of her book: to study how "power maintains subjects in subordination"; to examine the fact that the subject rescued from annihilation bears the mark of a lost and "inassimilable remainder, a melancholia that marks the limits of subjectivation"; and, finally, to explore how the site of constitution of the subject may simultaneously operate as a principle of emancipation. At its core, this project seeks to supplement the Foucauldian theory of the formative aspect of power with a psychoanalytical elucidation of the process by which "the subjection of desire require[s] and institute[s] the desire *for* subjection" (Butler 1997, 19).

How does this economy of emancipation and subjection play itself out in the realm of aesthetic presentation? The question is important because the aesthetic dimension embodies better than any other the specifically modern type of subjection. A first hint at this convergence between works of art and modern subjectivity comes in the way we pose aesthetic questions, which is practically indistinguishable from the way we pose the question of the subject. The reason for this convergence is made clear by Jürgen Habermas in *Philosophical Discourse of Modernity,* where he establishes that modernity is properly defined by the problem of self-foundation. This is why Hegel's philosophy of self-positing becomes, for Habermas, the quintessential modern philosophical quest. But Habermas also breaks away from Hegelian rationalism to pay increasing attention to theorists and theories of art. This displacement from the philosophical to the aesthetic, which seems, but only seems, to reverse the sublation of art into philosophy proclaimed by Hegel, is a natural consequence of the privilege that Habermas confers to the problem of self-foundation, since no object in modernity represents the question of autonomous immanence better than an object of art.

Something backfired in the aesthetic project. In *The Man without Content*, Giorgio Agamben distinguishes between a first period of aesthetic production dominated by a Greek conception of art and a second, modern one that arises in the passage from early modernity to the full-fledged Enlightenment. In the first period, the work of art is an objective production organically linked to the community, and its function is to open a space for the human habitation of the world. In modernity, on the other hand, the work of art is eminently subjective. It depends on the formative power of the artist, and since this power is nothing but the power to negate all content, the content of the work itself becomes negation. Separated from the world and identified with a content that now appears contingent and even capricious, the work of art, far from disclosing a human world, is consumed in its own rage. In this way, the project of aesthetic self-foundation that was supposed to bring to completion the enlightened ideal of a rational grounding of the self is threatened rather than confirmed by the collusion of modern subjectivity and art.

One of the outward, visible confirmations of this development lies in the split between the values of liberal humanism and aesthetic sensibility. According to Hegel, the best illustration of this split is the title character of Diderot's *Rameau's Nephew*, whose cynical persona is both aesthetically elevated and ethically irresponsible. However, it would be a mistake to accept the received narrative that regards the split between the values of liberalism and the critical subject of aesthetics as definitive and conclusive: literature remains a moralizing machine despite the critical function that came to identify its historical existence in modernity. The problem is where to locate this moralizing stratum. The obvious solution is to place the moralizing dimension at the level of content or meaning. Insofar as it relies on "representation," however, this solution remains both problematic and naive—problematic because every content can hermeneutically be interpreted in two different and opposite ways, and naive because it does not entertain the idea that the mechanism of representation is itself literature's moralizing element.[1]

This moralizing element that provided literature with its currency in a modernity dominated by bourgeois sensibility is not an element that can be easily separated from the literary project. In his "Fifteen Theses on Art," Alain Badiou proposes that "non-imperial art is necessarily abstract art" (2003). But is there a literary equivalent of abstract art? There are certainly some literary expressions that seem to cover this program, but they are for the most part poetic experiments that belong, properly speaking, more to the realm of *Dichtung* than to that of literature. It would seem that this element of figurality, which Levinas condemned as the thematization of a subject interrogated in the light of knowledge, is inescapable in the realm of narrative literature.[2] The figural survives every criticism and thus constitutes the hard kernel of our epochal experience of the literary.

It would be naive to point to a single name or event as the beginning of this pervasive identification of literature and the figural, narration and imperialism. More interesting, it seems to me, is an attempt to locate the general movement through which literary productions and art in general became a site for the repercussion of subjectifying effects that, moreover, are in the last instance agreeable to the project of modern governmentality. Hegel, with an insight that is still valid, renders the whole development of modernity dependent on the notion of subject. I think that we can borrow this Hegelian characterization to speak about literature. The equivalent of the logicization of the world is, in the literary realm, the subjectivation of the text. This literary subject, defined not only as character but also as plot, reader, or theme, is isomorphic with the modern (liberal) subject of politics. This isomorphism is a sort of deep grammar, not readily available for inspection or contestation. Tracing its historical constitution, however, is not difficult. Clearly, the philosophy of Immanuel Kant plays a foundational role in the creation of this order of subjection, in which subject and work become two sides of a single process. In this regard, it is more than a philological curiosity that roughly from 1780 on, philosophy and literature are filled with subjectivist categories that are practically indistinguishable from the prose of bourgeois political liberalism: *expression, will, spontaneity, opinion, point of view, identification, choice, sensibility, originality, imagination, enthusiasm.* Almost all of these words have a specific technical use in the *Critique of Pure Reason* and Kant's other two critiques.[3] In addition, almost all of these terms trace the contours of the subject of opinion of a bourgeois public sphere, a subject that not only sustains itself in its own system of judgments and predicates but also depends on a moral environment that mirrors its intentions so thoroughly that it is impossible to pinpoint which is the original and which the mirror image.

This circularity, which is the ultimate matter of this chapter, lies at the core of literature's entanglement with subjection. For this reason, attending to literature does not mean exiting the realm of primary subjection, as discussed by Butler, in order to enter a space of mere "consolidation." The subjected subject is not constituted once and for all. It needs, so to speak, to be constantly brought back into existence. Literature became the distinctive site for the constitution and defense of the project of autonomy against this backdrop of the endless production of subjection. So throughout the whole nineteenth century, the Kantian vocabulary of affection came to designate the intentional structure of the responsible subject of modernity in general; in the realm of literature, the transfer of the subject's transcendental nature had this uncanny result: while the universality of the subject of politics and even of the transcendental subject of knowledge have been brought into question by successive critical paradigms, the universality of literature has displayed a resilience that criticism and deconstruction have found much more difficult to dismantle.

The Romantic Age: A Point of Condensation

The articulation between subject and work of art, or more generally between subject and culture (I will tackle later the question of the ambiguity between art and culture), is a process played out entirely within the bounds of Romantic theory. This theory arises from the collusion between the philosophy developed in Germany between 1790 and 1810—from Kant to Hegel—and the literary elaboration of an aesthetic subject, a project carried out mainly in German, British, and to a lesser extent French literature. Kant has often been credited as the foundational figure of Romanticism, and his *Critique of Judgment* is claimed to outline the sphere of problems in which not only Romantic literature but modern art in general, and culture as a whole, unfold.

Recent years, in which criticism's attention has been directed as never before to the entanglement between culture and power, have added novelty. Kant's *Third Critique* is said to lie not only at the origins of the Romantic sensibility but also at the very source of modern Western politics. This claim seems exorbitant, and some important practical objections to it can be made. As Hannah Arendt points out, Kant "never wrote a political philosophy" (1992, 7). Moreover, most of Kant's political remarks are highly unphilosophical in nature. And when Kant does speak about politics, he does so from such a Manichean standpoint (politics for him is obviously just the site of coercion) that any problem of subjection seems beside the point. So in what sense is Kant the origin of the modern, hegemonic form of politics (according to Arendt herself, among others)? David Lloyd and Paul Thomas attempt to answer this question in *Culture and the State,* a book that synthesizes much of the current debate about the relationship between cultural forms and governmentality. For Lloyd and Thomas, Kant's conception of common sense underlines all our assumptions about society and the public sphere.[4] The paradox of taste—for example, the fact that we use a forceful expression such as "This is beautiful" to refer to a experience that is entirely subjective—reveals the existence of a presupposed commonality of all human beings. Universal communicability is the condition for the constitution of society, a condition anchored in the structure of human reason and fully revealed in the sphere of the experience of aesthetic productions, since the claim to universal validity in judgments of taste is legitimate only with the assumption of similar subjective conditions for judgment in all human beings.

Some authors also argue in favor of a *specifically* political role for Kantism in the conformation of the modern world. In *Enlightenment, Revolution, and Romanticism,* Fredrick Beiser claims that Kant's philosophy was instrumental in the wave of bourgeois revolutions that swept away feudal power in Europe. The debate over the bourgeois revolutions, Beiser adds, was "couched in Kantian terms" (1992, 3). Beiser goes even further in his portrayal of Kant as a sui generis political activist by concluding that "Kant's philosophy articulated the claims of reason for the revolutionaries" and inviting the reader to uncover the "cryptopolitical elements" in his philosophy. Beiser's passionate defense of Kant's revolutionary credentials misses the mark somewhat. After all, the assertion that Kant's philosophy "articulated the claims of reason for the revolutionaries" overlooks the fact that there were no revolutionaries in Germany. Even more, Kant's philosophy and its aftermath may indeed have had something to do with this conspicuous absence of revolutionaries, as Stathis Kouvelakis notes. It is possible, says Kouvelakis, to think that Kant—whose sympathies toward the French Revolution did not waver even when most German intellectuals deserted the revolutionary camp—displaces the question of revolution in a way that makes revolution itself superfluous. Kouvelakis reads Kant as advancing a propaedeutic that aims to produce the same subjective changes brought about by the (French) revolution, while simultaneously avoiding any revolutionary upheaval. This constitutes, in fact, the "distinct German path" to revolution, whose "results may well partially converge with the French equivalent, if only in a future as distant as it is indeterminate" (Kouvelakis 2003, 11). Later in this chapter, I will discuss how this "distinct German path" to revolution was enthusiastically embraced by different Latin American intellectuals at the end of the nineteenth century.

It was not Kant, however, but Friedrich Schiller who openly carried over the articulation between the realms of personal freedom and social determination demanded by "the distinct German path" to revolution. As a matter of fact, writes Beiser, it was only with Schiller that "the cryptopolitical elements of Kantian philosophy" acquired tangible consequences (1992, 8). In making this assertion, Beiser joins Paul de Man, who in *The Rhetoric of Romanticism* advances the essential connection between Schillerian aesthetics and modern political formations in the most unambiguous way possible: "The aesthetic, as is clear from Schiller's formulation, is primarily a social and political model, ethically grounded in an assumedly Kantian notion of freedom; despite repeated attempts by commentators, alarmed by its possible implications, to relativise and soften the idea of the aesthetic state ... that figures prominently at the end of the *Letters on the Aesthetic Education of Man*, ... it should be preserved as the radical assertion that it is.... For it is as a political force that the aesthetic still concerns us as one of the most powerful ideological drives to act upon the reality of history" (1983, 265).

Modern aesthetics—the only aesthetics, since the word itself is an eighteenth-century product—connects the realms of politics and society. It does so, however, not under the old feudal or absolutist model of obedience to a higher power. If representation is still the basic medium of aesthetic communication, it no longer seeks blind obedience to the image, but rather invites the incorporation of the image into the personal life of the beholder. The aesthetic claims to act upon a morally free and enlightened subject. To put it in Kantian algebra, the aesthetic is the mediation that allows us to be affected by the institution of the polis inasmuch as these institutions match our primordial (aesthetic) disposition: our drive to representation. De Man insists that this anchoring of aesthetics in everyday politics should be welcomed. If aesthetics still matters to us, it is because we find in it the venue and the force to act upon history.

But the road that the subject takes to act upon history is the same road that history takes to act upon the subject. Commenting on this duplicity in the opening pages of *The Ideology of the Aesthetic,* Terry Eagleton describes the aesthetic as being "from the beginning a contradictory, double-edged concept. On the one hand, it figures as a genuinely emancipatory force—as a community of subjects now linked by sensuous impulse and fellow-feeling rather than by heteronymous law, each safeguarded in its unique particularity while bound at the same time into social harmony." But simultaneously, Eagleton warns, "the aesthetic signifies what Max Horkheimer has called a kind of 'internalized repression,' inserting social power more deeply into the very bodies of those it subjugates" (1990, 28).[5]

One understands better, then, why de Man is extra cautious in his endorsement of the pedagogy advanced by Schiller in *Letters on the Education of Man* and why he later becomes openly critical of it. In the posthumous *Aesthetic Ideology,* de Man claims that if we follow Kant's aesthetic thinking to its limit, we find there not the conditions of the possibility of Schiller's project but, rather, the conditions of its undoing. While Schiller's intervention appears to de Man to be too complicit with the general project of culture as governmentality, Kant introduces in his aesthetic theory a principle of irretrievable materialism (de Man also calls this an instance of formalization—a reduction to the literal or to the letter, in a way reminiscent of Jacques Lacan) that Schiller's pedagogy seeks to cancel (de Man 1996, 129–62). However, in the same text, de Man introduces an important warning: "Don't decide too soon that you are beyond Schiller in any sense. I don't think any of us can lay this claim. Whatever writing we do, whatever way we have of talking about art, whatever way we have of teaching, whatever justification we give ourselves for teaching, whatever the standards are . . . they are more than ever profoundly Schillerian" (1996, 142). It seems worthwhile, then, to explore in more detail the ways in which our culture is still largely Schillerian.

The Schillerian Supplement

Schiller is central to any narrative of culture as subjection, because it is only with Schiller that expression and subjection become two inseparable sides of a single process. Of course, Schiller did not invent the logic of the double bind: it was in the spirit of the times, so to speak. One of its expressions was the anti-Enlightenment philosophy of embodiment, from which both Romanticism and Hegelianism sprang. Since the 1770s, authors like Herder had been developing an organicist philosophy stressing the mutual embodiment of world and subject in direct opposition to the crude and mechanistic "models" of the Enlightenment. The subject was conceived not as a preexisting marble statue animated by exterior forces, but as a sensitive body created in a constant exchange with the world (C. Taylor 1998, 12–27).

The central concept through which expression and subjection are knotted together in Schiller is, of course, the concept of *Bildung,* which stands for both education (as an individual process, and eventually as expression) and culture (a formative force applied upon the subject).[6] Schiller's idea of *Bildung* positioned itself squarely in the realm of the political constitution of society. Working against a long tradition linking citizenship to informed rational discussion, Schiller maintains that education in the virtues of citizenship depends on aesthetic empathy rather than on philosophical enlightenment. The aesthetic emphasizes the uniqueness of civil *paideia* and aligns it not with an ideal public sphere of discussion but, eventually, with the values of embodiment and spiritual affinity, a language whose importance only increased as modernity progressed. Finally—and this decisively connects the Schillerian system with emergent bourgeois political liberalism—the *Bildung* process is predicated upon militant individualism.

As letter 11 of Schiller's *On the Aesthetic Education of Man* reads, "The person . . . must be its own ground" (1967, 116).

What interests me in Schiller, especially in his notion of aesthetic education, is the constitutive ambivalence between *to affect* and *to be affected* that this logic of *Bildung* presupposes and that Terry Eagleton denounces as a form of social control. Eagleton's description, we must notice, seems to be based on an equivocal use of the word *aesthetic,* which in the first part of his description means "art" and in the second part, after his reference to Horkheimer, "culture." I mention this not as a fault, but as further proof of the ambivalence that our critical tradition weaves around these two concepts.[7] Even Schiller's work partakes of this ambivalence. Although Schiller is talking about art (*Kunst*) rather than cultivation (*Bildung*), his work stands at the crossroads of this common misunderstanding about the nature of the superstructural. The very concept of *aesthetic education* invites a blurring of the effects of art and mundane life. After all, art itself is not such a great thing for Schiller, who confesses that he feels ashamed to be busying himself with petty questions of taste when the times demand that one pay attention to "a loftier theme than that of art." And that element loftier than art is the creation of "the most perfect of all works of art—the establishment and structure of a true political freedom" (Schiller 1967, 5). The ambivalence between art and cultivation (or even civilization), with all the other minor ambivalences that it generates (art and craftsmanship, etc.), is grounded in their common belonging to the hermeneutic circle of culture, a hegemonic circle that attains historical density at the very moment at which cultural and artistic productions find in their interpellative-educational function the rationale for their historical existence. Like art, culture designates a two-way venue that represents the most perfect incarnation of the double bind that constitutes the subject, in the same movement through which the subject seeks to ground itself. Culture and aesthetics may be for the subject a site of constitution, assertion, and eventually autonomy. But nothing prevents aesthetics from turning from the production of autonomy into a place where the subject is composed through the disciplinary forces of society.

As with most post-Kantian thinkers, Schiller's declared goal was to supersede the tensions and dualities (nature and culture, reason and affect, morality and instincts) that Kant himself was unable to surmount. Schiller thought he could find a way to bridge these dichotomies by attributing to the idea of art/culture the power of sublating the tensions inhabiting the modernizing world of the ascending bourgeoisie. He borrowed from Kant himself the critical tool for this operation—none other than the transcendental element of unification in a philosophy of dualities. In the *Critique of Pure Reason*, the primary duality is the one between subject and reality (phenomenality). But a second duality arose for Kant within the subject itself, between its merely receptive (sensible) side and its active (categorical and dialectical) engagement with the data provided by sensibility. Now, sensible intuitions and categories are so different that the question becomes: what right do we have to imagine that such heterogeneous instances enter into any productive commerce at all? And if they do—as they should, if knowledge is to become possible—what medium is produced by such alchemy? At this point, Kant solves the riddle by proposing time as the element able to bridge sensation and judgment, insofar as it partakes of both intuition and conceptuality. This operation yields the famous "transcendental schema," through which world and subject are created by the spontaneity of the imagination. For Schiller, it is just a matter of "translating" the notion of schema into another, more malleable and verifiable notion, and he found this notion in the eighteenth-century ideal of organic culture. And although organic culture had been lost, the aesthetic became a medium to use in fighting for its return. This organic idea of a culture as embodied, fused with the expressive possibilities of the subject, operates as a transcendental schema in its own right. It comes to mediate between subject and world just as the transcendental schema mediates between subject and reality. The remarkable outcome of this process is, of course, the transcendental positioning of the cultural dimension, which is no longer a product but the most general condition of production of both world and subject. Like the transcendental schema, culture is said to come before the subject and to constitute its condition of possibility. Also like the transcendental schema, culture is an event we may call "prereflective." It is not the subject's product, but its foundation. At this point, it is worth recalling that for Schiller, art, not philosophy, was the appropriate medium of civil education. The main reason Schiller favored the aesthetic over the philosophical is, to my mind, the prereflective character that culture takes in his writings.

If through the schema Kant strives to show—as one exegesis of his work puts it—that in order to relate to the world we should be "immanently related to reality" (Gardner 1999, 34), then culture, which comes to occupy the same structural position, operates in modernity as the unsurpassable mediation between subjectivity and the symbolic universe. For a culturalist vision of society (and there is hardly any other), the subject is always immanent to the cultural configuration in which it was born and that condemns it, like a marked animal, to bear the imprints of that culture in its flesh.

A paradoxical result of the promotion of culture as the organic and unsurpassable horizon of meaning (whose modern version is, of course, the tautological conviction that "everything is culture") is that the autonomy of the subject, the basic tenet of both the Enlightenment and liberalism, is brought into question. Freedom itself becomes a dubious value once the hermeneutical circle of culture closes upon its own elements. The figure of the specular—evoked by Bill Readings as the very form of the relationship between subject and state—always already precedes all notions of culture and subjection. Through the double bind, the subject of *Bildung* becomes indistinguishable from the culture that nurtures him or her. Even more important, as de Man points out, instead of having shed this relationship with *Bildung*, modernity has witnessed the absolute generalization of this structure.

Subjection, Subjectification, and the Extimate Object

Subject and culture are not identical, even if the subject becomes indistinguishable from the culture that so defines it through *Bildung*. For the subject to be a subject, there must be a noncolonized space, a marker of the nonsutured gap separating him or her from the historical shape of the spirit.

This constitutive misidentification between subject and culture does not make the subject an inch more free, in the traditional humanist sense of the word. It only means that failure is an essential moment in the working of the system. And this failure is nothing but the subject itself. The subject is the element that by exerting its negating power brings uncertainty into the system and saves the idea of culture from auto-deconstructing into a mockery of the concept. There is no way for the aesthetic to "influence" culture or humanity if this space of freedom is not granted in advance. This interplay between a constitutive interpellation and resistant singularity provides further evidence that the double bind operates not so much by establishing frontiers between inside and outside, or expression and reception (the mark of a premodern theory of subject, art, and literature), as by blurring them. In this sense, the Romantic conception of culture as *Bildung* has the undeniable virtue of having grasped that the double movement of capture and resistance is essential to the process of subjective constitution. This conception thus also forced a reconsideration of the metaphysical distinction between subject and world, inside and outside, spiritual and material. But Romantic theory could not think the element of radical subjective incompletion in structural terms. It had only phenomenal access to it and could grasp its essence only in developmental terms. Its most conclusive formulation perhaps appears in Friedrich Schlegel's famous definition of poetry as infinite progression (1991, 31). It is only in the work of Jacques Lacan, and more precisely in his notion of *extimacy,* that we find a structural elucidation of the economy of subjection. Lacan used this notion of extimacy only sporadically, and most of what we know about it has been handed down to us by authors such as Jacques-Alain Miller and Mladen Dolar.[8] An extimate object is, in Dolar's words, "neither exterior nor interior, but not somewhere else either. It is the point of exteriority in the very kernel of interiority, the point where the innermost touches the outermost, where materiality is the most intimate. It is around this intimate external kernel that subjectivity is constituted" (1993, 78). Extimacy comes to disrupt the metaphysical separation between outside and inside that the Romantic theorization of the work of art had already put into question under what Jean-Luc Nancy and Philippe Lacoue-Labarthe call "the subject-work" (1988, xx). But in addition, because of its liminal position, the extimate object touches on the very ambivalence between assumed freedom and experienced cultivation. It is by virtue of this extimate character that the literary object incarnates the ambiguities produced by the double bind of subjection/subjectification better than any other form in modernity.[9] The literary object's extimate nature is the one that surfaces when reading is described in terms of a paradoxical moment in which the subject is inhabited by at least two consciousnesses—an account we find in critics of the Geneva circle, such as Georges Poulet and Jean Starobinski (see Poulet 1969). Once acknowledged, this character of extimacy of the literary has methodological consequences that far exceed the investigation of the ideological effects of the literary work. Any sociology of the literary or version of subjection that is inattentive to the extimate character of literature in modernity remains one-sided, and consequently, its explanation of cultural phenomena is only partial. Let us take, for example, the whole trend of cultural studies, which, following Foucault's lead, seeks to understand the literary as a particular instance of discipline, whose working (not "meaning") is completely "readable" at the phenomenal level of its institutional instantiation. Critics working under this paradigm contend, rightly, that signifying practices are always institutionally regulated (see Bennet 1990). However, as soon as one attempts to carry out an analysis capable of dealing with all the complexities of ideological production and reproduction, it becomes readily apparent that the stress on institutions and regulations can never offer a fully convincing explanation of the mechanism through which these aims are obtained.[10] It is not that pedagogy is not a moment of cultural domination; it is just that it is not enough. That said, I do not mean to "forget" about subjection through discipline; rather, I intend to supplement it. Normally, the opposite view is held: "material," "practical" disciplinarity appears as a corrective for the too "idealist" subjection. But this division between the material and the ideal is, as I argued earlier, too crude. It depends on a clear differentiation between inside and outside, interior expression and exterior language, that is itself problematic.[11] Routines, hygienic practices, and the enclosure or reform of popular culture: none of these methods of tying the reproduction of culture to the reproduction of power has the slightest chance of working in modern conditions if it does not have a decisive recourse to the logic of the double bind, that is, to the logic by which personal expression and cultural values tend to claim a common and indistinguishable ground or origin.[12] The logic of the double bind prevents the interpellative process from being a merely pedagogical or disciplinary enterprise. It would be impossible for the regulative institutions to "reveal" the identity of the subject if this subject did not reveal itself—freely, so to speak—through its own power of expression.

This logic, aptly captured in the Lacanian notion of the symbolic as pointing to both the exteriority of culture and the most intimate processes of subjective constitution, seems to greatly curtail any possibility of subjective revolt. In the logic of the double bind, the subject cannot openly negate culture, because given that culture is always embodied, this would amount to negating itself. It may be objected that we thus end up accepting an all-powerful symbolic that blackmails us with the threat of either submission or psychosis (your money or your life, as Lacan would say). But I would argue that the symbolic to which the double bind answers is thoroughly historical. True, Lacan says that his symbolic is also historical. But the historicity of the double bind is made of stuff far easier to theorize than the elusive historicity of the Lacanian symbolic: the double bind of culture always operates in the horizon of meaning provided by a given state-form. It seeks to perpetuate the most general form of society, its power relationship included. For this reason, the concept of interpellation is vital to our undertaking. Although Althusser's "Ideology and Ideological State Apparatuses" is really no more than the sketch of an essay, it spells out clearly the dynamics that obtain between the structural (eternal) nature of ideology and the historical embodiment of interpellations (as in the example of the three medieval orders turned into actions: plotting the land, waging war, and praying). Interpellations are the intentional acts of a historical form of subjection. If we give up this Althusserian intuition, the historicity of cultural practices of subordination disappears.

These implications were partially out of reach for Schiller, who lived and wrote in a context in which a cultural and holistic idea of the German nation carried more weight than a still-absent state. Schiller worriedly perceived that the state of his time was not an ethical state ("the state remains forever a stranger to its citizens' existence since at no point does it ever make contact with their feeling" [1967, 101]). For him, it was not evident that the state could eventually accommodate the pedagogy whose program we can map throughout Schiller's work, much less that "the state" would one day become the name for this process. For us, on the other hand, at least since Antonio Gramsci's redrawing of the concept of the state as "ethical state," the question arises of what right we have to make an analytical distinction, in bourgeois modernity, between culture (the apparatus of civil society) and state.

Latin American Actualizations

If we look for a point at which Latin American literature clearly displays a drive toward the representation of the expressive possibilities of the people, while at the same time acquiring the structure of a program of subjection, the period between 1880 and 1920 (varying somewhat by region) comes to mind as the culmination of this two-faced process. During this period, several important changes prompted deep cultural transformations. Social and economic modernization and expanding politicization fostered the need for a broad incorporation of mobilized sectors into the national community. A supplementary answer to this crisis of development came through the production of different forms of cultural nationalism that, throughout the continent, ethnicized the study and valorization of literature.

The ethnicization of literature and the rise of cultural nationalism are developments that we associate with names such as Pedro Henríquez Ureña, Carlos Eduardo Bunge, José Vasconcelos, and José Martí, and to a lesser extent—and in a more regional sense—Alfonso Reyes, Leopoldo Lugones, and Alberto Sánchez. All of these intellectuals acknowledged the formative influence that the Uruguayan José Rodó exerted upon the lettered culture of the time. For Henríquez Ureña, Rodó was the first Latin American intellectual: "Rodó is a teacher who educates through books; perhaps the first among us in influencing with the sole means of the written word" (1984, 58). Rodó's *Ariel* also marks the beginning of the discourse of Latin Americanism (understood as Hispanism, in recognition of a Hispanic heritage) through the establishment of a cultural and political agenda. On its cultural side, this agenda was a *paideia,* a virtuous education whose constant appeal to classical (mostly Greek) forms seemed to detach its productions from the practical concerns of everyday life. On its political side, it was marked by a relentless but mostly metaphysical anti-Americanism.

Rodó was not unique in assigning an educational and political role to classic culture. In fact, one of the most striking features of this new generation of thinkers, closely tied to the development of a hegemonic state in modern Latin America, was precisely their conviction that Greek culture provided the most comprehensible blueprint for facilitating the incorporation of the Latin American masses into the modernity that these thinkers were guarding. Wherever one looks in Latin America in the period from 1880 to 1900, one encounters a proliferation of Greek references and motifs, most of them organized around numberless institutions bearing the apposite name Ateneos. José Rodó's *Ariel* is shot through with references to classical antiquity. Roberto González Echevarría points out that Rodó gave his work the structure of a Platonic dialogue. I would note further that this dialogue is staged in front of a statue of Ariel, the genius of the air (later I will return to the question of the statue). In Argentina, Leopoldo Lugones beautifully translated some lines from *The Illiad* (the lines that Alejo Carpentier uses as an epigraph to "Semejante a la noche"). A couple of decades earlier, the local Ateneo in Buenos Aires had been created to favor classical culture and resist vulgar literary expressions. Calixto Oyuela, one of its founding members, proposed a "national expression" that might inscribe its meaning on "Hellenic marble" and build a "magisterial statue" ("Heleno mármol con afán busquemos / Y de la luz moderna a los fulgores / Estatua nueva y magistral labremos") (qtd. in Rubione 1983, 30). In Peru, Luis Valdelomar, taking Greek tragedy as a model, offered a strictly Schillerian version of culture when he defended the thesis that the universal relationship between human beings and the natural world is resolved through art. Valdelomar's vision is permeated by assumptions about the role of theater and culture that Nietzsche's immensely popular *Birth of Tragedy* had disseminated throughout Latin America. In Bolivia around 1917, Franz Tamayo published *La Prometheida*, a tragic lyric drama loaded with mythical Greek characters; he would later return to the issue of the value of classical education as the appropriate embodiment of citizenship in other writings. Latin American scholars have found it difficult to accommodate these expressions within narratives of Latin America's cultural past. In *La formación de la tradición literaria en el Perú,* for example, Cornejo Polar dismisses Adolfo Vienrich's theories about genealogical connections between Greek and Quechua (in *Azucenas Quechuas* [1905]) as "frankly delirious" (Cornejo Polar 1989, 124). Although Cornejo Polar's claim is correct, this passion for all things Greek still requires elucidation.

To the best of my knowledge, except for isolated essays, the many references to classical antiquity in these transitional intellectuals have largely been overlooked.[13] Such references have been read simply as a marker of distinction that further removed intellectuals from the people and from their own engagement with the development of the modern national state. But there is no cultural dandyism in these references to classical sensibility and the fine arts. They appear, as a rule, in the most resolute, engaged, and "serious" intellectuals of the time. It would be equally misleading to disdain the presence of Greek motifs as an imperfect reading of some trends that were active at the time in European culture and arbitrarily transposed to the Latin American context (what Roberto Schwarz would call "a misplaced idea"). Yet these insistent references to classical antiquity fit uneasily with the historical context in which proponents of classicism were acting. In *La tormenta,* the second volume of his memoirs, José Vasconcelos recounts a trip to London and a visit to the British Museum that had as its most important goal "the visit and adoration of Phidias's sculptures" (2000, 23). At this point, it is perhaps apposite to recall that ten years later, when Vasconcelos became minister of education, he launched a literacy campaign that was based, among other things, on the translation of Greek tragedies. And although much has been made of Vasconcelos's Hellenizing preferences, he was not even the most Greek of the Mexican Greeks. The *ateneistas* organized communal readings of Plato's *Symposium* and replaced the traditional Christian Christmas with a pagan celebration to honor Dionysius. After the revolution, the same intellectuals supported the revolutionary government and gathered forces to open the Universidad Popular as a tool for bridging the abyss between the cultural standards upheld by the group and the traditions of the popular revolutionary masses. The point is that there is no real break between those who gathered in honor of Dionysius or collectively read the *Symposium* and those who declared themselves the intellectual branch of the revolution, just as there is no real break between the Vasconcelos who was sincerely devoted to the revolution and the Vasconcelos who prioritized a visit to the British Museum over his immediate revolutionary tasks.

What is interesting here is not the merely anecdotal prestige of Greek culture among the intellectuals carrying out the project of informing citizenship through culture. The real problem is explaining the timing of this use of Greek motifs and the fact that such usage did not wither away but was instead transformed into different forms of nativism in the years to come. In his memoir "Pasado inmediato," Alfonso Reyes provides a clue to understanding the paradoxical actuality of Greek culture in turn-of-the-century Mexico: at the time, Reyes remarks, to be Greek (classical) meant to be modern (1960, 186). What sense of modernity is at stake here? Carlos Monsiváis answers this question when he notes, in an essay entitled "La toma de partido de Alfonso Reyes," that the essential task Mexican intellectuals like Reyes appointed for themselves was to guarantee governmentality through cultural persuasion (Monsiváis 1989). With unerring instinct, of all Reyes's texts, Monsiváis chooses "Discurso por Virgilio"—a text in which Reyes argues that culture is above politics—as the exemplary instance where Reyes declares his political commitment to the consolidation of the postrevolutionary state. Reyes's intentions are relatively irrelevant. The structure of the double bind and the reflective nature of the relationship between culture and state manage to capture the individual work of the philologist in the nets of state formation. Besides, Monsiváis's analysis of Reyes's "political option" reveals Reyes's thorough adherence to principles of cultural criticism that are deeply indebted to the work of Matthew Arnold, the British intellectual and educator whom Cornell West credits as perhaps the most influential voice in our modern concept of culture (1999, 119), and who, according to David Lloyd and Paul Thomas, was the first intellectual to completely carry out, in the sphere of state influence, the project of preventing violent conflicts (even revolutions) through aesthetic education. There is something more than chance at work here. Pedro Henríquez Ureña, the undisputed leader of the Mexican *ateneistas* and a personal mentor to the younger Reyes, never concealed the origin of his intellectual project: works by Arnold, which he read constantly and urged Reyes to read.[14] Through Arnold, we return not only to the essential project of culture as governmentality but also to the question of the revival of Greek culture, since, as Eagleton points out, Arnold's maxim is "to Hellenize" (Eagleton 1993, 24).

At the moment when culture takes the role of educating people into virtuous citizenship, Hellenism becomes a favorite tool for the moralization of politics and society. As Josef Chytry observes, there is nothing strange about the fact that a reference to the first successful experiment in democratic incorporation (Athens) should draw the attention of a whole constellation of intellectuals for whom the incorporation of the uncultivated middle and popular classes (in Europe), or of peripheral and indigenous populations (in Latin America), had become the most urgent issue on the social agenda. The emerging capitalist world system, and its attendant political form of subjection, liberalism, could borrow in good conscience from a form of civic education that foregrounded the value of persuasion over any form of dogmatism or authoritarianism.

The classical tradition could not be adopted wholesale under modern conditions. Some elements were embraced, others negotiated, and still others rejected outright. The collusion between politico-economic liberalism and ancient humanism constitutes one of the formative trends of a modern common sense in Europe. In the case of Latin America, classical education often articulated conservative interests, insofar as it served as a means of expression for the deeply rooted convictions of Latin American traditionalism. For there was a second vital element that the intellectuals in charge of the revival of Greek culture extrapolated from antiquity: the ideal of an integrated cultural life. The image of an organic culture spoke directly to the most urgent need of eighteenth-century intellectuals in Europe and nineteenth-century writers in Latin America. As modernization was tearing apart old regimes and creating new social actors, intellectuals desperately searched for ideals of society strongly impregnated by the values of communitarianism and patriarchal rule. After all, the distinctive feature of "modern" culture lies in its ability to figure a site for experiencing an organic wholeness directly opposed to the realities of capitalist development at a time "when it was already apparent that the division of intellectual and manual labor was increasingly formative of specialized or partial individuals" (Lloyd and Thomas 1998, 2). Hence the none-too-surprising embrace of nationalism and traditionalism in a consecrated Hellenist such as Leopoldo Lugones.

Although eighteenth-century European intellectuals were convinced that Greek art produced the most useful systematization of the project of civil education through culture, they were unsure as to what form of art was appropriate to carry out the project of an enlightened *paideia*. Even if we know that historically literature would perform a first experiment in symbolic enfranchisement, this option was not so clear in the early stages of the movement. After all, as the proponents of the aesthetic state knew, literature as a discourse was not available in ancient Greece. Baumgarten, for instance, thought of sculpture as the formative art par excellence, for obvious reasons. Sculpture is the literalization of *Bildung,* the material incarnation of a formative action. Here we should recall a series of "anomalous" turn-of-the-century references to sculptures, busts, and statues, such as the statues of Phidias adored by Vasconcelos and the bust of Ariel that presides over Prospero's speech. Its perfection and remoteness, along with its limited capacity for circulation, made it impossible for sculpture to play the role that Baumgarten had assigned to it. The pedagogical statue (a cosmopolitan marble statue, not the nationalist bronze) evoked, by its very presence, an unviable Enlightenment inheritance. But the trace of sculpture did not disappear from literature. Indeed, Oyuela proclaims his decision to represent modernity through a Hellenic marble. When Oyuela proposed inscribing the meaning of modernity in the form of a classical statue, he was speaking not literally, but literarily. He was describing the practice of writing poetry as if one were carving a statue—that is, writing poetry without renouncing the guiding project of *Bildung.* Although Oyuela was unable to give up an aristocratic longing for an enlightened direction of society, something else occurs in this substitution of poetry for sculpture. In Latin America, as everywhere else, the project of political enfranchisement through classical education was doomed to failure. It failed because classical culture and its constitutive categories could not become extimate objects, objects capable of abolishing the difference between outside and inside, subject and culture. Confronted with the literal appearance of the question of *Bildung,* the beholder can only stand in awe or adoration, as Vasconcelos did before Phidias at the British Museum.

Regionalism and the Subject of Extimacy

Despite the intense longing for an integrated life that many intellectuals experienced, the revival of Greek culture as a modeling force for capitalist development remained problematic. Modern life was simply inimical to the integrative project that intellectuals envisioned in the culture of antiquity. Persuasion itself, the basic category of communal relationship, seemed difficult even in modern European societies, not to mention in their prob-lematically hybrid Latin American counterparts. After all, as Chytry points out, "the art of speaking well, the laws of rhetoric, and the development of formal rules of disputation, argumentation, demonstration, and proof were made possible by a communal setting of face-to-face contact, of constant personal acquaintance and exchange" (1989, xli). Besides, the different in-tellectuals of the aesthetic state were not unanimous in their assessment of the political valence of ancient culture. Not surprisingly, the autonomy of the subject, a central tenet of Enlightenment and post-Enlightenment political theory, was the organizing principle of this disagreement. Liberals like Schiller continued to criticize the absence of a strong independent per-sonal life in ancient Greece. Hegel himself thought of Greek culture, based on the organization of the city-state, as parochial. Finally, the actualization of Greek tradition was hindered by an essential Romantic impulse: modern expression as the product of an autonomous subject is inimical to all forms of external authority. In an organic culture—that is, a culture where knowl-edge is remembrance—mimesis is productive. In modern conditions—that is, in a world where the subject is responsible for producing its own world (through spontaneity)—mimesis is either impossible (one cannot access the noumenal "real" world) or sterile. Kant was conclusive in this regard when he conceived of "genius" as wholly opposed to the spirit of mimesis.[15] If Romanticism engendered a modern subjectivity, this was not because it embraced a homeostatic balance between subject and world, but because it cast the subject against an irresolvable instability—an incompleteness that no pedagogy could cover up.

This epochal rather than historical character of Romanticism may help to explain some historiographical anomalies in the constitution of the liter-ary canon in Latin America and elsewhere. Scholars have often pointed out that the promotion of national problems in the Latin American literature of the first decades of the twentieth century marks a return to some presup-positions already laid down by Romantic authors like Esteban Echeverría and Domingo Sarmiento in the first part of the nineteenth century. It would be a mistake, however, to refer to this movement as a return to a Romantic aesthetic. Romanticism never ceased to be one of the dominant aesthetics of modernization in Latin America. Romanticism came to represent the most general conditions of the possibility of literature's engagement with the sociopolitical possibilities of the present because it fundamentally altered the narrative function inherited from the enlightened secularization of the aesthetic word. This break is aptly summarized in Murray Krieger's brief account of the development of the Romantic theory of art and subject: "The aesthetic, as it was made available to modernist theory by Kant's third critique, by its adaptation into Schiller's *Letters on the Aesthetic Education of Man*, and by the Schlegels, Schelling, and Fichte—all of these brought about into Anglo-American discourse by Coleridge—rested upon the humanist's definition of the artist's power to make many into one" (1994, 22). Krieger points to an epochal change in the nature of the aesthetic subject. In its passage through Romanticism, the nature of the agent of literary expression changes. This agent is no longer the writer or the intellectual but the poet, who, in line with Idealist philosophy, is defined as the one who holds the power of making many into one. The poet is the master of *Dichtung,* the first modern intellectual completely conscious of the instituting power of the aesthetic word. The poet, the genius opposed to mimesis, is not a moment of literature as an institution (not an author, in Foucault's sense), but, rather, the carrier of a divine force. This force, which is, properly speaking, poetic force, is, somewhat paradoxically, the foundation of the poet-writer's earthly efficiency.

The gains at the level of subjectivation that this movement achieved were by no means intangible. Living beyond classical mimesis, the artist becomes productive, but the condition of such productivity rests on the existence of a certain constitutive lack. As M. H. Abrams writes in his classic *The Mirror and the Lamp*, the eighteenth-century concept of genius underlined the paradox of those able to follow the rules without knowing the rules. The genius is the one who cannot give reason of his knowledge (this reason is always decentered in him: the unconscious, inspiration, etc.). Jean-Luc Nancy and Philippe Lacoue-Labarthe are quick to point out that Romantic theory expanded this lack well beyond the realm of the individual genius to cover the entire field of subjectivity. The famous fragment 116 of the *Athenaeum* is clear in this regard: the poetic activity through which the subject produces itself under the aegis of the subject-work possesses such a nature that this subject-work "should forever be becoming and never be perfected" (Schlegel 1991, 43). The incompleteness of this subject, it should be noted, does not harm the project of modern political subjection. Only a subject of lack can become a subject of hegemony. As a matter of fact, it is not difficult to see the origin of our still-dominant conception of self and society in Schlegel's notion of an ever-developing expressivity. In the work of Ernesto Laclau and Slavoj Žižek, the constitutive incompleteness of the subject (what Schlegel would have understood as its "fragmentation") is what produces a process of political subjectivation agreeable, in the last instance, to the establishment of modern democracy.

What Happened to All Those Latin American Greeks?

To return to our Latin American Greeks: on the one hand, their Hellenic fervor convinced them that, as the Mexican Antonio Caso phrases it in a book suggestively titled *Nuevos discursos a la nación mexicana,* "to persuade is the highest and most urgent of human activities" (1934, 242); on the other hand, their embrace of the *Dichtung* aesthetic reveals that they were equally aware of what we may call the "mystical foundation" of authority. The act of instituting is not consensual in nature but a moment of force, a moment when language ruptures and bursts into society. Not surprisingly, in the historical context of the turn of the twentieth century, poetic force was envisioned as a tool that was much more apt to map the new expressive possibilities of a changing society than were the stiff forms of classical education (which nonetheless found their habitat in the recently created school systems).[16] The merely pedagogical art of sculpture, then, gave way to poetry as the foundational instance of community. There is a graphic record of this movement in the history of Latin American literature: one can trace it in Rodó, Martí, Lugones, Martín Luís Guzmán, Teresa de la Parra, José Vasconcelos, the early Carpentier, and many others. In all of these writers, the image of the statue or the question of image itself is replaced by the singer-poet, the popular bard who sings the secret song of the land.[17]

Perhaps the best answer to the question of what happened to all those Greeks is *nativism,* the search for the vernacular. When the Greek vogue eventually withered, it was replaced by a *criollista,* an *indigenista,* or a *ne-*

grista sensibility. This aesthetic shift was not necessarily accompanied by a renovation in the intellectual cadres. True, the intellectual scene that had so far been dominated by fairly circumspect "intellectuals" now witnessed the tempestuous appearance of a whole group of "national writers": Rómulo Gallegos, Teresa de la Parra, Alejo Carpentier, Luis Guzmán, Lydia Cabrera, Jorge Icaza, Ricardo Guiraldes, César Vallejo, Clorinda Matto de Turner, Eustasio Rivera. These first national authors are all heirs of the Romantic aesthetic in that they revitalize the motifs of *Dichtung* and expression and link them specifically to political notions of selfhood and to practical problems of nation-building. Against all expectations, the relationship between the rising nativists and the old proponents of the aesthetic state was not antagonistic. As a matter of fact, the same intellectuals who had touted the potential of civil education through classical art were those who would now uphold the instituting power of "popular" *Dichtung*.[18] Henríquez Ureña no doubt continued to revere Arnold, but inasmuch as he considered a classical education the proper path to informed citizenship, he soon oriented his research toward the possible collusion of the popular with nationalist aims. Leopoldo Lugones exchanged barbarism for civilization, José Hernández for Homer, and proclaimed the until-then-disdained *Martín Fierro* to be the national book of Argentina. José Enrique Rodó became an advocate of *telluric criollismo* and praised Carlos Reyles. Alfonso Reyes became a relentless examiner of Mexicanidad. Luis Valdelomar put his Schillerian theory of theater at the service of the Inca theater movement that spread throughout Peru and South America in the early twentieth century.

This onslaught of nativism and nationalism does not imply a renunciation of the initial precepts of the aesthetic state. It arises, rather, from a negotiation between intellectual convictions and historical demands. Schiller had already clearly perceived something that the Latin American intellectuals would also come to realize: the masses to be incorporated into the rule of governmentality do not come to the political arena as a tabula rasa, devoid of experiences and preconceptions.[19] As I noted earlier, for Schiller the age demands an education that is not philosophical but aesthetic. If philosophy proposes itself as a search for truth, it also demands a conscious change in the subject of its propaedeutic. Aesthetic education, on the other hand, acts on sensibility, refining an already existing disposition.[20] In Latin

America, the turn from a Greek propaedeutic to a popular-nationalist approach (whether *indigenista* or *criollista*) became a necessity ruled by the law of the double bind of subjectivation once it was clear that the emergence of the masses in political life (immigration in the Southern Cone, the geographical mobility and increasing presence of the working class in the Andes, social revolution in Mexico) demanded that the protocols of recognition be swiftly rearranged. As much as the substance of representation changed, its strategic goal remained fixed for most of the modern period. The displacement from pedagogy to expression, from Greek *paideia* to intuitive nativism, did not break with the predominant theory of culture that had made the Greeks an appealing object of imitation in the first place. Wholeness, embodiment, originality, and organicity are all predicates that the late nineteenth century associated with both popular culture and the exemplary Greek past. José Martí, who explicitly opposed the Greek propaedeutic in favor of a *criollista*-nativist model, confirmed the deep similarities between the two when he presented the opposition in terms of "Our Greece / the Greece which is not ours" (1977, 88).

"Hispanism" was perhaps the most comprehensive label applied to this conception of culture, which, though still willing to navigate the different currents of hybrid modernization, simultaneously remained loyal to the ideal of a community built around the uniqueness of language and ethnicity, even at the cost of becoming reactionary and parochial. In the late nineteenth century, Miguél Cané wielded the utopia of an organic city against the plagues of modernization.[21] In the twentieth century, de la Parra's *Memorias de Mamá Blanca* relaunched the ideal of an organic culture tied, even if ambiguously, to the re-creation of a foregone patriarchal society. And, of course, right at the cleavage of the two centuries, José Rodó's *Ariel* envisioned a reduced pan–Latin Americanism as the spirit (or ghost) of a Hispanic heritage. Alfonso Reyes, who took from Henriquez Ureña the task of promoting Rodó's ideas in Mexico, disclosed the continuity between the injunction to Hellenize and the arising Hispanic paradigm. In "Pasado inmediato," he wrote, "To the love for Greece, we later added the love for Spain's letters" (1960, 186). The sense of continuity proposed by Reyes, however, hides a noticeable displacement. Greece was the name of a utopia, while Hispanism is already a portion of realpolitik. Hispanism attempted to rally the people behind its banner by proposing that the main historical contradiction was between the Hispanic spirit and Anglo-American imperialism. Since the values of Hispanism were identified as cultural in nature, Hispanism thus obscures the many social tensions underlying the fragmented Latin American societies at the very moment that the different regionalisms threatened to unveil the deeply fissured character of Latin American societies. For this reason, the writer-poets of Hispanism (like Oyuela in Argentina) had a difficult time turning the many into one, especially if this "one" was to be identified with the sociopolitical viewpoints of the dominant Argentine classes. Praise of Hispanism functioned as a tool of internal domination in societies where large sections of the populations were black or mestizo (Colombia, Venezuela, the Caribbean), indigenous (Mexico, Peru, Bolivia, Ecuador, Central America), or immigrants representing new political modalities like socialism or anarchism (Argentina, Chile, Uruguay). As a unifying characteristic of the different turn-of-the-century hegemonic projects, Hispanism was more than a corrective supplement to nativism (creolization, understood as Spanish heritage in America) and more than a celebration of commonality based on the Spanish language as a marker of transcontinental identity. It was a class project cast in the mold of a cultural assertion. The promotion of Hispanic identity coalesced with increasing attention to the secularization of society (which caused many frictions with the Church, while greatly expanding the authority of the state in areas previously considered private) and an exponential increase in education, bureaucracy, security, hospitals, and hygiene. All these changes relate to the establishment of biopolitical standards for managing the highly diversified Latin American societies. Hispanism served to legitimize these biopolitical procedures. From a racial discourse directed against encroaching North American imperialism, Hispanism reverted quickly to its true nature as a racist discourse directed against the downtrodden and the excluded. In this sense, Hispanism is the true heir to the subdued dichotomy between *civilization* and *barbarism* that the logic of cultural modernization was supposed to undermine.

Beyond continuities and ruptures, a certain figure asserts itself through all of these changes: the figure of the subject, which brings into full view the question of subjection as the most urgent of the time. From the Hellenic

dreams of nineteenth-century educators, passing through the hybrid textuality of writers like Ureña, Reyes, Vasconcelos, Lugones, Rodó, and Martí, and finally reaching the more organic and representational expressions
of the first *criollistas* and *indigenistas,* Latin American literature incarnates
the role that Roland Barthes attributed to the literary throughout modernity: the institutionalization of subjectivity. If the project of the aesthetic
state presupposed a model to be followed in one's personal *Bildung* process,
then the different nativisms likewise centered their attention on a specific
subject deemed representative of the national character. (And if these ideal
subjects had already disappeared from the historical horizon, like the Indians in the Dominican Republic, or were in the process of disappearing, like
the gauchos in Argentina, so much the better.) Although these representations were obviously stereotypes, they managed to position the question of
the subject at the center of cultural representation. This subject frequently
appeared to be elusive, impossible to apprehend, but also seemed to possess
the hermeneutical key to the land, despite its ignorance of the civil duties
that followed from such intimacy.

In attending to the too obviously representational character that Latin
American literature bestowed on the process of cultural subjection (mostly
through a parade of masculine national types), it is easy to forget such a
project's transcendental conditions of possibility: the modern theory of
culture determined by the double bind of expression and subjection. At
this point, it is important to note that "double bind" refers not only to the
fact that the subject is modeled through culture—a tautology—but also
to the notion that culture itself is modeled after a peculiar concept of the
subject: expressive, self-contained, communicative, responsible, able to
provide its own hermeneutic, and so on. It is because the subject is able to
lend its structure to culture (just as culture suggests the idea of the state
in Arnold) that subject and culture were thought to be indistinguishable,
since in this schema as in Kant's, subject and world consist of the same substance. In Kant, let us recall, what is left outside the connecting rule of the
schema is the noumenal, the inapprehensible perspective where only the
gaze of God lingers. Today we seem condemned to understand this excess,
which for Kant—as later for Heidegger—was a proposition strictly derived
from the Cartesian identification of God with the infinite, in more pro-

saic terms. Thus, for Slavoj Žižek—who does not fail to quote the appropriate genealogy of the noumenal—the "thing in itself" is another name for
the nonsymbolic, the Real. In this version, the noumenal is no longer the
"most intelligible" but the "monstrous."[22] Likewise, culture, as our schema,
comes to be an all-encompassing concept. Beyond its walls lies what can
only be thought under the guise of a meaningless war or imagined through
a "theoretical presupposition," which, since Jean-Jacques Rousseau, we call
"the state of nature."[23] There are of course other names for that outside: the
other, the subaltern, the heterogeneous, and, certainly, the spectral.

Guzmán, Campobello, Muñoz

Literary Strategies in the Face of Revolution

"They were not expecting it," reads the opening line of Aguilar Camín's and Lorenzo Meyer's *In the Shadow of the Mexican Revolution* (1993, 1), one of the most comprehensive and comprehensible books about the vast revolt that created modern Mexico. What arrives without announcing itself is, of course, the revolution, which was not only unforeseeable but also, if we trust its witnesses, the formless appearance of the present. It surprised the politicians accustomed to mulling over the tired formulas of their rituals as much as the generals educated to revere the European science of war and to underestimate the peasantry. It even surprised literature. Literature's function was to announce the future, but when the future finally came, no writer could recognize its face. In one of the most perspicacious studies of the literature of this period, John Rutherford concludes, "It seemed that, as far as literature was concerned, the Revolution might never have happened" (1971, 51).[1]

The so-called literature of the Mexican Revolution provided a belated and problematic response to the revolutionary upheaval. Most "novels of the revolution" appeared between 1930 and 1960—fifteen to thirty years after the events—and as a rule, they display a general antipathy toward the revolt. Authors as diverse as Martín Luis Guzmán, José Vasconcelos, Agustín Vera, Rafael Muñoz, and Mariano Azuela, and later Juan Rulfo, Carlos Fuentes, and others, found it extremely difficult to compose anything other than condemnations of the movement. In their works, the revolution is resolved through a language of abjection and a whirlpool of whimsical decisions portrayed as the fruits of petty passion and unrestrained ambition.[2] Most express such dismay at the lack of moral or ideological convictions involved in the revolution that one is forced to wonder in what sense these are novels *of* the revolution.

Perhaps literature's skepticism provides a clue to a more profound truth. One can always argue, with good Marxist common sense, that literature portrays the Mexican Revolution as chaotic simply because it was not *really* a revolution. It lacked programs and did not alter the form of the state in favor of those who carried on the fight. Given its lack of goals and direction, how can this revolt be considered a revolution at all?[3] Yet there is another sense in which the Mexican Revolution was everything that a true revolution should be. In *Marx for Our Times,* Daniel Bensaid posits that "a revolution 'just on time,' without risks or surprises, would be an uneventful event, a sort of revolution without the revolution" (2002, 54). Realizing a possibility, a revolution "is in essence untimely and, to some extent, always 'premature': a creative imprudence" (Bensaid 2002, 54). The Mexican Revolution was just such a creative imprudence. It opened a hole in reality that literary and other discourses strove in vain to close for almost seventy years. And even when it seemed that it had indeed been closed, it could still reopen in a burst of futurity. In *Cultural Politics in Revolution,* Mary Kay Vaughan writes, "When in 1994 the Indians of Chiapas rose in armed rebellion they spoke from the depths of the revolution's cultural legacy" (1997, 3).

Vaughan's book, on the educational policy of the Mexican Revolutionary state in Puebla and Sonora in the years immediately following Obregón's access to power, aptly introduces once again the problem of belatedness in the intellectual rapport with the revolt. As Vaughan explains, for more than ten years, the revolutionary government relied on textbooks produced by Porfirista authors, who tended to glorify the state of things that the revolution had come to destroy. Even under the dynamic leadership of José Vasconcelos, the Secretaría de Educación Pública (SEP) was notoriously slow to modify its curriculum to reflect the new reality brought about by the revolt. From 1917, when the new Mexican constitution was proclaimed, until the end of the 1930s, the old Porfirista textbooks were widely used in many states, creating an uncanny sense of disjointed temporality. Peasant armies were victorious everywhere, and a progressive elite was in charge of the educational apparatus, yet in the middle of this triumphal revolutionary march, the textbooks used to incorporate the peasant rebels into the logic of the state encouraged nostalgia for the old regime.

The origin of this analytical powerlessness, which equally affects the writer and the pedagogue, is not difficult to find. In fact, it fits on just one page of *Pedro Páramo*, the novel that Juan Rulfo published in 1955—the page with the dialogue between the landowner Pedro Páramo and a group of revolutionaries who arrive at his ranch:

> Pedro Páramo watched them. These were not faces he knew. . . .
> "Señores," said Pedro Páramo, when he saw they were through. "What else can I do for you?" . . .
> "As you see, we've taken up arms."
> "And?"
> "And nothing. That's it. Isn't that enough?"
> "But why have you done it?"
> "Well, because others have done the same. Didn't you know? Hang on a little till we get our instructions, and then we'll tell you why. For now, we're just here."
> (Rulfo 1995, 96)

Here Rulfo dares to undertake an ambitious project: to recount the arrival of the revolution, marking the exact moment at which the present begins. The fact that Pedro Páramo cannot recognize any of the revolutionaries' faces illustrates the huge territorial displacements, the rupture of confined, parochial life, that characterized the popular experience of the revolt. Yet when faced with the "novelty" of the revolution ("We've taken up arms"), Pedro Páramo asserts the repetitive nature of reality ("And?"). The revolutionaries, in contrast, stress the exceptionalness of the moment ("Isn't that enough?"). Pedro Páramo, the master of resignification, is surprised by the weird temporality of an event that arrives without arriving. The revolution is here, but in such a way that it cannot be grasped or contested. This much is clear when Pedro Páramo conjures up the revolution by reducing the event to the categories of will and interest: "Why have you done it?" The answer introduces the traumatic nucleus that the whole literature of the revolution strives to understand: "Hang on a little till we get our instructions, and then we'll tell you why. For now, we're just here." This statement defines the revolutionary moment itself as the instant when the present becomes absolutely predominant, no longer subject to the chain of the past and not yet territorialized in the demands of a utopian future. The absolute predominance of the present weakens both causes and teleologies to open an epistemological crisis that the writer, the pedagogue, and the landowner experience as the same anguished question: how could the revolutionaries have arrived *before* their consciousness? And how can the bond of recognition be reconstructed when bodies alone—but not spirits—make themselves present? Hence Pedro Páramo's question "What do you want?" For him, it is essential that the revolutionaries want something, because his power lies in positioning himself at the other end of the revolutionary demand—as a proxy of the instance of social recognition. I will give you this and that, he says to the revolutionaries, and by giving them this and that, he creates the demand whose absence so alarmed him.

The Role of Fantasy

What is the representation that literature failed to achieve and whose absence makes itself felt so intensely in literary texts, which leave us with the feeling that "as far as literature was concerned, the Revolution might never have happened"? We may find an answer to this question in the cinematographic rendering of Carlos Fuentes's *Old Gringo*. Neither the film nor the novel forwards a particularly powerful interpretation of the revolution, yet both—especially the film—offer an interesting reflection on the question of revolutionary agency as the kernel to be considered in any aesthetic rendering of the revolt. Aesthetics is in fact of paramount importance in this case, since *Old Gringo* provides a poetic picture of the revolution in the Aristotelian sense, giving us the world not as it is but as it should have been. Everything that in the literature of the revolution is whimsical, ungrounded, and capricious appears here as the product of a deep-seated popular wisdom.

In Fuentes's story, the Villista general Tomás Arroyo has taken over a local hacienda. He does not occupy the ancient master's quarters, and he is careful to order his soldiers to avoid any contact with the mansion's decadent luxuries. However, General Arroyo is too haunted by the past to carry out his revolutionary mission. So instead of leaving behind a small guard and continuing his military campaign, he becomes obsessed with proving that the hacienda's old landowners (the Mirandas) stole all their land from the Indian communities. He finally recovers the documents that would prove their expropriation (some primordial titles that the Indians hid in the church's bell tower hundreds of years ago). He gathers his people and ecstatically proclaims that the titles "prove that this land belong to us." He is here interrupted by the eponymous old gringo, played by Gregory Peck, who finds it amusing that Arroyo wants to use "meaningless" papers to prove the rights he has won by force. Arroyo answers that the papers are sacred, to which the old gringo replies that they may seem sacred to him because he doesn't know how to read.

Arroyo's answer to the old gringo's challenge is meaningful insofar as it marks a caesura in the exchange. He has been charged with ignorance and with revering items that are meaningless, but his reply is only loosely connected to these accusations: "Gringo, do you think that we don't know who we are? But I know who I am." This assertion is the opposite of the one in *Pedro Páramo* ("These were not faces he knew"). But why is an identitarian discourse rehearsed as an answer to a practical objection? While one may speculate that the old gringo has threatened the imaginary continuity between the indigenous community (which authored the papers) and the revolutionaries, the scene that follows demonstrates that this is not the case. Arroyo takes all his people inside the mansion (so far they have seldom gone past the front door) and directs them to a circular room whose walls are covered in mirrors. Here Arroyo proceeds to verbalize the process of reflection: "Come, look at yourselves. There you are. Look, I am the one that looks at you and points at you. Look at yourself, Ataulfo. You, Nicasio, are the one with the big mustache. Look, Leocadio, you are the short one. It is us."

The populist mirror stage portrays the joyful recognition of the fighters under a fiction of peoplehood. Revolutionary autonomy is preserved through the trick of staging a recognition that lacks a recognizing instance. The recently founded people see themselves in the mirror, their presence only authenticated by the joyful gaze of an American friend: Jane Fonda. The mise-en-scène of the interpellative call artfully avoids any charge of didacticism by representing the sequence as a process through which the people come to recognize themselves as who they already are, adding only two things to what each man or woman knows before entering the room. First, each now sees him- or herself as part of a totality, a people, and in this sense the scene works as a belated elaboration of General Arroyo's earlier challenge: "Do you think that we do not know who we are?" Second, the recognized and the recognizing instance appear, literally, on the same plane, only mediated by Arroyo's voice and the masterful movement of the camera, which circles around the people in such a way that it accentuates the figure of community while disavowing the eye of the camera.

As in the mirror stage, where specular recognition precipitates the subject into a dialectic of identity that is not sustained by reality, in *Old Gringo* the staging of popular identity is accomplished through a deceitful anachronism. At the historical moment represented in the movie, there were neither Mexican people nor circular mirror-filled rooms that could support their reflection. Regarding the first point, one must side with Alan Knight, who remarks that the idea of Mexico was the result of the revolution, rather than the condition of its possibility (1990, 1: 26). As for the second point, the mirror in *Old Gringo* allegorizes an element that is in fact utterly absent: the reflecting instance, the surface of inscription of the political, or more plainly the state as the guarantor of the circularity that makes national subjects out of disaggregated individuals.

The populist mirror stage names the primordial fantasy of political subjection. "Fantasy" is intended here in the specifically psychoanalytic sense that Slavoj Žižek has given to this concept. In *Looking Awry*, Žižek says that fantasy thus understood is "a scenario that realizes the subject's desire" (1991, 6). The stress here is on the verb—*to realize:* "What the fantasy stages is not a scene in which our desire is fulfilled, fully satisfied, but on the contrary, a scene that realizes, stages the desire as such" (6). The fundamental point of psychoanalysis, says Žižek, is that desire is not something given in advance, but something that has to be constructed—and it is precisely the role of fantasy to bestow the coordinates of the subject's desire, to specify its object, to locate the position the subject assumes within it: "It is only through fantasy that the subject is constituted as desiring: through fantasy, we learn how to desire" (6).

If the notion of fantasy is so instrumental to our understanding of the Mexican Revolution, it is because fantasy underlines the constitutive—instead of merely reproductive—nature of representation. In *The Plague of Fantasies,* Žižek probes more deeply into the use of fantasy as the constructive instance of the social world. In this text, he calls fantasy the transcendental schematism in its own right. The Kantian simile is taken further when Žižek theorizes fantasy, whose primordial function is the narration of an unnarratable kernel, as performing its work through the temporalization of experience (in Kant's first critique, temporalization is also the key to the connection between concepts and categories).[4] This notion of fantasy, we must admit, comes quite close to the concept of ideology, and as a matter of fact, Žižek regularly equates both notions. However, if the notion of fantasy seems more pertinent in the context of the Mexican Revolution, this is because, unlike ideology, fantasy does not need to presuppose intentionality as the causal connection between what calls for representation and the representation itself. In other words, fantasy seems more apt to capture the relationship between the unintentional assemblage of revolutionary forces that contemporary analysis recognizes as a fundamental trait of revolutions and the more intentionally organized sphere of political revolutionary outcome. Seen from the perspective of ideology, which posits a world of interests and determinations and then assesses how the shape of the world deviates from it, the Mexican Revolution appears as either a betrayed or a false revolution. Seen from the perspective of fantasy, the Mexican Revolution appears with a new legitimacy, the same legitimacy that obtains between the inorganic nature of drives and the organization of desire in the world of fantasy.

The present-day historiography of the revolution confirms the importance of the dimension of fantasy in the reconstitution of social and state power. Once the fight was over, the construction of the Mexican state was not just the business of state functionaries and the military; it took the form of an expanded conversation full of contradictions and ambiguities, in which many groups helped shape the face of the Mexican nation. The Mexican Revolution, as Claudio Lomnitz observes, was to a large extent a cultural revolution.[5] In this cultural revolution, different cultural idioms reacted differently to the constitutive event that caused their actions.

From very early on, painting took on the task of staging a revolutionary fantasy. Anthropology grounded the revolution in national history. And education—not law or the army—was the place where the revolution's disciplinary force took its preeminent form.

The Literary Mythology

What was literature's role in the vast collaborative project of state formation that Mexican culture embarked on after 1920? And what relation did the early literature of the revolution bear to the fantasy-making role that fell to art in this particular historical conjunction? Writers and literary historians have built a mythology that seeks to answer these questions. In this canonical view, the work of Mariano Azuela and the Ateneo of Mexico are often singled out as the earliest manifestations of a revolutionary consciousness in the terrain of literature. I find these assumptions disputable, even if I grant that Azuela and the Ateneo are essential to the development of a lettered consciousness of the revolution.

Azuela's novels of the revolution, like the cultural practices of the Ateneo, are an index of a crisis in the intellectual function in turn-of-the-century Mexico. In its most general outlines, this function is one of modernization. Intellectuals achieve this function by becoming mediators between people and state—the latter understood in a broad sense as the sum total of the bureaucratic and cultural apparatuses that favor social reproduction. Intellectuals in Mexico inherited a nineteenth-century ideal of progress and a liberal notion of accessibility to the realm of the universal. Since ideas come before actions and are supposed to govern them, it is perhaps correct to call their ideology of culture and society a modernized form of Platonism. In light of this tradition, the revolution operated an inversion through which those who should have been listening acted. The lettered intellectuals' paralysis in the face of the revolution exists in direct proportion to the peasant masses' activity. The peasants' autonomy, which condemns the intellectual mediation to irrelevance, is the element that lettered rationality cannot digest, much less render literary.

Retrospectively, one can see that the crisis of agency is the most recurrent subject in narratives of the revolution, starting with Mariano Azuela's first novels. In *Andrés Pérez, Maderista* (1911), this problematic is cast as the crisis of traditional liberal subjectivity. The eponymous Andrés Pérez is a vacuous character. He seems a secure person, a journalist, firmly set in his historical times. Inwardly, however, he reveals himself to be empty, moving from one capricious decision to the other. In an inversion of the process of subalternization, intentions are attributed to him that he never had. The question of agency reappears, though greatly transformed, with the revolutionary fighter Demetrio Macías in *The Underdogs* (1916). Critics have underscored Demetrio's inability to verbalize why he is involved in the revolutionary uprising. In what is perhaps the most famous scene of the novel, when his wife asks him why he keeps fighting, Demetrio answers by picking up a stone and throwing it to the bottom of the canyon and saying, "as he stares pensively over the precipice," "Look at that stone; how it keeps on going" (2002, 148).

Andrés Pérez and *The Underdogs* register the alterations in the rules of subjection brought about by the revolutionary moment in a purely negative way. Andrés Pérez is a character out of sync with the times, and his outmoded historicity is replicated in the novel's slightly anachronistic language and style. *The Underdogs,* in contrast, displays a much celebrated economy of words that critics have deemed appropriate to the representation of the revolutionary drama. This shift, from an overly rhetorical presentation of the revolutionary antihero in *Andrés Pérez* to a more circumspect revolutionary leader in *The Underdogs,* already reveals a profound change in Azuela's perception of the possibilities of historical agency. Yet neither Andrés Pérez nor Demetrio is a match for this historical event. In this sense, agency seems to remain a problematic issue for Azuela. But historical agency is not equal to the liberal ability to voice one's opinion in the public arena. For this reason, Andrés Pérez's lack of will can in no way be confused with Demetrio's resigned fatalism at the end of *The Underdogs.* While Andrés Pérez's actions have the fragility of a leaf in the wind, Demetrio's fatalism is as solid as the rock in which he sees, so accurately, a mirror of his destiny. Azuela reaches this point, but he goes no further.[6]

The Ateneo illustrates a second possibility opened to intellectual mediation in Porfirian Mexico. The Ateneo was a collective project in which what was at stake was not, as in Azuela, honesty of representation but survival of the intellectual class through alliance with state power. The problem for the Ateneistas was, of course, that the revolutionary moment canceled the authority of the state and weakened the formative powers of culture. The Ateneistas were slow to realize that the translation of a revolution into the realm of forms confronted them with unforeseen challenges. They could conceive of the revolution as either utter chaos or a sublime spectacle, but either characterization forced them into a peripheral and even estranged relationship with the event they sought to interpret.[7] Awe and confusion are, of course, the Kantian tropes that define, in the first instance, the experience of the sublime. We know that throughout the eighteenth century and beyond, the language of the sublime was transposed into political descriptions as a way to make sense of the most violent moments of the French Revolution (Paulson 1983). In Kant's view, the feeling of the sublime arises from the world yet can be explained only through reference to a power of the subject (Kant 1987, book 2).[8] Likewise, the problem of the revolutionary sublime is connected not so much to the actual experience of the revolution as a chaotic experience, as to the limitations of the regulative discourses that are mobilized to interpret historical events. In Kant, there is a schema or schematism of judgment that applies concepts to intuitions in order to produce, through their synthesis, a valid knowledge. Social discourses, such as literature and art, are also schemas in their own right, although they represent not primary or structural conditions of knowledge, but historical ways of configuring and handing experience. To better illustrate this problematic, we can talk, as the art historian does, about schema: blueprints, elements from the past that can be modified to represent the present. Norman Bryson observes that well after European travelers had brought back firsthand knowledge of a rhinoceros, European artists continued to draw the quasi-mythical beast according to a schema borrowed from Dürer's painting. Revolutions, however, do not have a Dürer, and the Mexican intelligentsia soon discovered that they were left with the doomed task of making sense of the revolt with schemas that were completely inadequate for understanding the extent of the changes developing before their eyes.[9]

The Ateneo's most lasting legacy is a series of conferences, the last one held in 1910 (still under Díaz), in which the Ateneistas voiced their culturalist and Latin Americanist credo. The same year the last conference was held, Francisco Madero launched his Plan de Potosí, calling for a general revolt against the government.[10] To the surprise of many, the proposed revolution triumphed, and Díaz fled to Europe. On June 11, 1911, Alfonso Cravioto, president of the Ateneo, organized a dinner to celebrate this triumph. A week later, the new president of the institution, José Vasconcelos, gave his speech "The Intellectual Youth in Mexico and the Current Historical Moment," in which he suggested a parallel between the political revolution led by Madero and the intellectual revolution sparked by the Ateneistas.[11]

After Madero's triumph, a group of Ateneistas founded the "Universidad Popular," offering hundreds of courses and presentations to workers and rural laborers. The Universidad Popular was directed by Alberto J. Pani, and Martín Luis Guzmán acted as its secretary. Its first effort to reach out to the groups that had previously been excluded from cultural instruction because of the prejudices of the *gente decente* took place on November 16, 1912, at the shoe factory Excélsior, in Tacubaya. On that occasion, Alfonso Pruneda (the organization's vice chancellor) addressed how to prevent infectious diseases, Martín Luis Guzmán read and analyzed poems by Manuel Gutiérrez Nájera, and Alba Herrera Orgazón offered a short piano concert. The politics that the Ateneo proposed to the revolutionized Mexican is a reflection of the policies with which Madero tried to solve a deep social crisis by reeducating the Mexican people. This program was almost immediately challenged by a Left that Madero had betrayed and a Right that his concessions did not manage to appease.[12] Besieged, Madero's government lasted two years. On February 18, 1913, a coup d'état led by Victoriano Huerta and backed by the U.S. embassy displaced Madero, who was killed the following day. His assassination ignited the second phase of the revolution, which was social and deeply agrarian. Some Ateneistas, such as Vasconcelos, Alberto Pani, and Martín Luis Guzmán, fueled this phase, while others, like Alfonso Reyes, whose father had died in the revolt against Madero, retreated into silence or exile. A third group of Ateneistas, deeply identified with a Porfirist ethos, joined the cabinet organized by Huerta. The core of the Ateneista project was devastated by Huerta's coup and the destruction of the imaginary that had sustained the life of the Maderista polis. Already in the early years of the revolution, Alfonso Reyes had tellingly described the bewilderment that the revolt had caused in intellectual circles. In a letter to Pedro Henríquez Ureña dated May 6, 1911, he wrote, "I always judge things Mexican with your eyes . . . so now I can't see a thing" (Reyes and Henríquez Ureña 1968, 168). Unable to understand the moment he was living in, Reyes complains of the most characteristic symptom of the liberal intellectual confronted by the revolution: blindness. It is perhaps ironic that he complained of this blindness to Pedro Henríquez Ureña, the most clear-sighted of the Ateneístas and also the first, as Enrique Krauze reminds us, to write "a retrospective analysis of the Revolution," as early as 1924 (1976, 186).

If the Ateneísta legacy did not fall completely into oblivion, it is because the pedagogical state apparatus mounted in Mexico from 1930 on had strong similarities with their project. As a matter of fact, insofar as the Ateneístas incarnated a classical relationship between intellectual mediation and govermentality, their actions remained paradigmatic of the relationship between culture and social power in modernity at large. Despite its self-constructed revolutionary pedigree, the Ateneo initiated its activities and came to maturity under Porfirio Díaz's government and, to an important extent, with its help. Porfirismo supported the Ateneístas not so much in order to co-opt them but out of a more profound conviction of the unavoidable affinities among class, education, and social interest. For the Porfiristas, it was inconceivable that someone educated at "la Preparatoria" (the Escuela Nacional Preparatoria, founded by Gabino Barreda in 1868 and attended by most of the Mexican intelligentsia) could entertain ideas or projects other than those of the ruling class.[13] In a certain sense, the Ateneístas both refuted and confirmed this diagnosis. They refuted it (and in the process refuted themselves) because they demonstrated that the realm of culture and ideas is not a pacific territory beyond war and antagonism. They actually introduced an agonic version of culture through their conviction that their spiritualist philosophy was irreconcilable with the positivism and determinism dominant among Porfirist intellectuals. However, this displacement was not enough to connect the thinking of the Ateneístas with the emerging social revolution. They favored an evolutionary politics, not a revolutionary politics. The group's history and actions fit squarely into what Stathis Kouvelakis calls the "German road" to revolution: the movement, initiated by Kant, Fichte, and later Schiller (all avidly read by the Ateneistas), that sought to carry out the work of liberation in the realm of philosophy as a way of "making further revolutions superfluous" (2003, 11).[14]

One may even argue that the revolution happened, precisely, because of the failure of the Mexican bourgeoisie (represented by the Ateneo) to modernize Mexico by broadening democratic and social rights. The Ateneistas were not, of course, responsible for this failure, not even as accomplices of the Porfiristas and their shortcomings. But if one examines closely the ideas the group championed, and the Ateneistas' wide-ranging reactions to the inception of the revolution, it is obvious that the Ateneo was firmly rooted in a Porfirista habitus that only the force of events, not the conviction of ideas, would be able to shake.[15]

...

The early literature of the revolution came into existence in three works published within a short time span: Martín Luis Guzmán's *The Eagle and the Serpent* (1928), Nellie Campobello's *Cartucho* (1931), and Rafael Muñoz's *¡Vámonos con Pancho Villa!* (1931). These novels practically exhaust the "novel of the revolution" genre; after them, very little was added to the understanding of the revolt from a literary perspective. *The Eagle and the Serpent* is at times a feverish exploration of the system of dual and sometimes even multiple sovereignties that ran through the fabric of revolutionary Mexico. *Cartucho* addresses a different problem: the constitutive fissure between people and peoplehood and, consequently, the distance between narrative redemption and the irredeemable nature of life as simply lived. I think that the political option Campobello presents, seemingly more accessible at the time of its publication than later, is best understood in the context of certain contemporary political thinking regarding the autonomy of communal logics vis-à-vis the bureaucratic organization of the state. *¡Vámonos con Pancho Villa!*, finally, offers a more traditional vision of the revolt as marked by a constitutive moral deficit. However, Muñoz's moral standpoint is punctuated by an uncanny awareness of the revolutionary nucleus that it is the destiny of any discourse, not just the literary, to shun. As if faced with Medusa's head, Muñoz turns away in horror from the abyss of morality that, to his eyes, is the revolution. But in seeking refuge in a nationalist ideology able to justify what is plainly unjustifiable, he catches a glimpse of the Real of the revolution.

The Reconstitution of the Schema in the Field of Literary Imagination: Martín Luis Guzmán

Martín Luis Guzmán was the first writer who, as a writer, confronted the fact that the revolution had totally transformed not only the political order but also the relationship between intellectual representation and social power. Throughout *The Eagle and the Serpent,* the reader confronts different modalities of power: There is the power that comes with the destruction of the bourgeois moral superego, the one that enjoys or suffers the anonymous mass that Guzmán heroically confronts one night in Sinaloa. There is the power of the bureaucracy, solicitous and inefficient, as the voices and memories of some old functionaries of Madero's government. There is the power that incarnates the sovereign link in its purity: the power of Villa, the terrible power that rests not on a contract but on an attachment that, if followed, implies the abandonment of all juridical command and tradition. There is the power of forms, which like the power of religion still has a secret hold over the souls of those whose bodies have rebelled. Guzmán believed that it is up to writers and intellectuals to organize this multiplicity of powers in a well-structured cultural idiom. For this reason, the central problem in Guzmán's early literature is reconstituting the interpretive schema in such a way that the literary institution might address an event that had left authors and texts mute and undecided. Such a project entailed a radical transformation of the intellectual function. In *The Eagle and the Serpent,* a travel narrative whose only consistent motif is, not by chance, the constant mutability of characters and scenarios, Guzmán jettisons the ethical-political baggage that characterized the Ateneista imagination, while embarking on a tentative and half-blind search for a new hermeneutics, one able to give reality its due and restore intellectual mediation to a commanding position.

Often in a novel there is a particular scene that condenses the whole intention of the text in a sort of narrative microcosm. In such instances, the text reads itself and exposes the fundamental modalities of its construction. In *The Eagle and the Serpent,* this declaration of intention comes in an episode entitled "Night Flight," in which Guzmán recounts his trip in a motorized handcar with the young and promising revolutionary general Rafael Buelna, who has rescued Guzmán from an uncomfortable journey via train and invited him to share his vehicle, a platform to which he has attached an engine and a couple of seats. During the first hours of their trip, Buelna and Guzmán talk, comfortably seated in the chairs that Buelna has secured to the platform. But then night comes, and the noise of the engine makes conversation impossible:

> There came a moment when Buelna and I could no longer talk. The motor, in complete mastery of its perfect rhythm, grew by what it fed on, and gave itself over to the full enjoyment of its finest hour. The "flying machine" really seemed to be flying. And there was something truly awesome in that wild flight, without purpose or objective, over rails of darkness. It was a unique experience, that vertigo of speed without any point of reference, under the impassive stars, the vertigo of pure speed, perceptible to the ear and the muscles. As immobile as though we were not moving, ahead of us shone the two arrows of light which the lantern cast upon the rails. (Guzmán 1965, 138–39)

Since time immemorial, intellectuals have granted meaning and intelligibility to a world based on contingency and uncertainty. Their function has been less to educate than to illuminate. For this reason, it is significant that Guzmán confronts his role in the middle of the night, from a moving platform that furthers his feeling of uncertainty. In "Night Flight," Guzmán recognizes the unprecedented agency of the peasant masses as the unquestionable, historically given element of the revolution. In this sense, the engine that accelerates until it gives "itself over to the full enjoyment of its finest hour" is an exact figure of the revolutionary forces. Of the peasants of the revolution, too, one can say that this is their hour. Although agency is clearly dissociated from the place of the narrator (the peasants' finest hour cannot be Guzmán's), Guzmán is far from condemning the vertigo that the machine imposes on the travelers, even if its roar forces him into silence. On the contrary, he finds that there "was something truly awesome in that wild flight." The passengers (of machine and revolution) are conscious of the danger entailed by this wild run, in darkness, guided only by two weak beams of light. But Guzmán also knows that "no man, for all his foresights, can outwit his destiny" (138). Like Demetrio Macías in *The Underdogs*, Guzmán welcomes the inertia brought by the revolution. But Guzmán is not Demetrio, and his abandonment to the revolutionary situation means, no doubt, something different from Demetrio's.

Throughout his trip, Guzmán's ignorance of his exact location has made him anxious. No matter how hard he tries to guess the name of the next village or landmark, he fails. The mad rush of the flying machine seems to confront him with the limits of his intellectual function. Yet it is as an intellectual that Guzmán resolves the scene: "My efforts to penetrate the darkness were finally rewarded. I could see as clearly as though the sun were shining: a perfect road, lined with trees on either side, telegraph poles, carefully laid ties" (1965, 139). Comforted, he adds, "It was a smooth, clear track on which one could not imagine the slightest obstacle" (140). Not only is the road perfect; in addition, despite the darkness, he is able to see "as though the sun were shining." Then, confident, after a sleepless night, he abandons himself to a deep, pleasurable sleep. But in the next sentence, the car is jolted, the engine falters, and the machine derails and stops. With great irony, Guzmán halts the all-too-smooth course of the revolutionary machine and the all-too-pleasant sleep of a no-longer-vigilant intellectual to ask himself the most urgent question in this historical context: what is the unexpected obstacle? The obstacle is, of course, none other than the emergent political function of the peasant masses in Mexico. But for us, words like *peasant* and *masses* have a secure meaning. They evoke an already naturalized system of connotations and have more or less defined affective overtones. This was not the case for a Mexican intellectual in the middle of the revolution. For Guzmán, rather, the obstacle takes the form of an enigma: it comes in the night of the intellect and overtaxes his ability to see and foresee.

The extended prejudice that assumes that testimonial texts do not demand much reading work to unveil their meaning has kept Guzman's novel in a sort of hermeneutical limbo. The laborious reinterpretation of postrevolutionary Mexico that *The Eagle and the Serpent* implies, with its formidable systematicity, has never been readily accessible to Guzmán's critics. The novel has been praised for its style (Monsiváis 1997), its mastery of language (Poniatowska 1988), its testimonial value (Leal 1960), and its memorable snapshots of the revolution (Martin 1989), but little has been said about how it advances a new and influential version of the revolution by confronting the most urgent task imposed on intellectuals by the actuality of the fight. Even an attentive reader like John Rutherford sees the novel as nothing but "a collection of well-written traveler's tales referring to the years 1913–1915" (1971, 43). The book's structure is not alien to this effect. *The Eagle and the Serpent* gives the impression, as Rutherford notes, of being a loosely connected series of stories. In addition, Guzmán's hermeneutic of the revolution was rather slow to evolve. In 1913, he had published a book that was still within the limits of the old Ateneista schema of social evolution through virtuous apprenticeship: *La querella de México* (The Quarrel of Mexico).[16] In *La querella,* political action is regulated by moral values. The country appears as already condemned, under siege, trapped between the moral bankruptcy of the mestizo and the stupidity of the Indian. Only a strong moral force can save Mexico. Although this moral discourse can still be heard, if more faintly, in *The Eagle and the Serpent,* the later novel's fundamental aim is to work out a new hermeneutics of historical reality. With unparalleled political realism, Guzmán assumes the destitute position of the intellectual as the starting point of his narrative project. This destitution is double. On the one hand, estranged from the actual agents of historical change, intellectuals remained blinded by events and cut off from a situation they should otherwise master, explain, or translate. On the other hand, having lost the authoritative status of the ideas that had platonically guided their labor, intellectuals now found themselves devoid of a reassuring belief in the truthfulness of discourse. In this sense, the lack of vision of which Alfonso Reyes complains to Henríquez Ureña describes an objective rather than subjective malady. Intellectuals could not see for the simple reason that the element that was the object of their contemplation, the world of ideas transmuted at the end of the nineteenth century into an ideology of progress or civilization, had vanished into thin air as an epochal inversion gave actions and bodies precedence over theories and ideologies.

The new schema is not offered up to the reader as a systematically arranged set of propositions. Rather, the reader needs to seek it, working through a text of multilayered significations that hardly seem to coalesce into a whole. Unearthing this schema is the task of the pages that follow.

Images and Spontaneity: Old Schemas and New Forces

Commenting on a photo of Madero and his followers taken shortly after the uprising, Carlos Monsiváis notices the informality and lack of ceremony that characterize the new breed of revolutionaries. "Orozco has his arm around Madero's shoulder. The photograph decrees what is ineluctable about the revolution. The monolithic pose has been broken" (1976, 15). For Monsiváis, the revolution marks the origin of the modern, specular, and even mass-mediatic body of Mexican politics, a body populated by signs that communicate a whole arrangement of values and attitudes. Guzmán also finds the key to understanding his time in an image of the revolutionary body: "I seemed to find some subtle meaning, something that revealed I hardly know what intimate essence of Mexico, in the movement of those men through the darkness, rifle on shoulder, and hip as though grown to the shape of the revolver" (1965, 75).

The options could not be more suggestive. Monsiváis directs his gaze toward a well-delimited historical figure: Pascual Orozco, one of the earliest and most faithful revolutionary leaders, who will nevertheless end his life with the stamp of the traitor. Guzmán, on the other hand, searches for the interpretative key to the present in a body that is fundamentally anonymous and unobserved. Moreover, while Monsiváis tries to capture the essence of the moment in the surface of a photograph, Guzmán aims for a depth and intensity of affect that have seldom before appeared in Mexican literature.

The first encounter with Pancho Villa provides an occasion for the rise of Guzmán's new hermeneutic of the revolution. Guzmán arrives at the meeting with two representatives of the recently overthrown Madero government: his personal friend Alberto Pani and a solicitous but inept bachelor named Amador. Most critical accounts of this first scene correctly stress the brutal subalternization of Villa that opens and closes the scene. Guzmán calls Villa "a wild animal" and sees him as "more a jaguar than a man" (1965, 41). Such rhetoric was more or less widespread among lettered intellectuals of the time. González Garza, for example, surpasses Guzman in ferocity: for the Maderista leader, Villa "was a troglodyte, a beast . . . a destructive force difficult to control" (qtd. in O'Malley 1986, 99). But unlike Garza and others, Guzmán sees beyond his own prejudice, and what he discovers in the figure of Villa is the rising of a new form of sovereignty whose exact formula *The Eagle and the Serpent* strives to decipher. I understand sovereignty traditionally: as the problem of the embodiment of a binding power. Constitutional order dilutes the problem of sovereignty in a net of mutually conflicting powers. In a revolution, however, since the legal stability of the state has been put into question and actually destroyed, sovereignty reverts to its initial relationship with body and force. This is the dialectic investigated in Kantorowicz's pioneering argument about "the king's two bodies." One, the body natural, perishes, but the other, the body politic, keeps living in the medium of the state. "The king is dead. Long live the King" means, then, that the chain of sovereignty can survive unbroken the death of the monarch. In the beginning, the body natural created the possibility of the body politic: this is the order of affairs that the revolution restates and that the first encounter with Pancho Villa admirably condenses.

As the gentlemen from Mexico City enter the room, Villa, who is lying on a cot, orders his aide to bring in some chairs, but only two are available. Questions of rank dictate that Pani and Amador take them. (Throughout the novel, Guzmán depicts himself as peripheral, almost inessential.) The revolutionary logic of the world turned upside down is instantly activated to bring those on the periphery of political power, like Guzmán, closer to the irradiating center of the revolt. At Villa's invitation, Guzmán sits "on the edge of the cot, a few inches from him" (1965, 42). Guzmán sits by Villa and then, in a revelatory sentence, adds, "The warmth of the bed penetrated through my clothes to my flesh" (42). Not only for Guzmán but for many others throughout the book, Pancho Villa is a negative figure of sovereignty: one whose mere presence perpetuates the exception of the law. Villa has gone even further and proposed mutual suicide. But Guzmán only submits to the evidence of the reembodiment of sovereignty as a tactic that will allow him the Promethean act of stealing the source of political life. The fact that the communication between Villa and Guzmán is intuitive and corporeal, not intellectual, is precisely in line with Guzmán's assumption that the revolutionaries represent a force devoid of autonomous form. As a matter of fact, it is only in terms of affection that Villa will become a key to the revolution, not only for Guzmán but for whole generations of Mexican intellectuals.

Neither image nor language, much less logos, this body in which Guzmán reads the essence of the revolution is a manifestation of affect and the placeholder of force. The body, with its enigmatic capacity for affect, appears resistant to capture in images and rituals. The opposition can be resumed as one between deepness and superficiality. If the image is shallow and its power always tied to well-established rituals, the enigmatic body of the revolution is characterized by unsoundable depth. This opposition reigns everywhere in *The Eagle and the Serpent,* as the field of the visible is occupied almost entirely by vacuous rituals (Carranza), meaningless photographs (like the photo of Obregón that Vasconcelos keeps in his wallet), or clumsy and anachronistic characters (like the *licenciado* Amador). The falsehood of the old schema is manifest in its dependence on image and on a merely mechanical, disaffectioned relationship to the world of forms. This is the agonic strategy that Guzmán deploys against Venustiano Carranza. The "First Jefe" of the revolution tempts Guzmán with a position on his staff, but Guzmán unhesitatingly rejects him. Carranza seems to actualize the schema of the old Porfirista regime too closely: "His appearance, besides, wakened in me the memory of the typical figures of the Porfirio Díaz régime" (1965, 47–48).

The banal persistence of the rituals of an old order does not make the revolutionary camp any more intelligible. In the novel, the revolutionary masses are mostly confined to the register of unpresentable and unpresented clamor. In other words, we know what is false, but we don't yet know what truth is. Once again, narrative dialectic will serve the purpose of bridging a perilous gap in the order of social imagination. Although Guzmán does not see a new schema arising readily from the mass of revolutionary events, he is also far from rejecting the unintelligible nature of reality as a deficient ontological mode of the social—as the Ateneistas would have done. Instead, he tries to discern the new face of the Mexican nation in the almost incomprehensible chain of events with which reality greets him at every step.

But how to reconstruct a reality that is no longer governed by the teleological presupposition of a cultivated minority and backed by the authority of the state? Confronted by this predicament, Guzmán actualizes perhaps the singular most pervasive strategy for coping with the revolutionary sublime: an immediate reliance on the actually seen and the practically lived. If no regulative discourse is able to take on reality, the safest option is to restrict oneself to peculiar accounts of "what really happened." Interpretations can go wrong and be refuted. But a minimal narrative of what has been seen and experienced remains beyond objection. Hence the marked insistence in novels, memories, reports, and histories of the period on presenting particular versions as *true* stories. The landowner Silvestre Terrazas writes *El verdadero Pancho Villa,* and Alfonso Taracena calls his very personal history of the revolution *La verdadera revolución mexicana.* Ironizing this trend, Friedrich Katz gives his 985-page study of Villismo a literary title: *The Life and Times of Pancho Villa.* What these examples teach us is that if the *truth* of the revolution cannot be enunciated, then the *true* of the event is always available.

   True and *truth,* let us notice, imply different epistemological claims. The *true* is anchored in the particular. *Truth,* on the other hand, is always severed from experience, since it aspires to the irrefutability that pertains only to the universal. Now, the only reason that this dialectic between *true* and *truth* is of any importance in this context is that Guzmán uses it to solve the problems posed by the scandalous simultaneous existence of a dying social form and an emerging revolutionary force. For every single event he witnesses, Guzmán proposes a hermeneutic that will give us not this or that particular true, but the truth of the revolution itself. The many critical readings that have seen in Guzmán's novel a series of "well-written traveler's tales," or a firsthand account of the revolution, linger precisely in the dimension of true, but they remain partial and insufficient insofar as they are unable to reveal the truth that, according to Guzmán, belongs to the nature of the event. In reading *The Eagle and the Serpent,* the reader must be subtle enough to follow this double path of *true* and *truth,* the constant subsumption of the particular into the universal. Linking the particular to the universal is also a definition of the intellectual function. For this reason, the reconstitution of the bond between the particular and the universal is the same thing as the reconstitution of the intellectual's authority. In the space between true and truth, the writer finds the historical role that he or she is called to fulfill. The writer becomes, as the Romantic definition of the poet has it, the one able to make many into one. To this, Guzmán would only add that the success of this project will depend on the intellectual's ability to look for the one in a different place—not in the realm of images, condemned to the falsehood of pretensions, but in the subterranean dimension of the secret.

Martín Luis Guzmán's Grammar of the People

Although, as a scandalized Vasconcelos relates in *La tormenta,* Guzmán not only showed a fascination with Pancho Villa but also professed perhaps a true admiration for him, Guzmán's real object of narrative redemption is not the solitary figure of Villa, but the vast masses of revolutionary men that Guzmán seeks to subsume under the notion of *people.* In Guzmán's eyes, the revolutionary masses do not constitute a people. Rather, they represent different bands upholding unarticulated demands. It is not only their dispersion that constitutes them as nonpeople but above all their unruliness. Guzmán knows, as Paolo Virno puts it in his reading of Hobbes, that in the absence of the state, there is no people (2004, 22). Guzmán is aware that at the time of narration (1913–15), there is no state to which the people can be translated, and, more problematically, there is no people to be translated. Guzmán can do nothing about the inexistence of the state, but he appoints himself to solve the second problem.

Although educated in the belief that only ideas embody the nation in its purity, Guzmán comes to admit that these "others" who act and fight possess the essential traits of the national culture. They are, however, unaware of this richness. The intellectual function should, precisely, reconnect the historical essence, which is sheer action, with its formal embodiment. But for this, Guzmán first needs to see this essence for himself. One night, at General Carrasco's camp in Sinaloa, he has his chance:

> As I neared the place where I had heard the shots and the screams, the noise—no less confused and blurred—grew louder. "There must be a lot of them," I was thinking when I stumbled against what seemed to be the legs of somebody leaning against the wall, and I fell forward in the mud. But as I threw out my arms while I fell . . . my hands miraculously caught hold of the clothing of another

body, and I hung on to it. . . . My invisible savior . . . squeezed my neck with unexpected affection, a sensation which speedily dissolved in me, giving way to a very disagreeable human smell. . . . The darkness blinded me now more than before, but, thanks to the awakening of some new sense, I became more aware of the multitude. Within its limits, which I could not see, but divined, there existed the soul of a collective unity. The mass began to move like one body, swaying about, stumbling, all in the heart of a thick, dull noise. The same low, vague murmur of the voices continued as before. Whatever collisions took place while moving were deadened by the mattress of mud. It was evident that the mass was guided now by a single will. A current of some sort seemed to flow from body to body. . . . The human mass of which we formed a part was moving toward the end of the street. Several tall silhouettes as of men on horseback formed the pivot round which the rest of us milled. . . . Every now and then there floated down from them shouts that had a tone of command, but to me they sounded confused and inarticulate. One of the queerest things was that in the midst of that sea of human beings I had not been able to make out a single intelligible word. . . . The only sound made by that whole mass was nothing but whispers, murmurs. . . . How long was I held in that nauseating embrace—one hour, two, three? When I jerked myself free, I seemed to rid myself of a greater oppression, both physical and moral, than if all the blackness of the night, converted into some horrid monster, had been resting on my shoulders. (1965, 91–94)

Carlos Monsiváis has already addressed the love-hate relationship that characterizes the writer's relationship to the people: "They try to fly from the people and yet they want to redeem the people. They strive to recognize the people but at the same time they deny its existence" (1997, 1477). Guzmán's visit to Carracasco's troops is a good example of this ambivalence. The account ends with an encounter with a barrier that opposes all concept, as well as all narrativization. Guzmán experiences again, as in his visit to Pancho Villa, the dimension of affect that, in breaking the liberal law that sees community as a sum of individuals connected by a common logos, threatens the autonomy of the intellectual mediator: "My invisible savior . . . squeezed my neck with unexpected affection." The people that Guzmán encounters do not offer a better understanding of the "essence of Mexico"; on the contrary, they work as a dark gravitational force that devours any effort by the writer to illuminate the world around him. Guzmán's words are sharp, precise: the mass, the multitude, is composed of bodies—bodies that in their sheer materiality are not yet a political subject. Although he gains "a new sense" in the middle of the night, this sense is still unable to transform the chaotic mass into an intelligible concept. The very pillars of experience are shattered by the encounter. Guzmán does not know how long he wandered through the mass of bodies, and the experience of failed translation is rendered in an utterly subalternist prose.[17] The night, the others—all is literally unintelligible: throughout all the minutes or perhaps hours that Guzmán spends in the camp, he is unable to understand a single word. Baffled and defeated, he recoils from the enigma, which is tantamount to saying that his intellectual function here reaches its historical limit.

State Fetishism

One episode in *The Eagle and the Serpent* is the mirror image, the perfect inversion, of Guzmán's failed attempt to grasp the essence of the revolt at General Carrasco's encampment. In this episode, entitled "Zapata's Troops in the Palace," Guzmán meets the agents of the revolution on his own turf. Now it is the revolutionary masses who have come to a space that is alien to them but completely familiar to the intellectual: the national palace. Here the bearers of Mexico's new essence confront the state-sphinx that silently prepares itself, from the depth of its indifference, to welcome the insurgents.

The joint parade of Villa's and Zapata's armies in Mexico City in November 1914 was one of the most dazzling performances in the modern history of the Latin American political imagination. These armies represented radically different realities. Zapata was a member of an agrarian society, profoundly indigenous in upbringing and worldview. Villa represented a vague view of justice that was widely held by hacienda pawns and independent cattle ranchers, in a space greatly influenced by the ideology of individualism and developmentalism promoted by their American neighbors. Villa's troops marched dressed in uniforms bought in the United States, showing off the almost mechanical efficiency of their movements. Zapata's men arrived in their traditional white cotton peasant clothing, each battalion holding a banner with the image of the Virgin of Guadalupe. This is the encounter captured by Agustín Cassasola on December 6, 1915: the mythical moment at which Emiliano Zapata and Francisco Villa met at the National Palace. In Cassasola's photo, Villa has taken the presidential seat. In a way, this is the closest that these revolutionaries will come to the emblematic and institutional forms of centralized power in Mexico.

Many inhabitants of Mexico City had never before seen a peasant when the forty thousand members of the North Division and the Liberatory Army of the South paraded through the streets of the capital. Neither had the peasants ever experienced the splendor of the Districto Federal (DF). The peasants' revolutionary occupation of the DF staged this deep fissure in Mexican social fabric. For Camín and Meyer, the occupation of Mexico City augured the rebels' inevitable defeat: "The true powerbrokers in the Convenionist alliance, Villa and Zapata, did not want to and could not organize a government at the service of their interests" (1993, 56). It is worthwhile to recall this analysis, since Guzmán stages the same defeat for his readers in a literary register. And although this characterization is certainly disputable in the light of some recent scholarship, such as Friedrich Katz's book on Francisco Villa, it is undeniable that, as Camin and Meyer put it, Villa and Zapata "lacked what Carranza had in excess: the notion of the state" (57). At the level of national politics, all the power of the revolutionaries lay in blackmailing the establishment and its politicians with the constant threat of revolutionary violence. Even this strategy would be reversed in Guzmán's account of this event.

The scant six pages that Guzmán devotes to the peasant armies' occupation of the National Palace are perhaps those with the greatest symbolic density in the novel. Guzmán arrives at the palace as a diplomatic envoy of the Villista group in the wake of Villa's and Zapata's encounter in Mexico City, and the first thing that he notices is the semiotic scandal created by the presence of men alien to any notion of government and etiquette in the Mexican bourgeoisie's monument to its own political legitimacy. Guzmán cannot help but observe the change that the disjunction between power and representation has wrought on the building itself: "That palace, which I had seen so many times and which always seemed the same, gave me on that occasion, practically empty as it was, and in the hands of a band of half-naked rebels, the effect of something new and strange" (1965, 326).

Guzmán and his friends—among them the recently named president of

Mexico, Eulalio Gutiérrez—are received by Eufemio, likely Emilio Zapata's brother, who offers them a tour of the palace, since he assumes that it must be as alien to them as it is to him. The narrative exhibits contempt for this popular insolence: "Eufemio looked like a stable boy who was trying to act like a president [como un caballerango que se cree de súbito presidente]. When his shoe touched the carpet, there was a clash between carpet and shoe. When his hand rested on the banister, there was an immediate incompatibility between the two. Every time he moved his foot, his foot seemed surprised at not getting tangled up in brush and undergrowth" (Guzmán 1965, 327).

The process of the subalternization of the peasant fighters is similar to the subalternization of the troops of General Carrasco in the scene analyzed above.[18] But on this occasion, the narration also opens onto a metaphysics of state power. Eufemio continues the tour of the palace with comments that make his illustrious visitors smile: "This is where the government meets to talk. . . . This is where the government eats. . . . This is where the government has its dances" (328). Guzmán perceives Eufemio's description as optimistic and naive, but he does enjoy the deconstruction of the spaces of governmentality. The tour ends in front of the presidential chair, the element that should inspire Eufemio's most absurd description. Eufemio, however, does not say, "This is where the government sits." Rather, resorting to the ontologically overwhelming language of deictics, he proclaims, "*This* is the chair" (328). And then, with what Guzmán describes as enviable candor, he adds: "Ever since I've been here, I come every day to look at it, just to get used to it. Because—can you imagine it?—I always used to think when I heard them talk about the president's seat that they meant his saddle" (328).

Amid the laughter, Eulalio Gutiérrez cannot help but put Eufemio in his place: "The day this seat becomes a saddle, you and others like you can all be presidents" (Guzmán 1965, 328; translation modified). The key to the passage lies in the words "others like you." Were these words, which Guzmán here puts in Gutiérrez's mouth, penned with the image of Villa sitting in the presidential chair still vivid in Guzmán's memory? Couldn't this whole scene have been written against Cassasola's photograph? Has not Eufemio climbed the stairs "like a stable boy who was trying to act like a president"? But Guzmán cannot content himself with this mostly reactionary outcome. Eulalio's words have created a deep gulf in the symbolic—the same gulf that devoured Porfirio Díaz. To Guzmán, it is ill advised to point out with excessive cruelty the barrier separating popular revolt from institutional power. He does not intervene but instead calls the reader's attention to something else in the scene: the way in which it reinscribes the aura of power. Eufemio's gaze is unable to exhaust the mystery of the chair, which is why he goes to watch it every day "to get used to it." What exactly is he getting used to? The answer can be found in the same scene. While Eufemio guides them through the palace, Guzmán observes two Zapatistas following them closely and notices that these Zapatistas keep "their palm-leaf hats humbly clasped in both hands." They behave as if they are in church, with an "almost religious humility" (328). The two escorts contemplate some paintings, keeping their distance from Eufemio and the visitors. Guzmán the beholder, unlike Guzmán the narrator, eulogizes these Zapatistas. Their almost religious attitude represents "something sincere and worthy of respect" (328). The Spanish version gives an even clearer indication of Guzmán's rhetoric of subterranean sympathies: these men "representaban allí una verdad." The schema able to subdue revolutionary force is a mixture of art (culture) and religion—a formula that the postrevolutionary state will expand to the point of a spectacular clash with the Catholic Church. True, Guzmán is not able to provide the exact form that the subsumption of collective unruliness into communal law will take (once again, literature was by and large unable or unwilling to propose this formula). He contents himself with offering the most general form that this subsumption will have to take in order to be operative. And on this point, the whole history of the postrevolutionary state proves Guzmán right.

The notion of *sincerity,* which Guzmán opposes to the old schema, expands throughout the novel until it becomes the key to the new subjective configuration. This sincerity is correlative to the mystery Guzmán experiences in his first encounter with Villa and finds again in the night of the intellect that follows his visit to Carrasco's camp. In this specular chapter, the forms of governmentality become the mystery of the revolutionary fighters. Through their rapport with these forms, the Zapatista escorts achieve something that Eufemio is always on the verge of grasping but that in the end always slips through his fingers. While Eufemio betrays incompatibility between hand and banister, foot and carpet, body and stair, the escorts attain a true rapport between the building as emblem of governmentality and their own bodies. The fact that Guzmán succeeds in portraying a fantasy of political subjection does not mean that he is actualizing the Ateneista program in which he was educated. As the many references to the religious sphere make clear, Guzmán thinks of the new obedience that the state commands in terms of a mystical rapport between the truth of the subject and the symbolic forms of government. This relationship to the secret, and its grounding power in the constitution of the social body, is the element that Guzmán wishes to steal, from the beginning, from the terrible aura of Pancho Villa. Although *The Eagle and the Serpent* continues for hundreds of pages after this scene, its narrative project has already been accomplished. The intellectual has discovered the void at the center of his figure, and by traveling to the terrain of a scandalous revolutionary agency, he has managed to recover the cipher of his own consciousness. On the other hand, the unruly members of a revolutionary pack have found in the banners of power a sign of the universal, a place where they can inscribe the truth of their existence.

Pancho Villa Dies a Second Time

On June 20, 1923, Pancho Villa fell, assassinated in an ambush. Fifteen years later, the last avatar in Guzmán's passionate relationship to Villismo appeared with the publication of *Memorias de Pancho Villa* (1938–40). By 1938, the revolution had become a dignified object of literary attention, even if unruliness and chaos were still the major components of its literary rendering. This change in perspective was accomplished, above all, in Lázaro Cárdenas's government, which nationalized oil, awarded land to landless peasants, and raised the moral standards of the revolution, allowing writers to reconcile themselves with their country's revolutionary past. Many of the canonical novels about the revolution (and those more sympathetic toward the revolt) appeared after 1936: Mauricio Magdaleno's *El resplandor* (1937); Miguel Lira's *La escondida* (1947); Agustín Yañez's *Al filo del agua* (1947); José Mancisidor's *Frontera junto al mar* (1953); Juan Rulfo's

Pedro Páramo (1955); and later texts by Carlos Fuentes, Elena Poniatowska, and Elena Garro, among others. *Memorias de Pancho Villa,* however, is not one of these important works. It has been eclipsed by the other novels that Guzmán published in the 1920s and 1930s. The book is crucial, however, for understanding how Guzmán completed his literary project, how the rhetoric of spontaneous and subterranean sympathy that characterizes *The Eagle and the Serpent* was transformed in the 1940s into a nationalist pedagogy. Read from the perspective of *Memorias,* the treatment of Villa and the popular in the earlier work seems a circumstantial detour, a maneuver forced by an unforeseen obstacle. Once the writer is done with the obstacle—that is, once the establishment of a strong state has washed away the anxieties related to the loss of power of intellectual mediation—Guzmán's treatment of the popular falls back into the aristocratic paternalism against which *The Eagle and Serpent* was written.

In the foreword to *Memorias,* Guzmán explains how several papers that belonged to General Villa (as Guzmán now refers to the revolutionary from Chihuahua) had reached him. Although these documents were "dictated" by Villa himself, Guzmán tells the reader that none of them are "written in Villa's own language" (1991, 7). The person who wrote down the memories (probably Bauche Alcalde) had "translated" Villa into an alien voice, and Guzmán vows in the foreword to retranslate him back into his simple and diaphanous idiom. To make this "translation" even more forceful, Guzmán narrates the novel in the first person. This authorial choice reveals an extensive change. In *The Eagle and the Serpent,* Guzmán presents Villa as a jaguar "whose back we stroked with trembling hand, fearful that at any moment a paw might strike out at us" (1965, 44). Now Guzmán lends his voice to the jaguar, to the man who was earlier a beast rather than a human being.

Although ostensibly a restitution, Guzmán's hijacking of Villa's voice has all the marks of an appropriation. In chapter 6, Guzmán reports a conversation between Pancho Villa and the Chihuahuan revolutionary leader Don Abraham González, who tutored Villa at the outbreak of the revolution. González tells Villa that it is time to take up the fight. Villa's response is eloquent: "Señor, be reassured that you will always be obeyed. We face the fight as conscientious revolutionaries who know that our fight is for the good of the people and the poor. We know that we are ignorant because nobody cared about us, and for that reason we need the guidance and the command of those who know better" (1991, 27). The Villa of *Memorias* always invokes the nation (*patria*) as the driving force of his fight and never tires of proclaiming that those with education must be in charge of politics and the general direction of the revolution. He is already wholeheartedly integrated into the constellation of nationalist ideology. In this way, Guzmán attempts the final territorialization of Villa as enigma. In *Memorias,* there is not even an enigma to be solved, since Villa is "read" by the situation from the very start. The obvious problem with this "solution" is that if the subjectivity that Villismo came to incarnate were really like the one that Guzmán depicts in this late novel, the revolution would never have happened in the first place. By 1940, Guzmán no longer needed to reveal the revolutionaries' secret system of allegiances to the motherland: they were already fluent in this discourse. By this point it was possible (at least for Guzmán) to believe that the construction of a powerful nationalist state apparatus could cancel and, more precisely, sublate the barbaric force of the many into the gigantic project of a national, integrative pedagogy.

Writing a Forgotten Afternoon of the Revolution: Nellie Campobello's *Cartucho*

Cartucho exists in two versions. The first, published in 1931 in Veracruz, as the inaugural book of the leftist publishing house Ediciones Integrales, contained thirty-one narrations, covering the historical period 1916–20—the years of the dissolution of Villismo and its reversal to a guerrilla warfare movement. The second edition, published in 1940, adds twenty-four new episodes and removes only one, entitled "Villa." Max Parra refers to the difference between the editions in these terms: "Whereas in the first edition the stories are based on her own and her family's immediate experiences during the war, the new stories draw from a wider range of sources, including material from her fieldwork on Villismo . . . as well as from her compilation of regional legends and corridos." This procedure authorizes the reader, according to Parra, to see the text as "not so much the product of a personal as of a social memory" (2005, 53–54). Jorge Aguilar Mora comments extensively on the stylistic and compositional changes that Campobello introduced in the 1940 version. His valuable reconstruction of the shifting ground of Mexican culture in this period and the evolution of Nellie Campobello's public persona suggests that the changes added in 1940 deeply affected the identity of the text. My reading of *Cartucho* is largely based on the first edition, although I do not consider the vignette "Villa" that Campobello excluded, perhaps wisely, from the final edition.[19]

Although her figure has become increasingly central to studies on narratives of the revolution, contemporary scholarship did not "discover" Nellie Campobello. Antonio Castro Leal included *Cartucho* among the works he selected for his ultracanonical *La novela de la Revolución mexicana* in 1960, and Campobello was already well-known in intellectual circles of the 1930s and 1940s.[20] Her stature dwindled in the 1960s, but her later sudden disappearance and death renewed interest in her historical persona. Finally, the post-1968 crisis of the Mexican postrevolutionary state allowed her works to be read in a completely new light, and critics turned an avid gaze in her direction. Elena Poniatowska complains that she "never received the recognition that would stimulate her vocation as a writer" (1988, ix), but one can also argue, as I will here, that there is in Campobello an active resignation from the field of literary production, a discomfort vis-à-vis the problem of narrating the revolution, which remained, nonetheless, Campobello's favorite subject.

There is a general agreement about the fundamental features of *Cartucho*. The narrative voice is that of a girl, the Nellie of 1916–20 (she was perhaps born in 1909), growing up in Parral, the stronghold of Villismo.[21] The text, which develops through a series of vignettes, is partly autobiographical, partly fictional. The episodes are, as a rule, quite short, some running to half a page, only a few reaching two pages. Although there is a strong narrative voice, the form sometimes resembles that of popular, anonymous narration, and despite the avowedly testimonial character of the book, references to recognizable events are scant or inserted into what can be described as a poetics of the prosaic that tends to weaken their "historical" significance. Stylistically, the most striking trait of the book is the narrator's matter-of-fact tone as she recounts the horrors of a revolution that she sees, literally, parading in front of her window. This parochial location of enunciation is essential to the narrative project. Unlike Guzmán, who narrates the revolution from the perspective of intimacy with its leader, or Vasconcelos, who reveals patches of what the reader imagines to be a more intense involvement with the secret scenes of revolutionary power, *Cartucho* describes the revolution from the perspective of a provincial street (La Segunda del Rayo). The dissimilar claims to narrative authority made by Campobello and Guzmán are revealed quite clearly in their books' titles: Guzmán's evokes the paradigmatic figure of Mexican nationalism, the mythical eagle and serpent that figure at the center of the Mexican flag; Campobello's, on the other hand, appeals to anonymity, since, as we learn in the opening chapter, it pays homage to a character who never speaks his name (Campobello 1988, 6).

This rhetorical arrangement creates a series of determinations for the reading of the text. We are so steeped in a logic of meaning indebted to hermeneutical exercises that it is very difficult for us to read something so evidently transparent that it can be grasped almost without interpretation. In contrast to Guzmán, here there is no deep grammar to be unveiled, no hermeneutical work to be done, and no symbolic surplus to be appropriated. If Guzmán chooses depth as the key to the subterranean solidarities that sustain the world of his book, Campobello makes an inverse choice in favor of a literal approach to the world that seems to mirror the revolution not only without fear but sometimes without affection. In this way, Campobello rejects the implicit difference between *true* and *truth* that populates the narrative of the revolution and claims that if there is any truth to the revolt, it can be found on the surface of the world-text. As a consequence, the symbolic operations that make *Cartucho* exceptional remain, like Monsieur Dupin's famous purloined letter, both unreadable and constantly exposed. In such a situation, the most straightforward description, like the following by Aguilar Mora, becomes a theoretical statement: "Nellie Campobello approaches events that appear fleeting, insignificant. . . . She does not describe battles or political positions. She does not rescue the voice of the warriors. She searches her memory in order to perpetuate the most forgettable instants, what is forgettable to others but most intense for those who lived through them" (2000, 12–13). It is the superficiality of meaning, not its hidden kernel, that solicits the attention of the writer. The true of everydayness has the upper hand against the colonizing truth of historical or nationalist territorialization.

Campobello's reference to the origins of the novel is no less unpretentious. *Cartucho* was an attempt, she says, "to write a forgotten afternoon of the revolution." The phrase does not lack ambiguity, but we can assume with some certainty that what was forgotten are not the circumstances of the novel's composition, but rather a particular afternoon, or all afternoons in their particularity. The novel would thus work as the recovery of a singularity that has been left untouched even by the busy scriptural machine of the revolution (so many stacks of books on its literature, history, ethnography!). This temporal and regional locus is an index of the intractable difference between the locality of the event and the dialectic implicated in any narration. I think it is fair to say that the relentless assertion of local autonomy encapsulated in this eulogy of an unsubsumable particular is the element that lies at the source of contemporary fascination with Campobello's work. In unassuming prose, Campobello sought to disarm the institutional appropriation of the everyday into the historical coding machines that organize meaning and power.

But Campobello also asserts that the book answers specific political demands. The novel appeared almost simultaneously with a journalistic piece in which Campobello defended Villa. Some critics believe that this piece, which appeared on July 20, 1931, in *Revista de revistas*, was the first public panegyric written in favor of Villa. It is also said to have provoked the wrath of the *entorno* of Plutarco Elías Calles. In the foreword to *Cartucho*, published only four months after the article, Campobello repeats her allegiance to Villa: I wrote *Cartucho*, she says, to avenge an affront. The affronted one is Pancho Villa, whose memory is constantly sullied by the lies of commentators. However, Villa is mostly absent from the pages of *Cartucho*, whose title refers to a secondary character in a novel in which all characters are, in fact, secondary. How can we understand a book in which Villa is mostly absent as a defense of Villismo? To answer this question, we must pay some attention to the text's formal properties.

Campobello's decision to remain on the surface of acts and events doesn't mean that her text lacks aesthetic pretensions. An enormous deployment of literary sophistication is needed to create the illusion of sincere platitude that critics have almost unanimously celebrated in *Cartucho*'s pages. An analysis of any isolated vignette, such as the one entitled "Nacha Ceniceros," would suffice to show how this sense of the prosaic is produced. The vignette in question retells the story of the final hours of Nacha Ceniceros, a *coronela* of the revolution enrolled in the ranks of Pancho Villa's army. Campobello explains that the version she is going to tell is not the true one: Nacha did not die, but left the revolution alive and went to live on a ranch. The moral of the untold true story, however, replicates the moral of the story that Campobello reproduces. In the vignette, Nacha accidentally kills her lover, Gallardo, who was also an officer in Villa's army. As was customary in these cases, and despite Nacha's rank and merits, Villa orders her execution. The narration of Nacha's final seconds is exemplary of Campobello's strategy of using a poetics of the prosaic to fight the appropriation of the everyday by a scriptural machine:

> She wept for her lover, put her arms over her head, with her black braids hanging down, and met the volley of the firing squad.
> She made a handsome figure, unforgettable for everyone who saw the execution. Today there is an anthill where they say she was buried. (1988, 21)

Three short, sharp, and apparently unpretentious sentences constitute the core of the narration. They could be a paradigm of popular circumspection. They may also represent the brief, almost speechless way a shocked girl might testify to incomprehensible violence. But these sentences also stage the movement of the dialectic. They even mimic the structure of a classical syllogism, parodying its form: by so inverting the classical purpose of the syllogism, Campobello's reasoning grants access not to the universal but to the singular. The first sentence represents an objective position, an image to be described. We see Nacha from a narrative outside (as we can see the generic man in "every man is mortal"), and this structure mitigates the otherwise uncanny use of an "adult," military vocabulary. The second sentence singularizes the figure of Nacha Ceniceros, rescuing her from any objective or authoritative discourse through aesthetic intensity ("she made a handsome figure"), while simultaneously underscoring the importance of actual witnessing: the figure of Nacha is unforgettable *for those who saw her death*. The final sentence represents the story's total relinquishing of narrative authority: taken over by a parodic impulse, it mocks the "monumentalization" of the execution site, marked now by an anthill. When the reader reaches this final sentence, all versions, even those of the witnesses, have been stripped of authority, and the prose of the world has been appropriated by the sphere of rumor ("dicen" / "they say").

It is time to return to our initial puzzle, since we now have all the elements we need to solve it. How is it that a book that scarcely mentions Villa was conceived and written as a defense of Villismo? *Cartucho,* an attempt, as Campobello said, to write a forgotten afternoon of the revolution, is a defense of Villismo by the very nature of its forgetfulness. The writing of the forgotten *is* the defense of Villa. Villa is seen by Campobello as an irruption of the everydayness of the people into the sacralized time of an overarching national reality. But the politics implicit in the novel is not just a politics of time but one of space, or, better said, locality. The revolution and the revolutionaries encroach and trespass. They break into history as they break into cities and ranches, occupying spaces that they often viewed as heterogeneous to them. The movement of uprooting is not only, however, a movement away from a place or toward a goal—it is also a passing by. In *Cartucho,* the revolution passes by without finding a proper place in which to take root. The tropes of displacement, travel, and uprooting so characteristic of the narrative of the revolution are somewhat inverted in the pages of *Cartucho,* where movement is seen from the perspective of a piece of world that in the middle of revolutionary turmoil remains faithful to its own essence, equal to itself. This is a utopian space that always, throughout the novel, means refuge. This is the enchanted world that the revolutionaries left to found Mexico.[22]

To articulate a defense of Villa means, then, to rescue him not only from the horrific stories told in the yellow press but also from any attempt to integrate him into the general current of a glorious history of the Mexican Revolution—a process that was already foreseeable in 1931 (see O'Malley 1986, 99–112). Nellie Campobello vindicates Villa in the singularity of experience, in the "this" and "that" of which history and literature know nothing, because they are born of their disavowal. What is an afternoon of the revolution—one already forgotten as Campobello writes—to the powerful discourses that order the brute facts of existence into the transcendental-

ism of a design? For the people who experienced the everyday of the revolution, as Campobello did, this afternoon is all they have. To narrate such
an unsubsumable afternoon (to sustain the gap between the locally lived
and narrative subsumption) offers the possibility of living the temporality of the event not from the perspective of an extra in the crowd, but as
part of the unanimous and inalienable experience of the everyday. To some
extent, sustaining such a reading involves shattering the too-comfortable
position of reading *Cartucho* as an innocent rendering of things that after
all, by virtue of the novel's parochialism, carry no weight compared to the
revolution's big events. It also means distrusting Campobello's professed
"sincerity" and reading her novel as a sly narrative of vindication.

There is only one moment in *Cartucho* when Campobello's decision to
keep her narration at a distance from the most recognizable national events
is compromised. This comes in the chapter "The Death of Felipe Angeles,"
where Campobello recounts the court-martial against Angeles that ended
with his execution. Angeles, a prominent soldier in the federal army before
joining Villa and the revolution, was greatly admired by many writers. In
The Eagle and the Serpent, for example, the first explicit formulation of the
poetics of sincerity can be found in a conversation between Angeles and
Guzmán at the headquarters of the insincere First Jefe. Only by considering
Campobello's passionate attachment to Villismo and to a figure like Angeles can the reader weigh the emotional restraint that she must employ in
her vignette in order to preserve the narrative voice as that of a girl only
obliquely concerned with the historical value of the facts she is narrating.

Campobello begins with one of the book's few representations of public
discourse, quoting Angeles: "I know you are going to kill me, you want to
kill me. This is no court-martial. For a court-martial you need this and this,
so many generals, so many of this and so many of that" (1988, 42). As if Campobello regrets the precision she has given to Angeles's voice, her narration
quickly acquires the vagueness of an ill-remembered scene. A few para-
graphs later, she offers her profession of literary faith: "They talked a great
deal. I don't recall what about. . . . [Angeles] mentioned New York, Mexico,
France, and the world. Since he was talking about artillery and cannons,
I thought his cannons were named New York, etc. The circle of men listened, listened, listened" (43). In a progression with which the reader is

already familiar, from the story of Nacha Ceniceros, Campobello mentions Angeles's execution but closes the story with an aesthetized portrait of his death. The vignette ends with a conversation between Angeles and a friend of Campobello's mother that completely removes the figure of the general from the battles, the cannons, the world (as Campobello says), restoring him to the stage of singular, personal, lived memory.

Campobello, who knew Villa personally, was obsessed by him for years. She collected all the information about him that she could and even wrote a book about his military genius. A stroke of luck put Villa's personal archive into her hands after his assassination in 1923, including most of his papers, the dictated memories, and his personal service record. In a sense, she now had all she longed for. But Campobello had no use for the archive and gave it to Martín Luis Guzmán, who, as noted earlier, used it as the basis for *Memorias de Pancho Villa*. The gift proved to be a poisonous one.

Looking the Revolution in the Eye

Revolutions as such seem to escape conceptual thinking. There are of course many approaches to and theories of the revolution: some are valuable; most, as Alan Knight once wrote, are useless.[23] Often the lack of mindful consideration of the revolutionary question responds to the methodological decision grounding the discourse. Still, some historians find the situation worth complaint. In the foreword to one of the most ambitious analytic efforts devoted to the Mexican Revolution, *Everyday Forms of State Formation*, James Scott admits that revolutions have hardly been a consistent subject of thinking for history: "Between the moment when a previous regime disintegrates and the moment when a new regime is firmly in place lies a political terrain that has rarely been examined closely. State-centric descriptions of this period typically emphasize its anarchy, chaos and insecurity." For the historical gaze, Scott concludes, revolutions are "an interregnum" marked by the absence of the state and the "collapse of sovereignty" (1994, ix). This analytic deficit is not peculiar to the historiographical discourse. Among the many registers and discourses that strive to approach revolutions, only a few, in exceptional moments, murmur a relevant insight. One finds a few pages by a political philosopher, an acute observation in a book of literary criticism, an improbable reading of a poem or a painting. As a rule, history, sociology, and anthropology have little to say on the matter—outstanding indeed, since by and large all of these discourses owe their existence to the age of revolutions. While literature and art, on the other hand, are often thought of as standing in a privileged position regarding change and revolutions, Trotsky complained that aesthetic representations of the big dramas of humanity (like revolutions) are as a rule notoriously poor.[24] The contradiction is only apparent. Modern art's relationship to revolution is not representational, as implied by Trotsky, but structural. Precisely because it is impossible to represent revolution *itself,* aesthetic forms seek to relive the revolutionary moment instead of portraying it. Art cannot reflect the revolution, but the revolution can happen in art. This is the not-so-secret nexus that links the avant-garde to the revolutionary ethos of the last century—a connection explored by Alain Badiou in *Le siécle.*

¡Vámonos con Pancho Villa! introduces a paradox to this dynamic between social revolution and revolutionary art. Muñoz's novel is not an avant-garde text able to point to an isomorphic relationship between the literary and the historical event. Muñoz's novel, rather, is a completely conventional narrative that assumes, more or less unproblematically, the task of portraying and representing Pancho Villa's adventures and character to the largest possible audience. However, this smooth text is interrupted here and there with scenes and episodes that cannot be easily subsumed within the current of the general narrative. It is in these sporadic moments that something like reflection on the nature of the revolution arises, and although isolated, these moments are not marginal. Rather, as I suggested earlier, they punctuate, organize, and in the end structure the text's overall message, acting, as I will detail later, like a political unconscious that Muñoz cannot ignore even if facing the revolution was perhaps the last thing on his mind.

¡Vámonos con Pancho Villa! tells the story of a group of friends, the Lions of San Pablo, who decide to enlist in the ranks of Pancho Villa's Divisón del Norte. The novel provides scant reasons for the Lions' desire to join the revolution. They don't seem to be particularly deprived in either economic or political terms. Notably, Muñoz's novel was adapted for the screen by Fernando de Fuentes in 1936. While the film version follows the book closely, the first scene is an interpretation—accurate, in my opinion—of some of the

novel's subterranean messages. This scene finds some of the future Lions walking arm in arm, singing a popular tune: "Si me han de matar mañana, que me maten de una vez" (If they're gonna kill me tomorrow, they better kill me right away). The movie thus begins with an immediate staging of the death drive—an element that, in the novel, comes to the forefront of the narrative in a slower, more oblique manner. Muñoz, incidentally, authored a book of short stories—pretty much in the style of Campobello's *Cartucho*—entitled *Si me han de matar mañana*.

Death for Being

Tiburcio Maya opens and closes the narration of *¡Vámonos con Pancho Villa!* He is the leader of the Lions of San Pablo and represents in several instances a serious conscience, casting a critical eye on the murky universe of revolutionary Mexico. Tiburcio Maya is the one who articulates the reasons the Lions join the revolution. He is the one who objects to their practice of playing Russian roulette, a game in which one of the Lions is killed. And he is the one whose disapproving eyes follow Villa when he refuses to approach a car train where Becerrillo, the youngest Lion, lies nearly dead, consumed by smallpox. Yet Tiburcio Maya is also the character who, in a parody of Hegelian teleology, embodies the anomic and clueless revolutionary spirit, such that his allegiance to the revolt translates into an almost total erasure of his consciousness and individuality. Tiburcio Maya is the figure subject to the blows of meaningless death and almost total subjective deprivation that run, as an undercurrent, throughout the novel's pages. The most intense of these blows come after Tiburcio, his Lions decimated, abandons Villa and returns to his ranch. Several years later, as Tiburcio is working the land, Villa returns for his loyal lieutenant and urges him to join the army he is gathering for an attack on Columbus in New Mexico. Tiburcio hesitates. He is flattered by the offer, but he has a young son, a daughter, and a wife. Then, in one of the most shocking scenes of the literature (and film) of the revolution, Villa solves the riddle with unparalleled ferocity:

> Yes Tiburcio. . . . How can you abandon them? But I need you. I need all the men I can gather, and you will have to follow me right away. So you know that they will not suffer hunger or suffer because of your absence, watch!

Quick as a whip he reached for his gun and with two shots he left the dead bodies of the mother and the daughter bleeding on the floor.

Now you have nothing and nobody. You don't need a ranch or an ox. Take your rifle and let's go. (1960, 728)

Confused and humiliated, Tiburcio brings along his young son and rides with Pancho Villa toward Columbus. While Fernando de Fuentes included this scene in his 1936 film, it never made it to the theatrical release, although the uncut version of the film was finally aired by Mexican television in 1982. This scene, in which Villa rids Tiburcio of everything hindering his potential for war, lends itself to a melodramatic reading, the essence of melodrama lying in covering up the senseless nature of suffering with a ready-made meaning designed to produce a well-contained reaction. Nonetheless, such a melodramatic take has been largely absent from interpretations of the murder in either novel or film. The scene seems to have been shocking enough to prevent the emergence of any moral interpretation. Instead we find a sort of displacement, a hermeneutical trick that causes the unviable melodramatic effect to emerge in a different location, namely, at the site of the author's political and moral responsibility. In this reading, *¡Vámonos!* is seen as a courageous text that dares to portray a revolutionary hero like Villa as a coward and a murderer. But does this interpretation allow us to come to terms with the destitution of meaning that we face in the murder? Clearly, it seems to allow the replacement of Tiburcio Maya's intentions with the author's. Although it is likely that Muñoz wrote this scene as a way of showing the immoral and sadistic side of Villa's appeal, we cannot escape the fact that Villa's action elicits a gesture of allegiance in Tiburcio. It is not that Tiburcio doesn't resent the killing of his family; he hates Villa and is ready to kill him. But in his destitution, Tiburcio yet incarnates heroically a tension between his individual and his historical persona. His individual body hates Villa and wants to be done with him. His historical body, however, follows the thread of the revolution to whatever destiny it may reach. It is because of this split that the connection between action and destitution, decision and anomie, that is the scene's final result cannot be approached from any moralizing or melodramatic standpoint. Rather, it requires an approach attentive to the drama of consciousness and decision that marks Tiburcio's life, from the beginning of the novel until its end.

Villa's deed and the way in which it immediately elicits loyalty from Tiburcio confront the reader with the vacuum that lies at the core of the revolutionary act. Murdering a women and her daughter in cold blood, of course, does not constitute a revolutionary act, but it does allegorize, with all the revulsion Muñoz can muster, the secret of dissolution and reconfiguration that is the condition of the revolution itself. This allegorical reading is authorized partly by the intense isolation of the scene's instance of death. Tiburcio does not bury his wife and daughter but simply leaves them where Pancho Villa put them: lying bloody and lifeless on the ground. Everything happens as if the murder has no consequences other than those that follow from Tiburcio's observance of Villa's call.

The scene of the murder, which seems to illustrate, if not Tiburcio's acquiescence, then at least his passivity, correlates to a scene toward the end of the novel in which the American forces that have entered Mexico to hunt Pancho Villa have only managed to capture Tiburcio. They offer him redemption in exchange for information:

> Do you have wife, children? . . .
> Wife? Children? Pancho Villa murdered them.
> The sergeant was confused and speechless.
> Pancho Villa kill them? You follow Villa?
> Yes.
> You obey Villa? You defend him?
> Yes.
> You crazy.
> Crazy yes.
> I don't believe you. If a man kill wife, I kill man. I do not defend man.
> I do. (1960, 775)

A certain admiration for Tiburcio Maya is manifest in the pages of the novel, including this scene, one of its most heroic. As I remarked earlier, the source of this admiration lies in Muñoz's attempt to capture Tiburcio's energy and his determined efforts to build a national program.

But nationalism is not the primary reason Tiburcio decides to withhold information about Villa's location. He cannot turn Villa in, he mutely reasons, because Villa's offense can be answered only in man-to-man combat. A second reason has to do with a nationalist pathos that subtends the whole narration and that emerges even more forcefully in the cinematic rendering of the novel. These dual loyalties determine the specific form of Tiburcio's resistance to the American's inquiries: a series of sharp, contentious *yes*'s and *no*'s that, like the "nevermore" of Edgar Allan Poe's famous raven, exposes the automatism that grounds and at the same time undermines all discursivity. After the useless interrogation, the Americans leave Tiburcio on a road near a city dominated by the Carrancistas, the sworn enemies of Villa and his supporters. Tiburcio does not attempt to hide his Villista identity, and the Carrancistas hang him some moments later. Hanging, as Claudio Lomnitz observes in *Death and the Idea of Mexico,* was a form of execution reserved for the *clases ínfimas* and the rank and file.

Muñoz presents Tiburcio's death as both the conclusion of a tragic life and the logical outcome of revolutionary allegiance. Death, in its multiple forms, but above all as death drive—as embraced destiny and sacrifice to a pantheon without gods—is the *other discourse* that traverses a narrative that would otherwise be completely conventional. This discursive undercurrent should not be confused with the popular thematization of death that has been the subject of many studies.[25] In these cases, death is linked to a particular ideology (nationalism, militarism, nativism, etc.). The abrupt emergence of death in Muñoz's novel, on the other hand, carries none of these meanings. If anything, it conveys the total vulnerability of life to chance. Thus, the gesture of uprooting and the motif of travel—so powerful in the narrative of the revolution at large—take on new meaning in Muñoz's novel. Wherever he goes, Tiburcio carries with him the mark of an initial commitment to death—a death that awaits him at the end of the road. Travel, invasion, escape: any movement returns the subject to the same place it was before. And what always returns to the same place, says Jacques Lacan, is the Real.

The previous description of two moments in *¡Vámonos con Pancho Villa!* rests on two implicit arguments that now need to be clarified. The first relates to the constitutively ungraspable quality of the revolution, the void that is the essential feature of the revolutionary time and for which the Real is, if not a model, at least an apt metaphor. The second relates to the subjectivity that can be constructed at the innermost circle of this void.

The revolutionary moment as such cannot be conceptually thought.

No reduction will be of use here—no phenomenology of the revolution is, strictly speaking, possible. The subtraction of state power, for instance, cannot give us the formula of the revolution. If that were an appropriate formulation, the revolution *in itself* would be identical with civil society in the classic Hegelian sense. And even if we purge civil society of all the elements that, as part the ethics of the state, compromise the purity of its moment, revolution would at most coincide with the reestablishment of a primeval everydayness; Campobello's *Cartucho* seems to advance in this direction. Nothing in these possibilities can account for the moment of the deanchoring of social relations evoked by the *¡Vámonos!* of Muñoz's title and lived by Tiburcio Maya to the point of subjective destitution. Simultaneously, we know that this pendulum of destitution and reconstitution has something to do with the elusive revolutionary moment we are trying to pin down. It is one of the forms assumed by the crisis of sovereignty and the arising of more than one sovereign power.

What the movement of subjective dissolution reveals is the same anomic element that James Scott strives to think under the guise of the interregnum. It is interesting to recall at this point Giorgio Agamben's observation that the word *interregnum* designates a well-established institution in Roman law. Agamben discusses this concept as he develops a genealogy of the "state of exception" (2005, 83). For Agamben, the state of exception points to the suspension of the law, as in the state of siege. He is interested in the paradoxical structure of the exception. When one element is excluded from a particular order, its status is neither inside nor outside that order. If I say "all colors can be worn except black," it is clear that "black" is included in the norm "color," although its actual realization is forbidden. For Agamben, the actors in the drama of the state of exception are law and force. The state of exception reveals a dichotomy that has always inhabited the realm of the law and its most persistent mythologies. In the Hobbesian state of nature, to mention the foundational political myth par excellence, everybody battles with everybody, and brute force reigns supreme. The law sublates the state of nature by incorporating its unbounded force into the sphere of the state. The sublated force now guarantees the enforcement of the law. In the state of exception, the law and its force are again separated, and it is not law but force that guarantees whatever social cohesion can be achieved. If this is interesting to us, it is because, besides the state of siege, the other two modalities that can reveal the disentanglement of law from its force are, in Agamben, resistance and insurrection (2005, 1).

The preference for death as the exemplary punishment in the state of exception is for Agamben proof that what is at stake is life itself. Likewise, in the revolution, obstinate fidelity to death is a way of domesticating and making available a surprising surge of life. Life—or rather, the possibility of its unbounded energy—keeps haunting the social body. It is not by chance that the disposition for war exposed by Tiburcio and his friends should be framed through an animal metaphor: "the Lions of San Pablo." However— although the revolutionary moment can be structurally akin to the state of exception, although it is itself a state of exception—death means completely different things in the two different situations. Borrowing words from Walter Benjamin, we can say that the state of exception imposes a law-preserving death, while the revolutionary wager is, at least ideally, for a law-creating death. Death in the revolution is not just a figure that allows us to point to the obscene essence of the revolutionary act; it is itself the real condition of the possibility of revolt. The condemnation of the senseless killing machinery inaugurated by the revolution is a theme that runs through all the writers contemporary to the revolutionary event. But few of them go as far as Muñoz in showing the intimate connection between death and freedom. Doesn't the murder of Tiburcio's family represent a horrendous instance of the cancellation of economic and social interest that grounds the possibility of the biopolitical at the level of the family? What else could be the meaning of Villa's cold words—"You see Tiburcio. You have nothing now. Take your horse and let's go"? The allegory of the revolutionary instance unambiguously shows that although we may think of death in the rhetoric of finality, it is in fact the rebellion's efficient cause. The promise that death holds is essential to the revolutionary moment because it annihilates, as mere possibility, the world of interest, all excuses for conservation. It fictionalizes the whole social body with a radicalism that other ways of envisaging possibilities (as the *als ob* that mediates and makes possible the Kantian moral imperative) only imperfectly match. The possibility of death is the real cipher of the revolution, because it elicits the freedom that comes with the loss of everything. Death, then, reveals freedom as the revolution's essence. It is the fiction, and yet the real possibility, of a lapse into autonomy. We find this interpretation confirmed by Maurice Blanchot. At times, Blanchot writes, one "encounters those decisive moments in history when everything seems put in question, when law, faith, the State, the world above, the world of the past—everything sinks effortlessly, without work, into nothingness. The man knows he has not stepped out of history, but history is now the void, the void in the process of realization; it is *absolute* freedom which has become an event. Such periods are given the name Revolution" (1995, 318).

The revolution, in our imagination so often a form of negative theology, stages once again the death of God. (The activity of dragging the saints out of churches and shooting them with a firing squad may find here its metaphysical grounding.) The void created in this theological debacle is the abyssal ground that sustains the revolutionary decision as an instance of freedom, because in order to be possible, the revolution must *first* elicit a moment of no-law, a regression to a foundational violence (or to a foundational force; here indecision reigns), which, as Kant saw so well, shatters the idea of immanent progress under which the minds of the Enlightenment begot the science of history to the future (Kouvelakis 2003, 10–23). As soon as the event gathers the force needed for the new political project to get under way, revolutions tend to cancel the moment of freedom that lies at their root and constitutes their conditions of possibility. This initial force released by revolt (the force of law, Agamben would call it) is not conservative or progressive; it is just indistinct force, the primary material of any revolt and the only foundation of human self-determination. Its convocation is, as I have said, almost simultaneous with its cancellation. Programs and proclamations (Planes de Ayala, Agua Prieta o San Luis), ideals (agrarian reform, universal rights), songs (*corridos* and popular tunes), routines, and disciplinary formations are all techniques that seek to capture the original Dionysian outburst of force in some Apollonian sort of container. Fantasy, whose result appears under the guise of the utopian, is never, strictly speaking, the vehicle of revolution. It belongs, rather and already, to the sphere of its subsumption.

The subjectivity that can be built in the innermost circle of this void can only be, therefore, a form of readiness: readiness for war and destruction but also for creation and reinvention. (As critics from Judith Butler to Giorgio Agamben have noted, Hegel discusses both revolution and culture under the heading of Terror.) Once we enter the realm of fantasy, we have already abandoned the territory of pure revolutionary violence. Pure violence and fantasy are structurally alien to each other, just as an instinct is alien to the form of its satisfaction. This structural difference between the efficient cause of revolution and its later embodiment explains, to a certain extent, that all revolutions are, by necessity, betrayed revolutions. Readiness announces itself as the necessary dispossession needed to make the whole of history and society available for political intervention. "If they're gonna kill me tomorrow, they better kill me right away," the Lions of San Pablo sing, well before taking up arms. What is shocking about the Lions' statement is their desire to speed up what we struggle to postpone. This desire, which strikes us as incomprehensible, defines, according to Alain Badiou, the militants' position in the twentieth century. Badiou's hypothesis is bold yet obvious: the twentieth century is the century of the Real. It is the century in which militants experienced the terrible attraction of the negative. "I am convinced," writes Badiou, "that it is the Real that fascinates the militants of this century. There is an exaltation of the Real that does not stop short of horror" (2005, 35). The nineteenth century, on the other hand, was for Badiou the century of the imaginary, the century of beautiful forms to be realized in the realm of politics and art (I earlier characterized the Ateneistas and their politics as a form of Platonism). For Badiou, art and poetry provide the truth of the philosophical dictum, while Brecht and Mallarmé seek in art what the militant seeks in politics: the limit, the last configuration of reality. Unlike Badiou, we cannot call for the avant-garde to help us corroborate the revolutionary courting of the Real. The novel of the Mexican Revolution—and Latin American revolutionary literature in general—is not prone to build an isomorphism between social revolt and formal innovation. But this is no reason to completely disavow the emergence of the question of the revolution in the more "conservative" and "provincial" (Muñoz's novel has not been translated into a single other language!) style of the early novelists of the revolt. "I saw nothing, I heard nothing," says Guzmán after his first encounter with—now we can say it—the Real of the revolution. So we ask: what about this nothingness itself?

Such nothingness is all there is to see, even if most Mexican writers felt uneasy when confronted by this void.

The discovery of the void as the essence of revolution, and the description of the twentieth century as the century that evokes the militants' love for the Real, are obviously complementary. One can take Badiou's argument further and say that it is because, in the twentieth century, the revolution reveals itself in its nakedness that the militant can embrace it as a noumenal event. In the case of Muñoz, I have tried to isolate the episodic moments in which the writer comes face to face with the radiating center that commands a movement away from all centers. The dominant rhetoric of the enterprise is, as in Guzmán and Campobello, regressive, and the search is for an origin; the inversion of the Platonic heaven of morally and politically good ideas that was the benchmark of nineteenth-century enlightened reformers becomes palpable here. Revolutionary fantasy, which was brought to completion in the works of the muralists and the first great ethnographers of Mexico, continues and deepens this thread. However, the project of excavating the past in the search for a primordial or essential moment when freedom and decision are not yet covered with the garments of a contingent history seems condemned to failure. One jumps almost imperceptibly from the layers of text and phenomena to the noumenal kingdom of the Real. At the bottom of the ark of culture and texts, there is only more culture and more texts. The regressive method—beautifully exemplified in Agamben's archaeology of the state of exception—discloses a fundamental if difficult truth that Agamben himself puts in these words: "Life and law, anomie and nomos, auctoritas and potestas result from the fracture of something to which we have no other access than through the fiction of their articulation" (2005, 88).

The task of looking the revolution in the eye is a futile one. If the center and the radiance of the revolution can nonetheless be encountered, this encounter takes place outside the coordinates of the symbolic. It is always poorly translated into the language of beautiful forms, but an encounter is what it is. We cannot know "what a revolution is" by inquiring into the depths of this void—not because there is no answer awaiting us there but because, like the Platonic sun, the radiance of the discovery would be enough to blind us.

The Cross of Literature in Paraguay

The Critical Legacy of Augusto Roa Bastos

Confronted by the work of Roa Bastos, critical reading stands in disavowal. Not that Roa Bastos lacks critical attention: the bibliography on his work, especially on his two great novels, *Son of Man* (1960) and *I the Supreme* (1974), has increased year after year. But these readings have been marked by what Gerald Martin calls an unwillingness to draw conclusions that, although inescapable, are also "unacceptable to the great majority of writers, critics and other intellectuals concerned with the problems of contemporary Latin America" (1979, 169). Hence the wearisome insistence on the novels' formal traits: How many voices compose *I the Supreme*? Whose authorial voice is the last? Is *Son of Man* a novel or a set of isolated tales? Formal aspects are, of course, essential to an understanding of Roa Bastos's literary project, but only insofar as they illuminate the sociohistorical determinations that forced upon the works an unprecedented crisis. By overlooking these determinations, critical reading ends up entrapped in a purely superficial, imaginary engagement with the text, one in which, to recall a poignant image used by Roland Barthes, the critic, like a child, takes a watch apart to figure out what time is.

Gerald Martin's concerns lie in the sphere of the relationship between the intellectual and the popular, and more specifically—to use a word that was not available when Martin wrote his piece—in the sphere of the relationship between literature and subalternity. Martin's indictment of literary criticism still retains some of its vitality today, even if several of the conclusions that he deemed "unacceptable to the great majority of writers, critics and other intellectuals" in 1979 were drawn in the wake of the promotion of *testimonio* as an internal criticism of literary studies. What Martin introduces—and my analysis of Roa Bastos retains—is the institutional dimension of the problematic of subaltern representation. The persistent unwillingness to read the consequences of Roa Bastos's novels is puzzling given that Roa Bastos wrote about his literary practice at length in a series of essays that established the basic coordinates guiding his aesthetic pursuit. In all these essays, the impasse that blocks the writer from his or her historical task is thought in institutional terms. It is, then, in terms of the institution of literature that we should pose the question: where does criticism's resistance to what is unambiguously advanced in the novels come from? In my opinion, the answer lies above all in the nature of critical analysis itself. Critical reading does not explain literary works; it does not look to unveil their secrets. Rather, it assumes the problem of the work as its own problem. It thinks through this problem in its own language. In order to do this, critical thinking always has an idea of what it is looking for in a particular work. It follows a "guiding question" or model based on an assumption about the work's essence, in this case, its *literary* essence. This is where Roa Bastos's entire project is revealed in its immense complexity and scope: the author proclaims that his works are produced in a country without literature.[1]

In 1989, after more than forty years of exile, Augusto Roa Bastos returned to Paraguay as the country's undisputed principal intellectual figure—a status that was galling to the many declared anti–Roa Bastos Paraguayan intellectuals of Asunción. A few months later, he initiated a resounding debate when he used the pages of the weekly *Hola* to make a tactless declaration: *there is no Paraguayan literature.* The ensuing polemic managed to obscure the whole discussion. After receiving a dozen or so letters from offended writers, and a similar number of novels and collections of short stories, Roa Bastos retracted his words. Although it was thus cut short, the polemic was instructive. When Roa Bastos said that there was no Paraguayan literature, he did not mean that there were no novels or writers in Paraguay, only that these novels and writers, for complex reasons, had not managed to become intermediaries between a modernizing state and a disenfranchised population. Roa Bastos had proclaimed the nonexistence of a national literature long before 1989; he had made this argument in the 1940s and repeated it in different essays throughout his life. In a 1987 interview, he had explained that the lack he identified referred to "the absence of a set of texts linked by common denominators. There is a lack of a system of fictional works able to translate the character of a collectivity, the distinctive traits of its history, its peculiar ways of being, its physical and sociocultural image. In other words, what is lacking is a series of texts able to represent what goes under the name of 'national identity'" (1987, 16).[2]

The weakness of the literary institution in Latin America (the problem of literature's autonomy) is often related to such issues as the low literacy rate, insufficient access to education, the lack of free expression, and the difficulties of printing and distributing literary works. It may seem that Roa Bastos's account of the conditions leading to the nonexistence of Paraguayan literature are sociological in nature. Besides, these conditions are not that different from those in other Latin American countries. But in addition to these widespread problems, Paraguay exhibits the "historical perturbations" experienced by a country "devastated in its material structure" (1983, 14). These devastations started with the War of the Triple Alliance, waged by the combined forces of Argentina, Brazil, and Uruguay against Paraguay (1865–70); were perpetuated by the Chaco War against Bolivia (1925–32); and culminated in the chain of dictatorships that has made the organic development of independent civil society in the country almost impossible. The War of the Triple Alliance was particularly disastrous for Paraguay. It is said to have killed more than half of the Paraguayan population, estimated at some 550,000 people at the outset of the conflict in 1865. The dictatorships, which began in the nineteenth century with figures like Gaspar Rodríguez de Francia and Francisco Solano López, peaked in the twentieth century with Alfredo Stroessner, whose brutal regime lasted from 1947 to 1988.

These traumatic events caused a collapse of national memory, and Roa Bastos's strategy for overcoming the trauma involves a popular subjectification of history. As in any subjectification, what is at stake here is a process of disalienation, of appropriating one's own history for oneself. In this case, the popular sectors must understand *that* history as *their* history. They must make it their own, in their own language and imagination, and validate their views in the larger context of Paraguayan society. It is precisely at this point that the most acute problems arise, because in Paraguay, popular imagination itself is a fractured realm. Paraguay is afflicted with what Roa Bastos calls a "linguistic pathology": the coexistence of two languages, Spanish and Guaraní. Why call this coexistence (a happy one, by many accounts) a pathology rather than celebrating it as an index of diversity? Roa Bastos explains that this linguistic particularity has pushed Paraguay toward schizophrenia in terms of social communication (1983, 17). Moreover, this linguistic divide exerts an almost unbearable pressure on the literary institution. Given that throughout modernity every theory of culture has considered the identification of a national language and a national literature a building block of cultural consolidation, Paraguay represents a striking anomaly: the language of literature and the language of the people do not coincide. This divergence leaves all Paraguayan writers in an uncomfortable situation. When Roa Bastos asks, "In what language should the Paraguayan writer write?" and he answers, "In Spanish," he is actually saying that the Paraguayan writer should write in a language that is not a national-popular language (i.e., not entirely a national-popular language).[3]

The student of Latin America knows that this multilingual situation is not exceptional and that Roa Bastos seems to be exhibiting an outdated monological attitude. Powerful national literatures have thrived in countries sharply divided along linguistic barriers, such as Peru. In the European tradition, not only did multilingualism not hinder the development of literary genres; it is in fact often cited as one of the sources of their development. At this point, a more sober consideration of the bilingual status of Paraguayan society is in order. Unlike in the Andes or Mesoamerica, in Paraguay Guaraní and Spanish are not clear-cut indicators of major social entities that we can refer to as colonizer and colonized, creole and Indian, and so forth. Guaraní is not the language of an ethnicity or social group. Although Guaraní is an "indigenous language," a speaker of Guaraní is not necessarily an Indian. The fact that somebody speaks or is addressed in Guaraní does not provide any certitude about social status or condition. While it is true that Guaraní is basically the language of the peasant or

of the migrant to the city, it is also the language in which the police officer addresses the cab driver who is taking you to the airport, the language
that the architect uses to communicate with his workers, the language of
frustrated public employees complaining about their salaries, the language
that the journalist uses to give a popular slant to her discourse. Guaraní
traverses sociolinguistic barriers and makes inroads into the professional
world and the media, territories that according to traditional diglossic theory should be the realm of a Spanish-language sensibility.[4] Yet surprisingly,
throughout this long and complex history of hybridization and exchange,
Spanish and Guaraní have remained two distinctly separate ways of inhabiting Paraguayan culture and history. At times, their difference appears to
be nothing less than irreducible.

Above all, Roa Bastos argues, the split between Guaraní and Spanish
mirrors the more lived separation between the oral and the written. Guaraní does not easily translate into written form. In fact, there is stark opposition between Guaraní's oral vitality and the striking poverty of its written
expressions, even though there are many texts written in Guaraní; such
texts have existed since colonial times, and no other indigenous language
of the Americas possesses such a wealth of written documents. Colonial ar-
chives in Spain and the Vatican are abundantly supplied with letters written in Guaraní by indigenous people of the region addressing the king or
the pope. So how did this sharp divide between the richness of its orality
and the poverty of its writing come about? Faced with this question, Roa
Bastos points to the fact that Guaraní and Spanish organize different and
incommensurable regions of Paraguayan cultural experience, producing
through their rift a cumulative series of fractures (of which tradition/mo-
dernity is only the most obvious) that makes it difficult to reunite these
two structures of intelligibility under a common form.[5] A language divide
and a history of frustrated constitutions of the social as a unified field are in
a relationship of mutual overdetermination. Thus, the element that hinders
the development of a national literature is not so much the existence of two
vital languages in a country, but rather the way in which this coexistence
points to deeper fractures in the experience of the social.[6]

In terms of a cultural and literary project, a comparison of the multilingual situation in Paraguay and the one that existed at the end of the

European Middle Ages is again instructive. In the case of Europe, the beginning of the novel is seen as reducing the multilingual universe of reference to a pluriphonic and pluri-ideological medium. But Mikhail Bakhtin
can borrow the medieval carnival as the matrix of operations that will later
characterize the novel only because medieval plurilingualism had already
been reduced around a common structure provided by Christianity and
the universal reach of its values and worldview. Despite linguistic differences, a more general cultural "language" created a shared set of presuppo-
sitions, and the fact that multilingualism gives way in Bakhtin to different
ideological valuations of the world proves that the world has already been
established as one—as a common ground and horizon for these processes of
ideological interpretation. So although local speech genres were often codified in different languages, the novel could always sublate riddles, prov-
erbs, and different forms of storytelling, because it was commensurable
with them in their totality. Thus, the differences between popular speech
genres and novelistic representation could always be negotiated to some
extent. In Paraguay, on the other hand, many of the elements that may constitute a national lore are not only expressed in Guaraní; more decisively,
they circulate according to a logic of communication, inheritance, and validation that is alien to the Spanish part of the linguistic universe. As a consequence, the gap to be bridged between Spanish and Guaraní appears wide
enough to seduce the literary enterprise into some form of ethnographic
exoticism, and literature—at least what is designated literature in modern
Latin America—cannot tolerate such an outcome. Strictly speaking, then,
it is not bilingualism that ruins the project of literature, but rather the impossibility of translating from one language to the other, given that what
must be translated are not signs or meanings but complex interpretations
of ways of inhabiting the world and making sense of historical time. For
Roa Bastos, Guaraní is silenced by the very incompatibility between its
enunciations and the distribution of speech in accordance with power. Its
words do not enter the economy of exchange and recognition characteristic of a hegemonic field of sociality. Significantly, Roa Bastos calls Guaraní
an "unformed discourse," an "absent voice," and even an "absent writing."
If, as Borges said, the writing of a poem requires centuries of a sedimented
memory of language, the problem in Paraguay is that Spanish and Guaraní

remember different temporalities, different intonations of a common and yet divided history. One language is the language of literature, the other the national-popular language. Literature cannot remember what the national-popular language remembers. Even worse, literature does not know what it is that the national-popular language remembers. It is unaware of the way in which it selects its objects and the forms in which its memories endure.

Son of Man condenses these problematics as no other Roa Bastos novel does. This is the novel in which Roa Bastos most openly and persistently addresses the problem of the linguistic divide between Guaraní and Spanish. Even before the first word of the novel appears, the whole novelistic project falls under the sign of double expression, as we can see from the two epigraphs Roa Bastos places at the doorway of this text. The first comes from the Bible. The second, from the Guaraní "Hymn to the Dead," encapsulates the promise that is at the origin of *Son of Man,* even if it is a promise that the novel can never deliver: "My voice shall be heard again among the dead . . . And my word shall once more be made flesh . . . When this age is over and a new one begins" (Roa Bastos 1988, 14).

Precursors

Although Roa Bastos insists on the nonexistence of a literary tradition in Paraguay, he recognizes a precursor to his work in the figure of the Spanish anarchist essayist Rafael Barrett. Roa Bastos sees in Barrett the figure of the committed intellectual whose only oath of allegiance is to the popular.

Rafael Barrett arrived in Paraguay as a correspondent from an Argentine newspaper to cover a liberal revolution in 1904. In December of that year, he entered Asunción along with the revolutionaries and decided to stay.[7] He lived in Paraguay for four years, becoming one of the capital's most important intellectual figures. His attacks on the authoritarian practices of the Paraguayan government finally sent him into exile toward the end of 1908. He died two years later, at the age of thirty-four, in France, where he had gone to seek a cure for his tuberculosis. During his brief time in Paraguay (and in Montevideo and Buenos Aires after his deportation), Barrett wrote a series of essays that constitutes, among other things, a sweeping interpretation of Paraguayan cultural and political life (Barrett 1988). Roa Bastos sees Barrett as incarnating two attitudes that would guide his own professional career. The first is his "ethical commitment" to the Paraguayan people: as Roa Bastos put it, even if he were to write fantastical literature, that literature would still have to make reference to the inequities and devastations that mark his country's history (Roa Bastos 1983, 19). The second is more transcendental, since we can recognize in it the core of Roa Bastos's narrative strategy. For Roa Bastos, in the history of delusions and false attributions that characterizes Paraguay, only Barrett and a handful of intellectuals like him had the composure to keep their eyes fixed on Paraguayan reality. In terms of literary history, Barrett was a realist, but not in the sense that he deployed a rhetorical apparatus able to simulate the real (a procedure that begs the question of the real as a solid, stable dimension), nor in the sense that his narrative of Paraguay was sanctioned by scholars or academies. Barrett was a radical realist, a realist able to follow the movement of the real in its sheer irrationality, because, as Roa Bastos is so fond of remarking, it is Barrett who for the first time defined Paraguayan life as a "delirious reality." To define reality as delirious means precisely to contest its presumed objectivity. It means to disclose the deficiency of the hegemonic grasp of the real to such an extent that this deficiency reveals itself not only as an interpretative lack (the hegemonic form cannot convince others of the value-description conveyed in its worldview) but as effectively impotent in the shaping of reality. Such is the reality that the reader encounters in *Son of Man*, a reality without a stable center and with no illusions of permanence, but also refractory to domestication by the powers of narrative, even the narrative of Roa Bastos.

The Question of Subalternity in *Son of Man*

Son of Man first appeared in 1960 in Buenos Aires. In 1982, a revised version appeared that contained an extra chapter and some other modifications. According to Roa Bastos, this revised version constituted "a wholly new work" (Roa Bastos 1986, 3)—an exaggerated claim, by and large. The English edition, published in 1988 with a foreword by Ariel Dorfman and a critical afterword by Jean Franco, is a reproduction of the first version and does not contain Roa Bastos's 1982 additions. The stories constituting the book span a period of almost fifty years, and although carefully knitted into a general, novelistic structure, they are discontinuous and may be read as independent narratives. Critical readers have often pointed to the work's complex structure as one of its most salient features.[8] Because *Son of Man*'s form has received so much critical attention, I will refrain from going into a detailed description of it. About the novel's composition, I will only point out that most of the action in *Son of Man* unfolds between two political geographies: one concerned with the life of the people in almost complete independence from state forms, the other with the life of the state in almost complete obliteration of the autonomy of the people. The first geography focuses on the histories of villages like Sapukai and Itapé, which lie dispersed across an imprecise geography and are traversed by characters who have been expelled from history, such as Old Macario, who remembers his childhood spent alongside the Supreme Dictator Francia, and Alexis Dubrovsky, a Russian doctor cast adrift by the tide of the Bolshevik Revolution. Other characters, ironically, lack the necessary symbolic density to qualify as subjects of grand narratives. I say "ironically" because the strategic question that the novel leaves hanging in the face of what we may formulaically call the nation-state is this: under what conditions can the popular sectors become intelligible to social forms of power (state and culture) and consequently become the recipients of its representational work?

The second geography deals with the Chaco War between Bolivia and Paraguay. The various characters that populate the first part of the novel come together in the second within a single regiment, around a single strategic military objective—the capture of Boquerón. Almost all of them have been outlaws; the few who have not been leading clandestine lives have been in prison. The point of articulation—but also profound differentiation—between the novel's two geographies is the positioning of these subjectivities in relation to the discourses that define them as subjects, either by omission or by inclusion. War is the historical event par excellence. It is customarily linked to the enfranchisement of marginal populations, although this is not what happens in the novel. Here, the forgotten characters that traverse the Paraguayan landscape—the outcasts of many revolts, who in the first part seem only reactively incorporated into the discourse of history, in the guise of guerilla or peasant-revolutionary movements—end up assuming a full historicity. Those most outlawed among the revolutionaries eventually embody the most heroic values (Cristóbal Jara, Aquino); the prostitutes take on the worthiest social virtues (Salu'i); the most insignificant and hardworking peasants manifest the most steely military resolve.

The fashioning of subjectivity that takes place during the war, reinscribing a proscriptive past in a heroic present and sublimating the contradiction between the popular and the state within the war machine, converts these subjects into subjects of history. This is achieved, however, only through the expropriation of their symbolic universe. Therefore, a narrator who wishes to bear witness to a difference that cannot be subsumed into the discourse of the nation must draw out those elements that appear to be irreducible to the linear, regulated discursivity that serves the realist precept of historical expression. As agents of a disruptive and evocative force in the narrative, these subjects rarely enter into history, and when they do, their power of disruption is domesticated and dissolved. Their condition of existence is clearly constituted as subaltern.

Roa Bastos's literary project bears a strategic resemblance to the set of historical investigations that inaugurated the subaltern studies group in India and some parts of Latin America, as well as among U.S.-based Latin Americanists.[9] Although the historian Ranajit Guha developed the term *subalternity* from the writings of Antonio Gramsci, subaltern studies endeavors to go beyond Marxist social analysis. The point of contention between subaltern studies and Marxism arises with regard to the problem of peasant consciousness. For classic Marxism, the development of the popular sectors is measured in terms of the consciousness that these groups acquire vis-à-vis their historical situation. From a subalternist standpoint, this formula is objectionable in at least two respects: first, insofar as a recourse to the "historical situation" aligns itself dogmatically with developmentalism and a historical teleology founded on the universalization of the movement of capital; and second, insofar as it presupposes that an oppositional consciousness must necessarily be situated a priori in the gnoseological terrain (the "historical situation") produced by the state apparatus and the dictates of modernization that it opposes. The problem, subalternists contend, is that these rules of engagement displace the autonomous politics of the subaltern to the region of the irrational or prepolitical—hence the early subalternists' famous denunciation of a prose of counterinsurgency that refers to subaltern actions through a metaphoric representation that underlines the nonpolitical nature of their emergence into history.[10]

I earlier introduced a discussion of subalternity while commenting on some aspects of Martín Luis Guzmán's *The Eagle and the Serpent* (see chapter 5). But the differences between Roa Bastos and Guzmán are fundamental. Guzmán subalternizes the peasant fighters in order to define them within a set of relationships that will assure his group, and the values it represents, control and direction of public affairs in Mexico. Roa Bastos, on the other hand, is a subalternist writer, a writer who brings to literature the same kinds of questions that the subalternist critic brings to bear on history and culture: How is a particular form of subjectivity or communal organization eliminated as a valid form of inhabiting the world? What is the relationship between subalternity and the relative development of state forms and their representational apparatuses? How does literature or any other representational practice enter into this dynamic of attributions of legitimate actions and colonization of alternative ways of worlding? In brief, a subalternist writer poses the question of subalternity.[11]

Posing the question of subalternity is not without well-known risks for the writer. The writer may fall prey to the fantasy of portraying the world through the eyes of the other, while he or she sees only with his or her own eyes. Yet the writer is not condemned to a sort of idiotic monolingualism. The writer may try to present an account of social power relationships using *almost* nothing but the framework of values and beliefs of subalternized people.[12] A monumental accomplishment in this regard is George Lamming's novel *In the Castle of My Skin*, which is to my mind a paradigmatic subalternist novel. Now, important as the issue of the worldview represented in a particular literary work may be, the subalternist writer does not simply look for validation of the subaltern perspective; even more fundamentally, he or she strives to make visible the social mechanisms that are responsible for the production of subalternity. What can this project mean when the subalternizing agency is the literary institution? Jean Franco expresses her bewilderment before the paradox encrypted in Roa Bastos's criticism of the lettered function when, in her afterword to *Son of Man,* she asks, "If literature—represented not only by the narrator Miguel Vera but by Roa Bastos as well—is unreliable because it originated outside the struggle, how can it then speak of the struggle?" (1988, 278). Franco's argument begs the question of the intrinsic right of literature (or the writer) to speak of the struggle even from a privileged standpoint. This position is not very distant from the claim, forwarded by institutional politics, that all politics must unfold according to the hegemonic rationality embodied in institutional politics itself. Roa Bastos, on the other hand, raises the question of the priority of literature, of its right to speak of the struggle in the first place. In practical terms, this means that the element that is most persistently interrogated in the novel is the privilege of the authorial voice, the intimate relationship between the author's right to tell and the real effects of the language of literature. Such an interrogation begins by thematizing all those elements that the literary institution takes for granted, disavows, or makes transparent as operations lying prior to and beyond the textuality of the text. I will call these elements, evoking a pictographic metaphor, a framework. A framework is the work of the frame; it both reduces a world and contains it. In the novels without borders that Roa Bastos is so fond of writing, the framework itself becomes a thematic element, not in that it contains a mise-en-scène that refers the text to the text itself, but in that it constructs a porous frame, constantly assaulted by an exteriority that the work cannot keep at bay, that the work *does not want* to keep at bay.

History and Subalternity

The subalternist position immediately taxes the writer. In his essays, Roa Bastos tells us that the catastrophes that obstructed the development of literature as a social consciousness in Paraguay are linked to national events like the War of the Triple Alliance and the string of dictators that marked the life of the country. In *Son of Man*, the original catastrophe that serves as the ambiguous foundation of memory appears in relationship to an event that belongs almost entirely to the space of popular, to subaltern—it is impossible to fix these terms—consciousness and politics. This event is the agrarian revolution quelled on the night of March 1, 1911. Atanasio Galván, a telegrapher, betrayed the revolutionaries and alerted the military, which sent a train loaded with explosives that met the insurgents at the train station where they had congregated for a final, utopian assault on Asunción. The explosion left its mark everywhere in Sapukai. The church's tower was almost destroyed, the population decimated, the houses deserted. All that remains of the incident is an enormous hole now covered by railroad track.

The novel's second chapter, entitled "Wood and Flesh," contains a brief and horrific description of the explosion site: "Little by little, gangs of labourers are filling in the cavern left by the bombs, but it seems to be a bottomless pit. In it lie the victims of the explosion: some two thousand men, women and children. Cartloads of earth and stones have been emptied into the hole, but it is still not quite level. Every time a train crosses the crater, the rails, supported by temporary piles, sway ominously" (Roa Bastos 1988, 42). The hole itself impels remembrance. It is full of women, men, children, and yet is empty. No amount of dirt suffices to fill it up. The dead insatiably suck the waste up as if the work of the rail crews were a sort of libation, an awkward homage prompted by fear and remorse: "It may be that the bottom of the pit has sunk since work began. At all events it is obvious that much more rubble will have to be thrown in before the buried village of the dead will be pacified at last" (35). This hole is the Real that convokes language and signification in the novel. It is its origin and its telos, although it must remain beyond the grasp of the writer, just as it remains beyond the grasp of the historian, because a second element complicates the picture: the revolt that Roa Bastos uses to introduce the peasant characters and their worldview is not recorded anywhere in Paraguayan history, at least not as a popular revolt. As Jean Franco observes in her afterword, the 1911–12 revolt was in fact a "military uprising, a *cuartelazo*" (1988, 271). Faced with this evidence of the revolt's "nonexistence," some readers have denounced the novel for lack of historical accuracy, charging Roa Bastos with being unfaithful to history. (A bemused and confrontational Roa Bastos remarked that Paraguayans had finally grasped the concept of fiction.) However, another solution—a properly subalternist solution—is also possible. In his essay "The Nation and Its Peasants," Partha Chatterjee argues that the emergence of a subaltern politics is normally linked to its superimposition upon bourgeois or hegemonic politics. When a subaltern group is mobilized or mobilizes itself, two different political domains come together, so that "while peasants [become] aware of the hitherto unknown world of nationalist agitation, they [make] sense of it not in terms of the discursive forms of modern bourgeois politics but rather by translating it into their own codes" (Chatterjee 2000, 10). Is it not conceivable that Roa Bastos's "invented revolt" is another instance of this phenomenon of a subaltern "force" using institutionalized and reified political venues as its means of expression? One should remain alert, however, to the impossibility of supplementing historical narrative with a subaltern perspective, which would give us something like "total history" or "history from below." Historical narrative and subaltern actions belong to different forms of relating actions to institutionally organized time. History works as a legitimizing discourse able to endow actions with meaning; subaltern actions, on the contrary, always represent a work of interruption, a system of dehiscences.[13]

The writer stands besieged by a double impossibility: the absent voice, the subaltern people. Since catastrophes are foundational in Paraguay, the need arises to remember the grievous moments of national history by working through the maze of fossilized memories and unspoken sorrows, thus inverting Renan's famous admonition to forget history in order to have a history (1990). *Son of Man* is itself the remembrance of an original disaster. But if the goal of the narrative is remembrance, piecing together, truth, how can we explain its disjointed architecture, its many interruptions, its incomplete allusions, its self-rebutted assertions? Literature, Roa Bastos seems to say, has to remember, not in the all-powerful model of an unbounded system of signification, but from the humble awareness of itself as only one voice among many trying to testify to a shattered reality. Roa Bastos writes as one who is observed, interrupted, belied by all the voices that literature must silence in order to exist.

In *Son of Man,* the only voice that can bring the old stories into the world belongs to Macario, the narrator that Roa Bastos always strives to imitate. Macario "always spoke in Guaraní. The soft, slurring Indian language made the horror bearable, domesticated it. Echoes of echoes. Shadows of shadows. Reflections of reflections" (Roa Bastos 1988, 18). Nowhere does Roa Bastos claim to translate Macario. Vera, the narrator of the novel, who comes closer to incarnating a sort of alter ego for the author, always insists on the impossibility of carrying on Macario's narrative legacy: "My testimony is not altogether reliable. Even as I write these recollections, I am aware that the innocent wonder of my childhood is colored by the disloyalty and neglect of which I have been guilty as a man" (18). Roa Bastos's initial strategy, then, lies in making the reader aware of the existence of another voice, the Guaraní voice. This voice is of paramount importance for the project of suturing the gap between literature and the popular, because Guaraní is the language that must remember the devastations of the past. One factor, beyond its effective vitality, grounds Guaraní's privileged relationship to memory: Guaraní is always already the memory of the catastrophe because it was itself born from one. The catastrophe in question, however, has robbed Guaraní of its own historical unity. Guaraní is not only the language of a subaltern voice but also a subalternized language, or, as Bartomeu Melía puts it, a reduced language (see Melía 1996).

The subalternization of the indigenous language was accomplished through the medium of religion, which presupposes the entanglement of some half-lost, half-present Guaraní worldview with elements introduced by the colonizer. In one of the most frequently quoted passages from *Son of Man,* Vera reflects: "The conditioned reflexes of the New Testament operate at full tilt in the furrowed strata of religious sentiment which is the real leavening of our mestizo culture. All of Castilian and Guaraní language, or a mixture of them, has been 'evangelized,' has been taken prisoner in the Saintly Sepulchre, within the miasmas of Redemption. We cannot escape" (Roa Bastos 1988, 177).

The Jesuit intervention that caused the reduction of the original language has canceled the idealized moment of the one (the nonmestizo, the unmixed ideality before the act of leavening). Instead of the plenitude of a beginning, we are left with utter indecision. Guaraní and Spanish are held together by something that is in fact inessential: a sentiment. Yet this sentiment ultimately functions as a prison. Vera says "we cannot escape." But the deictic attribution of his discourse is imprecise. Given the lack of distinction between the two languages, who are *we* in this sentence? Which language persecutes? Which one is persecuted? This indistinctness is crucial because throughout *Son of Man* there is a constant reinscription of the colonizer's religion in the cultural arsenal of popular imagination. Gaspar

Mora, the character who comes to incarnate the life of the people in its autonomy from state sanctions, is a carpenter, and carpentry was one of the trades that the Jesuits taught the Indians to promote their *reducción*. Mora's last work, which inaugurates a form of *des-reducción*, contains another Christian reference: a carved figure of Christ. The movement of *des-reducción* incarnated by Mora becomes even more radical insofar as it appears mixed with elements belonging to the never really subsumed Guaraní heritage. Once Mora separates himself from the world and goes to live alone as a leper, he refuses the help of those who go to see him, proclaiming that he is already dead. This reference to the dead bringing new life to the community recalls the Guaraní "Hymn of the Dead," which serves as one of the novel's epigraphs. It stages its promise even though the sedimentation of historical layers forces upon it an ontological quality that can only be named spectral.

This syncretism that complicates the distribution of roles and the genealogy of consciousness began with the cunning and savvy of the Jesuits: "With their usual cleverness and tact, the Jesuits had superimposed the Christian legend on the old Indian one, which said that the god Zumé had appeared there in the days when the sun was still a less important god than the moon. The Indians pretended to believe the Christian legend. . . . Today . . . no one cares anymore about the legend's origin" (Roa Bastos 1988, 53). In its popular incarnation, religion is a palimpsest where all intentionality is always already lost. It is only logical, then, that the religious sphere—devoid of clear or dogmatic subject positions—is where the antisystemic and anti-identitarian politics of the people find their expression. As is well-known, Roa Bastos often elevates these syncretic religious elements to a dramatic key able to lend historical events a depth that transcends the straitjacket of the historical record. But religious imagery can also be the site where the death of the transcendental reveals itself in its nakedness. In the late novel *El fiscal*, Roa Bastos has Brazilian troops crucify Mariscal Solano López on an improvised altar at the end of the War of the Triple Alliance: "Solano was there, nailed to a cross made of branches still covered in bark, as in Grunewald's alterpiece of Christ" (1993, 34). Unlike Grunewald's Christ, however (and Roa Bastos calls the mysterious German painter's panel a "frightening representation" born from the dark depths of the artist's soul), Solano López, the Christ of Cerro-Corá, lacks any transcendence. If this Christ is more tragic than Grunewald's figure, that is only because it evokes a pure abjection, a total reduction of life to the flesh in a hecatomb without gods or offerings.[14] Only when it borrows its meaning from earthly matters—that is, only when it exists alongside a practical promise of deliverance—does religion acquire a historical and transcendental meaning that justifies its existence. Thus, religion, at first a discourse that colonizes the subaltern imagination, becomes a tool with which the colonized can think its own conditions of existence. In *Son of Man,* a novel whose very title plays with the religious motif, this movement is best represented by the history of the hilltop Christ.

The Hilltop Christ

The two epigraphs that open *Son of Man,* one from the Bible, the other from a Guaraní hymn, represent the two pieces of the Paraguayan cross. The latter asserts a utopian moment of rebirth located beyond the present, *when this age is over and a new one begins.*

According to the dominant conception of time, which identifies the collaboration between historicism and modernity as the only possible interpretation of historical development, the "Hymn to the Dead" is pure nonsense. Modernity tends to destroy alternative temporalities by reterritorializing space. In *Son of Man,* the railway constitutes the most potent and representative synthesis of the modern spirit. Its presence as an emblem of modernization is a temporal marker through which life itself is metaphorically constituted as if through a process of awakening: "After the railway was finished, the village began to stretch itself. But"—the narrator adds almost immediately—"one relic of former times remains" (Roa Bastos 1988, 16). This relic or remainder, an element of time and space that is not subsumed by the temporal divide introduced by the railway, is the hilltop Christ. However, its permanence is a product not of the historicist logic of the residue—of the fragment that time in its carelessness neglected to transform—but of a confrontational and unsubsumable logic. The hilltop

Christ did not earn its place in the world as the reward for a strategically passive existence. Rather, it inhabits a space that is symbolically constituted, a locus from which and for which to fight.

Gaspar Mora, alone in the jungle, a leper isolated from the world, carves a life-size wooden Christ figure. When the villagers of Itapé suspect that he has died, they go in search of him and instead find the carved figure, which appears to be made of both flesh and wood. Their machetes raised, the villagers threaten the motionless figure that greets them with outstretched arms. But once the hallucinatory moment has passed, they realize the exact nature and dimensions of Gaspar Mora's last labors. Later, the hilltop Christ becomes the object of a displaced liturgy: "Eager, trembling hands were stretched out toward the crucified figure. They took him down almost roughly, with a sort of angry impatience. Then, with the figure on their shoulders, they went down the hill, their rough voices raised in a mournful chant. . . . In these annual rites the villagers seemed to regard the Christ as a victim they wanted to avenge and not as a God who has died willingly for men" (Roa Bastos 1988, 17). The narrator describes this ritual as the homegrown, heretical, and defiant liturgy of Itapé. The villagers refuse to recognize the syncretism of a God-man, so they proclaim him man and, as such, a son of man. Macario professes this belief at the beginning of the novel, when describing Gaspar Mora's death. After insisting that Mora died a virgin, he adds:

> "But before that he had the child."
> "What child?" someone asked him.
> He did not answer. His head sank to his breast. He gave a deep sigh. (24)

This is the scene that gives the novel its title, but not without leaving behind a significant trace that relates *Son of Man*'s problematic to a Christian imaginary deeply woven into Paraguay's popular culture. In the Old Testament, "son of man" functions sometimes as a reference to "man" or even "humankind" (as opposed to the divine). Thus, the Greek version of the Old Testament frequently renders the expression "son of man" as "anthropoid."[15] In a sort of inversion, the novel stands the divine on its head, proclaiming the human source of divinity. Christ becomes a son of man as the whole Christian imaginary is reworked by Paraguayan popular imagination. The identification between Gaspar Mora and the carved Christ is so strong that the narrator says the multitude carrying the crucified figure gives the impression that "the man whom they really wanted to avenge, or at least to exculpate, was Gaspar Mora" (17).

When, after Gaspar Mora's death, Macario and others carry the life-size Christ in procession to the church, the priest refuses either to bless it or to take it in. It is the handiwork of a leper—a tainted Christ. But the priest's doubts are of no avail. The Jesuit fathers had perhaps insisted too well on the advantages of transculturation, which the priest of Itapé now finds working against his church. The Christ figure becomes the catalyst for a polemic that ends up reversing the usual hierarchies: "Soon Macario's hut was surrounded at all hours by a noisy crowd. The old pauper became the real patriarch of the village. A schismatic and rebellious patriarch, revered by all" (Roa Bastos 1988, 34).

The curia is finally forced to relent, and Father Fidel Maíz is sent to baptize the figure. As the law's representative, Father Fidel Maíz performs the ceremony that effectively wrests all agency from the popular sectors: "It was not difficult to convince the people of Itapé that the Son of God, in his infinite humility, had permitted his image to be made by the hands of a leper, just as two thousand years before he had been willing to be born in a manger" (Roa Bastos 1988, 40). The minor battle over symbolic hegemony culminates in a further inversion that restores to God the power to produce transcendent and foundational meaning:

> "This privileged hill of Itapé," said the preacher, "will be known from this day as Tupá-Rapé, because the way of God passes through the most humble places and fills them with his blessing." And that is still what it is called today—Tupá-Rapé, which means Way of God.
>
> "I don't agree with the preacher," said Macario, after the ceremony. "There was no need to change the name. In any case the Christ's hill should have been called Kuimbaé-Rapé." And that is what Macario called it: Way of Man. (45)

Macario goes so far as to challenge the source of the entanglement between power and representation: the act and meaning of nomination. When Gaspar Mora's Christ appears on the scene, Macario and the priest are confronted by a transcendence of *this world* that not only inverts the transcendental schema implicit in religious discourse but also puts the value of work and production at the forefront of any idea of transcendence. Gaspar Mora transcends himself through his work (we are told later that the whole village bears the traces of his labor). By its very nature this inversion resists the colonization of the people's space; it is a gesture that finds a more radical supplement in the stubborn antifoundationalism to which Gaspar Mora's death gives rise. As the villagers approach the church, the priest forbids them to bring the image into the church: "Think of the man who carved this image. . . . A heretic, a man who never entered the church, an impure man" (34). Macario interrupts the priest's diatribe: "'Gaspar Mora was a good man! . . . There was principle behind everything he did. All over the village there are examples of his work. . . . This was the last thing he did . . . ,' he said, pointing to the Christ. 'We brought it from the *monte,* as we would have liked to bring Gaspar himself. . . . And look at it! Its wooden mouth is speaking. . . . It is saying things we must listen to. . . . Listen! . . . There was something he wanted to tell us through this image of his . . . when he knew that he would never come back, when he was already dead!'" (34–35).

We know that the various forms of transcendence singled out by the movement that associates itself with the "critique of metaphysics" are identified with terms "related to fundamentals, to principles, or to the center," terms that have always designated "an invariable presence—*eidos, arche, telos, energeia, ousía . . . aletheia, transcendentality, consciousness,* God, man and so forth" (Derrida 1978, 279–80). Macario's unveiling of a transcendence of this world, however, implies not a presence but a flaw in the mechanism of representation. The subsumed and subalternized elements of Guaraní culture resurface everywhere in the cracks of an impossible domination. Macario, we discover, is also a witness, a man aware of a calling that he does not understand, one that could quite possibly be unintelligible but confronts transcendence of this world with a post-Nietzschean God who, according to Macario, speaks, though no one can understand him. No character in the novel goes as far as Macario when he attributes to Gaspar Mora the principle of intelligibility, a principle the world increasingly appears to lack. Nor does any other character go so far as to identify this principle of intelligibility—aptly described as a foundation—with a desire to speak, or with an imminent speech that may never be voiced.

In Macario, Roa Bastos is finally able to discern the challenge that he faces: How to acknowledge the call of the subaltern? How to respond? Especially if this call comes in a language that the narrator doesn't name but in which *he* is constantly called? Once again, Roa Bastos's prologue to the second edition may offer some clarification: "For more than 20 years, for the whole of my life, I have unwittingly been imitating old Macario, and I feel that any author, even the most obscure and untalented—and perhaps for that very reason—should take up an ethics and a poetics of variation" (1985, 3). The writer thus acknowledges the call and resumes his storytelling. *That* is his answer and his responsibility. But this attitude does not grant the writer access to a secure realm of facts, memories, and words. Even when uttered by Macario, words describe deeds that are only shadows, echoes, reflections. The author must resign himself to this elusiveness. By interrupting the master discourse here and there, Roa Bastos disturbs its impossible order, and a new formula for addressing reality unfolds. I refer to this strategy as a rhetoric of spectrality—the necessary complement, at a textual level, of what Roa Bastos terms a *poetic of variations.*

Spectrality in Language and the World

Against centuries of ontological thinking, a rhetoric of spectrality asserts the power of the displacement of foundational discourses: such is the power that comes to the fore in the interrupted discourse of Gaspar Mora's Christ, which Macario exhorts the villagers to listen to. The notion of a rhetoric of spectrality implicitly refers to the modalities of manifestation and appearance. Manifestation, however, is always denied to subaltern force. Subalternists understand this denial as a negation of agency. In *A Critique of Postcolonial Reason,* Gayatri Spivak specifies that the word *agency* designates only "a socially validated action" (1999, 71). It is the transcendental sun of institutional power, the one that always gives body, visibility, and reason to the people's actions.

Roa Bastos, however, stubbornly refuses to cast light on the people from any position other than the position of the people itself. In *Son of Man,* the deployment of a rhetoric of spectrality serves only to protect the characters from any alienating illumination by attempting to name or allude to the agency of marginal subjects, while simultaneously dismissing any claim to representational accuracy. Examples abound: Nati and Casiano, escaping the plantation, are referred to as "spectral silhouettes" that "were nowhere visible" (1988, 65). No rhetoric of light—and literature is the most powerful rhetoric of this kind—can adequately "illuminate" them, even when they act by the light of day. When Vera, the intellectual narrator, is guided by a couple of peasants into Casiano Jara's old train carriage, he says of one of his guides: "I was following behind the last of the three. I could see his scar-rutted back. But even though I was watching him move—a man of flesh and blood—this still felt like a ghost story, incredible and absurd" (126).

But doesn't defense of spectrality imply the writer's flight from political responsibility? Although the word invites a certain confusion, *spectrality* is not an idealist concept. Far from eliciting escape from the materiality of history, the spectral speaks of an intense opening to a materiality of the world that is always in excess with regard to ontology. In his apposite commentary on this term—introduced in Jacques Derrida's *Specters of Marx*— Fredric Jameson insists on this connection between the spectral and the material: "Spectrality is not difficult to circumscribe, as what makes the present waver . . . [is] a temporary weakness in our grip on things: on that reality which is supposed to rebuke us by its changelessness, the 'en-soi,' being, the other of consciousness, nature, 'what is.' . . . Solidity corresponds to ontology. . . . How to describe what literally undermines it and shakes our belief? Derrida's mocking answer [is]—hauntology. Spectrality does not involve the conviction that ghosts exist. . . . All it says, if it can be thought to speak, is that the living present is scarcely as self-sufficient as it claims to be" (1999, 85–86). Spectrality reveals itself as a disruption of the feigned self-sufficiency of the dominant, as an opening into another history that is also the impossible history of others. As a refutation of the imperial forms of reason, spectrality denotes the impossible closure of the "real," or, to put it another way, disproves the notion of an end to history in a time without otherness. Meanwhile, for the writer, accepting elusiveness is not a vocational requirement, though it may appear to be so. The call comes from without, from the world. If the formulation of this call constitutes a poetics, it is a poetics that is finely attuned to the vagaries of the "real."

Popular, People, Subaltern, and the Work of Spectrality

The allegiance to the popular that Roa Bastos identifies as unavoidable for the intellectual is intimately and necessarily connected to the rhetoric of spectrality that works as the literary correlation of the definition of Paraguayan reality as a "delirious reality." Before proceeding to a discussion of this connection, we need to clarify the use of the terms that strive to name this elusive form of agency. So far I have been using the words *popular* and *subaltern* interchangeably to refer to those whose emergence is marked by an antagonistic relationship to representation, power, and the state. But *popular and subaltern* are in fact quite different concepts. The word *popular* refers implicitly to the concept of *people*, which, as Paolo Virno reminds us, appears always and necessarily correlated to the existence of the state.[16] The notion of subalternity, on the other hand, appears to exclude the appeal to the state.[17] Yet just as there is no clear-cut boundary between hegemony and domination, neither is there a sharply defined distinction between the popular and the subaltern. *Son of Man,* we can say, hinges on the imprecision between the subaltern and the popular. At least twice, the novel advances the question of the passage from one state to the other: in the case of the Chaco War, we witness an attempt to create the popular from above; in the case of the failed revolt betrayed by Vera, on the other hand, we see an attempt to create the popular from below. Both attempts end in failure—or, rather, in the dissemination of their original intentions. In both cases, an important measure of the failure can be attributed to the weakness or near-nonexistence of a Paraguayan state.

As the rhetoric responsible for representation of or simply allusion to the popular and the people, the rhetoric of spectrality serves the immediate end of imagining the emergence of a subaltern force not as the mere reverse of a hegemonic pressure, but in its autonomy, so to speak. Such is the idea that we find codified in one of the most powerful narrative images of the novel: the railway carriage that Casiano, Nati, and Cristóbal remove from the rails to bury deep within the jungle. When he encounters it for the first time, Vera describes his surprise, not unlike the surprise one might have on seeing a ghost: "When I least expected it, the coach suddenly appeared in a clearing in the *monte*" (Roa Bastos 1988, 126). Exploring the carriage, now decayed by the jungle, Vera comes across a chiseled inscription left behind by Casiano Jara: "Sgt. Casiano Amoité—Ist. Company—Battle of Asunción." The narrator remarks that "half the name had been changed, just as half of it had been destroyed by the verdigris of forgetfulness. Instead of Jara there was this Amoité, which means something far away—not just physically distant, but beyond the limits of vision and comprehension in space and time" (127). This spectral space, with its inscription that points to an inscrutable beyond (and to a beyond that actually never happened: there never was a battle in Asunción), is also a locus of politicization and resistance. It is there that a group of peasants will summon Vera to join a nascent revolution. When the revolt ultimately fails, the military will react with what seems like incomprehensible fury against the old, decayed carriage, setting it alight and excavating the earth around it in search of weapons. The whole of *Son of Man* is condensed in the trajectory traced by Casiano Amoité's railway carriage. The course it travels attests not only to the problematic of subalternity—a carriage in the jungle is the counterpoint, the inverted inscription of an emblem of modernization—but also to the constantly renewed capacity of the subaltern to emerge in nonstriated spaces within the networks of power.

The work of negativity incarnated in the principle of spectrality reaches even the most primordial intuitions: time and space. Anybody who has attempted to write about or merely recount the events related in *Son of Man* knows how imprecise the most familiar words—"before," "after," "later," "in the same place," "on the center," "on the margin"—become in this novel. The old modernist trope of the "fragmented novel" fails utterly to do justice to *Son of Man,* which goes well beyond the fragmentation of consciousness or of the textual form. As a matter of fact, there is no consciousness or narrative gestalt from which the fragmentation of time and space can be "reconstructed," because Roa Bastos's point is precisely that any hegemonic homogenization of primal and pure "intuitions" is arbitrary in the first place. In *Contravida,* Roa Bastos revisits the sites of his early fiction to tell the reader about the town of Manorá, whose people emerge, in spectral form, in the interstices between the spaces inscribed by power and those that are not. Actually, it is hard to distinguish Iturbé from Manorá. Indigenous and Spanish voices cohabit the same space, and Iturbé and Manorá themselves "occupied the same space. The property register was the same." However, "there were no authorities in Manorá. No priests, no political or military leaders. This was the pride of Iturbé and the source of all its ills [la causa de todos sus males]" (1995, 175). And how can we avoid reading here a reference to the ancient myth of the *land without evil,* the promised land of plenitude and immortality of whose existence the Guaranís were so sure that they charted almost the whole continent, in a series of legendary expeditions that invariably ended in disaster and self-extermination?[18] The atopic myth of a land without evil aligns the negating power of theology with the rhetoric of spectrality and is perhaps the only indication of the origin of the structural distortion of the Christian utopia among the Guaraní people. This dystopia seems to lend its resources to Roa Bastos, in whose narrative the disturbance of the established order never enjoys a positivity greater than that which the word *displacement* may accommodate: "Iturbé and Manorá were really indistinguishable the one from the other, although they were not identical.... For example, sunrise was a little earlier in Manorá, sunset, a little later. The time it takes for a falling grain of sand to reach the ground" (175).

Frameworks

It is only appropriate that we should come back to the question of the frame to close this exegesis of Roa Bastos's vision. I do not use the term *frame* in the sense of the formal literary elements that have been the concern of many critics of this novel. These structural determinations are no doubt legitimate philological concerns, but they exist under the shadow of a formal purposiveness of art that Roa Bastos's narrative seeks to destabilize. To some extent, "frame" is a faulty metaphor that invites us to think of the structural conditions of literature as lying outside or at the limits of literary discourse. The frame is not a context, but rather a principle of extimacy that brings the formal conditions of production in line with the ontological complexity of the work of art.[19] One of Roa Bastos's more dazzling propositions is that, far from dealing with these conditions under the ideology of the *genius,* the writer can and must police these determinations in an almost sacrificial modality of self-criticism. So although the question of the frame is not restricted to the narrator, the narrator is the best embodiment of its predicaments.

The narrative function in *Son of Man* moves from the purity of Macario's way of remembering to the impurity of Roa/Vera's account of the same stories. (As in the case of the paradox of the liar, the domain of this impurity includes, of course, the purity that the impure narrator attributes to Macario.) Roa Bastos insists that only Macario is truly able to tell the old stories. In telling them, he is able to recuperate that which resides in their residue. These are often stories whose meaning has been lost or that narrate an unsuccessful quest for meaning. Roa Bastos's avowed intention is to take up Macario's storytelling legacy, even if that means being subject to the same limitations. Potentialities and limits are brought together in the novel to give an account of the necessary historicity of experience, to reveal in the apparently stable background of the real an intimation of what might be, or perhaps of what might have been. The figure of the narrator combines with the rhetoric of spectrality as the only rhetoric able to name or allude to a delirious reality. Whether he is a shadow or a reflection, Macario is the spectral narrator. Perhaps it is more than just coincidence that in a prologue written twenty-one years after *Son of Man* was first published, Roa Bastos finds it necessary to use the word *spectral* to describe his foundational character: "Old man Macario . . . constantly varies the voices and the dreams of the collective memory that is made incarnate in that diminutive, skeletal and spectral body" (1988, 3).

The project of the popular subjectivization of history, then, first and foremost takes the form of a criticism of the frame, a criticism of literature as the authoritative word on the world. To thematize literature as such from within the literary discourse implies letting the stories be, while keeping an eye on the storyteller. The storyteller is not, of course, a person, but a function of the framework. Especially in Paraguay, it is the frame that distributes the roles of the internal and external, the witnessed and the merely seen, the certain and the hypothetical. It is toward the frame that Roa Bastos directs his best "deconstructive" efforts. The quest is not without complications. I earlier noted Jean Franco's complaint about the irresolvable tension in which Roa casts the relationship between literature and struggle: "If literature—represented not only by the narrator Miguel Vera but by Roa Bastos as well—is unreliable because it originated outside the struggle, how can it then speak of the struggle?" (1988, 278). Franco aptly adds that far from being circumscribed to *Son of Man*, this problem "haunts Roa Bastos throughout his writing" (265). Perhaps literature cannot speak of the struggle; perhaps it can only allude to it. One such allusion can be found where the literary discourse allows itself to be interrupted by the absent voice, the absent discourse that literature is unable to portray but in whose shadow the entire historical meaning of its being unfolds.

This interruption also belongs to the order of the frame, for the visor effect does not condemn the writer to the solipsism of the observer. Roa does not posit the popular as a mute, inexpressive realm composed of fugitive sensations. In chapter 9 of the second edition of the novel, entitled "Burnt Wood" (a chapter that the English edition lacks), Vera interviews a nun from Itapé about Melitón Issasi, the former political chief of the village. The nun begins reporting in respectful but familiar language, only to stop halfway through to assert: "You, sir, were born and educated here, in this town, and you know the whole story. . . . You don't need to be reminded of things that nobody here has forgotten" (1985, 271). As he becomes a state official and narrator, Vera breaks away from a community of knowledge and speaking. The function of writing separates him from this primordial hermeneutic circle, and he feels the need to return to the community in a desperate attempt to restore a popular ground to the stories alienated by the process of writing. It is only through writing, the very instrument of alienation, that he can undertake this return, but the criticism of this instrument remains relentless in the Paraguayan writer's work.

In 1967, Roa Bastos, who makes a creative habit of revisiting his stories, published "Moriencia," a short story that resounds with special force for the reader of *Son of Man*. Its first lines read:

> La oí nombrar hace un rato a Chepé Bolivar. ¿Lo conoció usted?—pregunté a la mujer en el mixto.
> —¿Al telegrafista de Manorá? !Eá, cómo no, si hasta su ropa yo le hacía!
> Miente la vieja palabrera, dije entre mí, acordándome de que el telegrafista anduvo casi siempre en cueros. . . . (2000, 11)

[You just mentioned Chepé Bolivar. Did you know him?—I asked the woman.
—The telegraphist in Manora? Why, of course, I even used to sew his clothes!
The old hag lies, I thought, and I recalled that the telegraphist was always
almost naked.]

Roa again begins with a framed narrative: an educated person, perhaps a
writer, interviews a humble peasant woman. Perhaps this is Roa Bastos, collecting material for a novel, perhaps *Son of Man*. But the woman lies, or the
writer wants us to believe that the woman lies, in which case he himself
lies. The story itself is about Chepé Bolivar, the telegraphist who should
have been on duty the day that another telegraphist betrayed the revolt and
caused the almost total destruction of Sapukai.

Is it true that in the agrarian revolt the forces loyal to the government
tried to force Chepé to send a false message in order to draw the rebels into
a trap? And is it true that he resisted bribery, blackmail, and a direct threat
on his life and stubbornly refused to deliver the message? As the conversation progresses, facts become blurrier, less distinct. "Moriencia" tells us
that the revolt happened in 1912, while the year given in *Son of Man* is 1911.
The novel and the short story offer different spellings of the same places,
and even the site of the original catastrophe is confused. The interviewer,
the writer, has to set the record straight: "La estación no voló en Manorá
sino en Sapucai, veinte años atrás" [The explosion wasn't in Manora but in
Sapucai, twenty years ago] (15). To which the woman replies, "No importa"
[It doesn't matter] (15). This reply calls to mind Roa Bastos's description of
the Indians pretending belief to the Jesuit fathers: perhaps they believed,
or perhaps they only pretended to believe, but it no longer matters which
of the two is correct. The reader of *Son of Man* might side with the woman:
it really doesn't matter whether the train exploded in Manorá or Sapucai.

Here Roa Bastos stages fragments of the popular imaginary that the
writer must collect and appropriate if a national literature is really going
to emerge from the whispers of popular memory. The popular subjectification of history is carried over, but not in a way that allows it to yield an
imaginary, stable identity, whether popular or subaltern. It is presented,
instead, as fidelity to call and as unyielding attention to its partial, fragmented existence. This subjectification takes place not at the level of the
popular itself, but in the realm of literary writing. Yet the function of this

subjectification is neither a mirage nor a consolatory compensation for a real and irresolvable contradiction. It is simply an intervention, and as such its highest aspiration lies in being the seed of possible change.

Painting in the City Deserted by Literature

Asunción, the political and cultural center of Paraguay, is a well-ordered and pleasant city. As one strolls through its streets, Angel Rama's image of the organized lettered city comes readily to mind. Yet in this architectural prototype of the lettered metropolis, there are no more than a couple of good bookstores, and they are scarcely visited by a limited readership. This paucity contrasts with the (relatively) high number of art galleries, those epitomes of bourgeois sophistication. This merely statistical reference finds an important correlation in the fact that plastic artists, rather than writers, played a leading role in the democratic consolidation after the Stroessner dictatorship. In the early 1980s, Paraguayan plastic artists served as an important component of international missions that denounced the dictatorial regime, and years later, when Stroessner was ousted, many of these artists helped establish and consolidate democratic rule.[20] These artists not only played an important role in the emergence of democratic culture in Paraguay but also took over Roa Bastos's legacy of mapping a history of popular conception of the Paraguayan nation—a popular subjectivization of history. This latter development bears witness to Roa Bastos's enormous influence on these artists, whose work and institutional endeavors stand today as the best reading of Roa Bastos's complex and multifarious work.

Before addressing specific works, I would like to comment on two institutional projects that imply a vast national reimagining through the recovery of popular traditions. The first relates to the creation and organization of the Museo del Barro, the second to the recovery and publication, by the same museum, of facsimile copies of popular newspapers that circulated among Paraguayan troops in the War of the Triple Alliance. Both undertakings reveal a cohesive cultural policy directed at overcoming the divide between the popular and the national that so obsesses the narratives of Augusto Roa Bastos and that today seems to have been inherited by some of Paraguay's leading plastic artists.

The Museo del Barro

In 1989, the Museo del Barro received international recognition from the United Nations as an institution organized around non-Western principles and subjects. It served as a point of consolidation for a long project that had begun thirty years earlier, when the painter-poet-novelist-architect–cultural organizer Carlos Colombino founded it in San Lorenzo, along with the lawyer, art dealer, ethnographer, and art critic Ticio Escobar and the British activist Ysanne Gayet.

Although the Museo del Barro today houses important pieces by contemporary Paraguayan and Latin American artists, it was created as—and still largely remains—a museum devoted to popular and indigenous cultures. The museum's displays of art are organized into three areas: urban, peasant-popular, and indigenous. The urban collection contains works by representative Paraguayan and Latin American painters and sculptors. The peasant-popular collection holds some four thousand pieces dating from the eighteenth century onward, including ritual and festive masks, ceramics, wood carvings, and gold and silver pieces. A good part of this collection is now housed in a special gallery sponsored by a private bank in downtown Asunción. The indigenous art collection gathers together some two thousand pieces made by the different ethnic groups that comprised Paraguay's aboriginal population (Zamuco, Chamacoco, Ayoreo, Guaykurú, and others). Adjacent to the Museo del Barro is the Center for Research and Documentation (CDI), which defines its goal as the recovery and preservation of indigenous and peasant art in Paraguay.

In 1998, the CDI published invaluable facsimile editions of two newspapers that circulated among the Paraguayan troops during the War of the Triple Alliance: *El Centinela*, which appeared in April 1867, and *El Cabichuí*. The museum's interest in these newspapers is based above all on their anonymous xylographic illustrations, in which many Paraguayan artists recognize a formative principle of their own activity. In a way, these newspapers embody the cultural divide between Spanish and Guaraní that so obsessed Roa Bastos: *El Centinela,* with its Spanish title, was published in Asunción by the national press (Imprenta Nacional), close to the central government; *El Cabichuí*—"The Black Wasp" in Guaraní—was produced in the trenches of the Cuartel General del Paso Pucú.[21] *El Cabichuí* is more prolifically illustrated, and Guaraní is more prevalent in it than in *El Centinela*.

In the foreword to the facsimile edition of *El Centinela*, Osvaldo Salerno proposes a reading of the significance of this publication that cannot fail to bring to mind Roa Bastos's project of a popular subjectification of history:[22]

> With this publication of the facsimile edition of *El Centinela*, the Museo del Barro seeks to promote and preserve some moments of our collective memory that not only possess a special expressive charge but also punctuate the history of our culture. Always remembered through the lenses of tragedy and horror—real components of the event—the War of the Triple Alliance has presented a somber and adverse face. But every historical time harbors within itself the forms of its own interpretation: the Museo del Barro wants to recover and propagate images that, emerging in the midst of the misfortune of the war, do so with such force and conviction that they become symbols and documents able to foster a different interpretation of our history.

As Salerno makes clear, what makes the publication of these old newspapers interesting are the abundant drawings created by popular anonymous artists. These images attest to the existence of a whole group of popular artisans who not only conceived of the publications' iconography but also, and more importantly, mastered both the printing process and the detailed procedure of carving the wood models. It is through these images (most of them satirical) that Salerno tries to glimpse a vision of history that is not doomed to repeat the received version of the war's meaning. Even if devastation was its sign, Salerno observes, the past also contains its own interpretation, and the fact that this self-interpretation testifies to a popular vision is not a minor detail. It would be naive to pretend that *El Cabichuí* gives us access to a perfectly constituted popular vision. Furthermore, especially in the case of a war journal, whatever consistency the popular may acquire, it will be always on the horizon of an ongoing dialogue and confrontation with the dominant elements of sanctioned culture. Critics have noticed in the figures the collusion of local, popular motives with European iconographic elements.[23]

We can view these attempts at cultural rewriting, undertaken by critics such as Escobar, Salerno, and Colombino, as part of an endeavor to make

popular culture the catalyst for any project of representational incorporation of the popular into the imaginary of the nation. It may be asserted
that such a project is far from original, even that it reveals Paraguayan intellectuals' belated awareness of a problem that had been dealt with decades earlier in other Latin American countries. Yet this very belatedness
no doubt affects the Paraguayan mode of incorporation by making it more
sophisticated in technical terms, more responsible in its ethicopolitical empathy with the downtrodden, and more conscious—from a political point
of view—of the strictures that link power and representation.

A Plastic Critique of Representation

Like many of his multifunctional plastic colleagues, Osvaldo Salerno is not
only a collector and historian of Paraguay's arts and crafts but also an important artist in his own right. In this context, I would like to comment on
a series of Salerno's installations, featured in an exhibition curated by Ticio
Escobar, who also edited the exhibition catalog, entitled *La Cicatriz* (The
Scar). This exhibition is part of a project Escobar presented in various metropolitan museums in South America, Europe, and the United States under
the title *The Shapes of Power*. Escobar's essay introducing Salerno's works is
entitled "The Absent Writing"—an unmistakable reference to Roa Bastos.
For Roa Bastos, let us recall, "absent writing" (la escritura ausente) is paradoxically the only kind of writing that a Paraguayan writer can produce
when faced with the evidence of an absent voice—the Guaraní voice—in
the repertoire of literary and symbolic hegemonic production. The cura-
tor's introduction of Roa Bastos is not simply a whim: "From 1994 on," as
Escobar explains, "Osvaldo Salerno collaborates with . . . Roa Bastos, in this
search for the boundaries between text and image" (1999, 97). One of these
collaborative works, entitled "The Re-presentation," dramatizes the intervention (the description of the work is "intervened book") of a worldly
hand (or rather, fist) into the lettered domain of the book. A whole series of
these "interventions" insists on the hand's encroachment into the book or
even on the uncomfortable subsumption of fingers into the now-disturbed
structure of the letter. Moreover, the hands here are the molded hands of
either the artist or Roa Bastos. Although the series claims to question the

relationship between text and image (writing and showing, literature and painting), this opposition does not proceed through a crude conflict between *Lebenswelt* and representation. The image is no less a representation than is the written text. It is possible for the spectator to read a few words of the intervened book, but the intervention of/on the book has nothing to do with the "content" of the book. Re-presentation is necessary as a new engagement (half complementary, half oppositional) with the assumed transparency of communicational rationality. Salerno's coming to terms with representation, even with his own representation, recalls Roa Bastos's ethics of variation. Also, as in Roa Bastos, the artist's re-presentation becomes an embodiment of a critical gesture. At its base is the insufficiency of any representation, the radical incompleteness of any presence.

"The Basin" (1997) also aims at questioning the self-sufficiency of representation. In this "intervention," Ticio Escobar explains, a white canvas was immersed in a long container filled with water. The piece was "embroidered with Roa Bastos's . . . aphorism: 'I walked out of the confinement with the smell of the open' [Salí del encierro oliendo a intemperie]"—words taken from the novel *El fiscal*. As Escobar points out, the sentence is full of political connotations. As important as these connotations is the destiny that the artist imposes upon the words, first because "embroidered time and again . . . the very sentence becomes . . . an embossed ornament, a trivial reference" (Ticio Escobar 1999, 98). Moreover, the fact that these words are submerged in a container of water makes them almost unreadable. Ultimately, the submerged message is dissolved by the water with the passage of time. Not even Roa Bastos's authorship can secure an essential, second, and eternal existence for these words.

Carlos Colombino is another plastic artist whose exploration of Paraguayan history and culture corresponds to the strategy of cultural recovery forwarded in Roa Bastos's literary works. Perhaps the most distinctive trait of Colombino's works is the fact that they are actually painted, carved surfaces. The predominantly brown tonality of these pieces accentuates their relationship to carving, one of the most widespread popular artisanal forms in Paraguay. (We have already seen how wood represents a basic element in Roa Bastos's textual universe: the references to carving, Mora, the carpenter, the hilltop Christ, the crucifixion of Solano in Cerro Corá, the references to wood in the chapter titles, etc.) The meaning of the material (wood, color) and the style of Colombino's painting is far from exhausting itself as a reference to popular expression. Its figurative dimension unmistakably belongs to a more universalized set of concerns, one in which the Paraguayan political situation often takes the upper hand. In this sense, carved wood gives most of Colombino's paintings a feeling of slowness, a barely oblique reference to the many obstacles that confront critical and intellectual labor in Paraguay on a daily basis. The obtrusiveness of this style has not prevented it from being relatively popularized, used in the cover designs for many books and cultural events (among them *Los duendes de la rebeldía* and the complete works of Rafael Barrett). But as in Salerno's case, Colombino's figural elements are never captured in a representational strategy, which these intellectuals, like Roa Bastos before them, tend to avoid. The modality of Colombino's paintings functions mostly at the level of allusions—allusions that, like the informed discourse of the Guaraní language, never subject themselves to the strictures of art as a form of either expression or propaganda.

Manifestation in the Field of Visibility

In one of his most frequently quoted essays, "Notes on Deconstructing the Popular," Stuart Hall concludes his Herderian-Laclaudian description of the popular by saying that the popular interests him only as a cultural constitution of the people opposed to the "power bloc." Outside this function, Hall concludes, "I don't give a damn about it" (1981, 36).

In Hall's vision, the popular has completely fused with the people. Popular and people are, however, two different concepts. There is a sense, for instance, in which the subaltern approximates the popular, but never the people. The schism between people and popular is one of the most obtrusive manifestations of the dysfunctional dynamic between people and the state in Paraguay, a dynamic in which nation-state and people do not exist for each other. Paraguay, of course, has been an independent state since 1811, existing alongside a vibrant popular culture and, hence, a Paraguayan people. But they are not the people of a state, and the state is not the state for the people.

Sometimes the visual register captures this dissociation between the popular and the people with such pathos that is difficult to ignore. The book *Los duendes de la rebeldia,* for example, recounts the trip to Spain made by several Paraguayan politicians, social activists, and intellectuals in 1987, with the patronage of Roa Bastos, to discuss avenues for the democratization of Paraguay. It contains a significant number of photos whose content seems to reproduce, once more, as in an infinite gallery of mirrors, the divide between peoplehood and representation, on the one hand, and the popular and the unnamed, on the other. The photos superimpose recognized and recognizable figures—from Willy Brandt, Felipe González, and Mercedes Sosa, to Gloria Giménez Guanes and Carlos Colombino—with other figures whose anonymity is hardly mitigated by the captions informing us that the photos depict "police repression" or a meeting of "landless peasants" (Giménez Guanes 1987, 8). The people are presented under a utopian, politically undivided visual rhetoric—a fact that can be institutionally explained in part by the fact that the two traditional actors in Paraguayan politics, the Liberales and the Colorados, seem more like movements than political parties. But the first page of *Los duendes de la rebeldia* contains, opposite the page that holds the opening quote by Rafael Barrett, a striking photo that itself appears to be an homage to Roa Bastos's ghostly aesthetics. In this photo, scattered groups occupy the front of Asunción's cathedral. The expressiveness of their gestures—above all of their limbs—speaks to an invisible power to which they seem to relate only tangentially; this tangentiality is emphasized by the absence of signs or banners. The powerful appeal of the photo comes, no doubt, from the woman at the forefront, standing with her arms open, who would look like a Christ figure were it not for the purse she carries, which restores her to a more mundane worldliness. She is a figure offered up to representation just as she seems to offer herself up to an official rage that may or may not reach her. Each society has its peculiar way of iconographically ordering the realm of the spectacular. This photograph is not only a valid reproduction of the Paraguayan specular imagination but also an unmistakable assertion of its uniqueness in the field of Latin American visual representations.

Finally, it is worth delving further into the realm of the anonymous. In the summer of 2000, I had the opportunity to see a series of anonymous installations that were set up in the plaza directly in front of the Paraguayan congress building. Actually, the characterization "anonymous" is inappropriate because they were never meant to have an author. These street installations, located in downtown Asunción, are original yet at the same time deeply rooted in popular traditions, and their presentation requires some historical contextualization. Salerno's work, like these installations, belongs to the context of postdictatorship Paraguay. The newly reestablished democracy faced a severe test in 1999, when the vice president of the republic was assassinated. Public demonstrations were organized, and the government responded with a far-reaching and uncontrolled repression that left several wounded and dead. Where protesters fell, these anonymous "installations" were set up in commemoration. These installations—which often are as large as two feet by four feet—are formed by a kind of bricolage, a wild assortment of signs and messages. They are set against the background of public buildings and are often covered by a tent which protects them from wind, sun, and rain. They lack signatures, and no political faction has ever claimed their authorship. Their political aim, however, is clear: they commemorate sites of repression. I do not know why the government did not remove them, and moreover, nobody in Asunción seems to know who created them. Very likely, they started as the solitary demonstration of one person or family, others joining in later, most probably without any relationship to the initial builders. Any attempt at "reading" these works makes it clear that no integrated discourse is being uttered here. The few written messages ("assassins," "heroes of the Paraguayan March") do not manage to override the overwhelming indeterminacy created by the bricolage style of the composition. Their different elements simply enter into felicitous conjunction. Despite the scarcity of words, some elements seem to have a communicative intention: a flower, a crucifix. Others, however, only make an attempt at expression and trust the effects of solidarity to the laws of metonymy: a phone book, a clipping of an ad selling a car, an old photograph.

When I remarked earlier that these anonymous installations are no doubt related to popular forms of cultural production in Paraguay, I was thinking of the *retablos* that even today populate the Paraguayan countryside—small boxes with backdrop paintings and one or two detachable carved saints. Even in the most modest families, it has long been a tradition to own a *retablo* carved from wood. Nowadays, private collectors and museum officials from abroad tramp across the countryside buying *retablos* from impoverished peasants. With limited resources but inexhaustible tenacity, the Museo del Barro has collected hundreds of these pieces and now exhibits them. Here I want to recall the significant role the *retablo* plays in Roa Bastos's fiction. In *El fiscal,* as mentioned before, Roa Bastos ties the story of the death of Solano López to the religious figuration represented in Grunewald's *retablo.* And in *Son of Man,* although the *retablo* itself is absent, the story of Gaspar Mora and the hilltop Christ reenacts the primordial elements of this figuration: Christian imagery and carved wood. In *Son of Man,* the inhabitants of the countryside expect a message to be delivered from this Christ, and their political revolt is not altogether independent of their relationship to this image. If there is a lesson to be drawn from Roa Bastos's novel, it concerns the importance of appropriations of Christianity in the development of popular and subaltern struggles in Paraguay. Roa Bastos's readers know this much: the power of the subaltern lies not in expression but in its absence and resilience. The carved Christ that Roa Bastos places at the center of *Son of Man* remains a silent and enigmatic figure. Likewise, a message is absent from these installations, these other altars. They convey no particular logic, no clear syntax. In the deserted streets of downtown Asunción, few look at them; nobody seems particularly interested in their presence. Their creation and reception cannot be approached, much less exhausted, by the constitutive categories of the literary and the aesthetic. They do not offer a terminus in the search for an expansion of the mutual engagement of cultural forms and critical thinking; neither can they provide an escape from the supposedly paralyzing effects of the criticism of representation, into an ethical haven opened up by the immediacy afforded by the image. In their unterritorializable expressions (and the word *expressions* is a misnomer), Latin Americanism can only produce itself—to continue with words from Roa Bastos—as fidelity to another voice, to an absent voice and an absent writing. Its critical discourse emerges precisely in the ex-centric and peripheral site of the oppression of people whom no discourse can represent and who for this reason demand, along with a practice of solidarity, a questioning of discourse and representation.

The

End of

Recognition

Arguedas

and the Limits

of Cultural

Subjection

On the back cover of the English edition of *The Fox from Up Above and the Fox from Down Below* (2000), Alberto Moreiras characterizes Jose María Arguedas's novel as "epochal" and "intense enough to arrest our world, and any world." Today few critical readers would object to that description, but when the novel was published in 1971, reactions were mixed. The novel's form and content, the wild proliferation of unpredictable characters, and what was perceived as a deep-seated pessimism were all difficult to reconcile with the image of Arguedas as a major cultural icon of progressive Peruvian culture. Martin Lienhard was perhaps the first major critic to fully acknowledge the extraordinary conceptual break accomplished by Arguedas's book. For Lienhard, *The Foxes* organized such an assault on literary norms that "only debris is left of the realist novel" (1981, 26). By "realist," Lienhard refers to the novel's recognizable, hegemonic form in the twentieth century. Whether realist or avant-garde, the Latin American novel has mostly produced an objectified version of the other any time it has had to deal with indigenous people. The originality of this novel lies in Arguedas's treatment of the indigenous population as subjects, no longer reduced to the status of a theme or a referent. Arguedas's strategy, as Lienhard points out, makes possible "the active intervention of a sociocultural strata thus far completely alien to literary production" (1980, 177). This centrality acquired by the indigenous subject represents such a break in the history of literary expression that its appearance marks for Lienhard the beginning "of a new form of production of the novel in Peru and, no doubt, in Latin America at large" (1980, 177).

Cornejo Polar, too, describes *The Foxes* as "a novel of extreme experimental modernity" (1992, 304). But Arguedas never considered himself the forger of a new paradigm. He despised professional writers and was said to have mastered Spanish later in life, only to yearn forever for the transparency of the indigenous language he had been taught in childhood. Why was this "traditional" author, among the many exceptional writers who populated the literature of the twentieth century, "the one to write an epochal novel that brought the hegemonic order of the literary to a close" (Lienhard 1981, 25) and arrested the progress of its time (Moreiras)? For there is little doubt that Arguedas is a culminating figure, a turning point beyond which things are never the same. He is the writer who inaugurates the closure of the historical project of Latin American literature, because he is the first to effectively address the question of subjection as the underlying grammar of literary representation. He achieves this only insofar as he is able to identify in *recognition* the dead center that molds the subjection of subjects to the hegemonic universe of their time.

The path that closes with Arguedas was opened by the *indigenista* project—a project that Arguedas is said to have variously completed, superseded, or destroyed. *Indigenismo* attempted the comprehension of the indigenous difference, but this recognition was abstract, demanding its object's total submission to the cultural and sociopolitical parameters of the dominant culture. The other, then, was recognized, but only at the limits of the generosity that the dominant culture grants to itself under such designations as "cultural difference" and "cultural relativism." One cynical aspect of this configuration lies in its immediate connection with the realm of political subjection. As I discussed earlier (see chapter 1), the recognition of subordinated people by the dominant society requires the prior recognition of the dominant forms of social power: this moment constitutes the recognition-granting instance of the social exchange. Thus, the same link that instantiates recognition and respect for the downtrodden works as the hegemonic link that guarantees the subjection of the subject. The force of Arguedas's narrative—and also the element that left even his most sympathetic readers perplexed for more than half a century—lies in its explicit refusal to validate this logic of recognition. For Arguedas, the indigenous community need not reveal itself in any other light than its own. It is not that recognition is not a valid element in his narrative universe (to the contrary: recognition dominates his writing up to *The Foxes*), but here Arguedas pushes for an unconditional recognition of indigenous people and their ways of inhabiting the world. Meanwhile, in *The Foxes*, even this claim for unconditional recognition is transformed as Arguedas engages with the most general conditions of subjection in Peru and, from the heart of the indigenous experience that now universalizes itself as the strategy of a whole people, goes on to claim that the bond of recognition itself holds no power in the subjective constitution of the popular.

But Arguedas's decisive break with the whole practice of literature becomes visible only against the background of the historical development of the literary institution in modern Peru and, more specifically, against the background of the development of twentieth-century *indigenismo*. Following is a very brief exposition of this history.

Modernization, National Integration, and *Indigenismo*

Unlike the case of Mexico (see chapter 5), there was no dominant modernizing project among the Peruvian intelligentsia at the end of the nineteenth century. In the Andes, issues of social and cultural integration were particularly difficult to address, much less resolve. Reflecting on this situation in *Seven Interpretive Essays on Peruvian Reality* (1928), José Carlos Mariátegui described Peruvian society as constituted around a deeply fissured duality. Unlike in other parts of the American continent, the indigenous population of the Andes remained largely unincorporated in colonial and later republican rule. Historical differences joined with the strictures of colonial power to create a strong split between indigenous and Creole people. As a result, any modernizing and nationalist project necessarily faced the challenge of ending the long "transition from dual colonial to unitary postcolonial forms of nationhood" (Thurner 2001, 1).

According to Peruvian historian Baltazar Caravedo Molinari, it was not until 1919, and then with remarkable weakness, that the Peruvian state gained a level of coherence that allowed it to intervene in local affairs. Before that point, its ability "to act upon the whole territory of the republic was precarious or almost nonexistent" (Caravedo Molinari 1978, 203). In this context, all the issues that usually pertain to the realm of political antagonism were "restricted to questions of control or manipulation" (215). In 1919, the same year Caravedo cites as the onset of change in this situation of social stasis, the young José María Arguedas visited Lima for the first time, and his recollection of this trip confirms Mariátegui's description of the dual structure of Peruvian society: "When I visited Lima for the first time, a *serrano* [highlander, equivalent to Indian] was immediately recognized and looked at with either curiosity or contempt. They were not looked upon as fellow citizens. In most of the small villages of the Sierra, on the other hand, the meaning of the word *Peru* was practically unknown. Illiterate people used to take their hats off when the flag was raised, as before a symbol that needed to be respected for mysterious reasons, because not doing so could bring devastating consequences" (1966, 1). Arguedas goes on to ask if there really was a country at this time. He concludes in the affirmative but immediately adds, "But it was not a nation." Arguedas's first visit to Lima took place the same year that Mariátegui embarked on a trip to Europe that would put an end to his personal "stone age." By then, the whole landscape that had kept Indians and Creoles apart was about to change, and Arguedas (and literature) would be decisive in the stormy transformation of Peruvian society.

Finally, 1919 is also the year that President Augusto Leguía came to power, breaking decades of oligarchic rule. Leguía's tenure coincided with a rapid process of modernization, great social upheavals, and the first appearance of a significant Peruvian press.[1] In this context, Alberto Flores Galindo writes, Peru became thinkable as a totality for the first time in its modern history (1979, 153). The first years of Leguía's presidency were marked by bitter confrontation with the regional oligarchies (*gamonales*).[2] It is impossible to refer to the *gamonales* without a mention of the hacienda, a complex socioeconomic unity that both inherited and perpetuated certain traits of rural colonial society. Manuel Burga and Flores Galindo describe the hacienda system as characterized by "the private appropriation of the land" (many times at the expense of indigenous communal land) and "the freezing of the circulation of labor power, feudal rent, almost nonexistent invest-ment [of capital], and poor development of the productive forces" (1980, 11–12). This world, composed of haciendas and *ayllus*—indigenous neigh-borhoods or communities—is a privileged site of *indigenista* fiction not only in Peru but throughout Latin America, and many of Arguedas's fictional works remain opaque to those who do not care to gain some knowledge of these peculiar institutions.[3]

From their haciendas, the *gamonales* concentrated land, as well as po-litical and even military power.[4] As the presence of the Peruvian state in the countryside was almost nonexistent until well beyond the 1920s, the *gamonales* felt free to mount their own private "armies" and did not hesitate to use these forces to punish revolting peasants or outspoken members of indigenous communities (see Burga and Flores Galindo 1980, 12–15). Since *gamonalismo* was based on an economy with almost nonexistent reinvest-ment of capital, the *gamonales* reacted to every expansion of commercial demand (particularly from foreign markets) with an intensification of the exploitation of indigenous labor and an extension of the exploited surface, which led to increasing conflict with the communities whose land the *gam-onale*s began to assault. *Gamonales* and *mistis*—a Quechua word that Argue-das uses to refer to white people and to mestizos with power and money—played an important political role in the highlands. Often they represented the only literate and Spanish-speaking segment of the population in remote and inaccessible areas. They became the "natural" depositaries of the repre-sentative function of the state and, as a matter of fact, the only ones able to perceive the state as an instrument that could further their own interests.

Leguía's confrontation with *gamonalismo* included the somewhat sur-prising promotion of a state-sponsored *indigenismo* in the first years of the regime. Interest in the indigenous question was concurrent with an explo-sion of texts from literary, juridical, and anthropological quarters that cen-tered on the fate of the Indian masses.[5] These expressions were far from unanimously progressive.[6] Many authors and publications reproduced, perhaps unwittingly, the liberal rhetoric of personal improvement and self-assertion that Mariátegui would criticize bitterly in *Seven Essays*. The pa-ternalism in these publications is clear: while they speak for the Indians or the growing mestizo population, indigenous people and mestizos are notoriously absent as authorial voices. The defense of the Indians is then, strictly speaking, a Creole achievement. In the terrain of literary studies, nobody has summarized this position more eloquently than Angel Rama. For Rama, *indigenismo* can be explained by a dynamic in which

> a new social group of variegated traditional background, urged by moderniza-
> tion and economic development, . . . advances clear demands upon society. Like
> any mobilized group . . . they voice their particular demands as if they were
> the demands of all the oppressed sectors and become thus the representative
> of their grievances. . . . In such a way, they manage to gain a popular force that
> does not correspond to their original limited number. No doubt, they felt strong
> solidarity with those underdogs, but they also used them as masks; since in the
> underdogs injustice was even more visible. . . . Finally, they counted on the pres-
> tige of having forged in the past an original culture. . . . The offended multitude
> was silent and for that reason easy prey to the ventriloquizing activity of those
> who were in total possession of the right tools: the written word, the graphic
> expression. (1987, 154)

Although Rama's description may be accurate, it betrays a top-down theory of culture that carries questionable results. Historically, the development of Peruvian *indigenismo* is far more complex than this too-schematic divi-sion of socially active agents and merely passive characters may lead us to believe.

The Revolt of the Southern Provinces

When Mariátegui's *Seven Essays* appeared in 1928, it reorganized the whole universe of discourses about indigenous people. Compared to *Seven Es-says,* the writings of González Prada, Luis Valcárcel, and Uriel García seem erratic and inconsistent.[7] The firmness of Mariátegui's position stems from his materialist methodology and his clear identification of the social agent of political praxis in Peru: none other than the Indian masses, which Mariátegui assimilates to the working class. This is the agent that Rama bypasses in his definition of *indigenismo.* Creole *indigenismo* tends to be be-nevolent and patronizing, but the subordinate masses in Peru were not idle or subservient. As a matter of fact, different peasant revolts had occurred with amazing regularity for at least four hundred years. In this context, it is important to note that the development of modern *indigenismo* in Peru coincides with a powerful social commotion: a largely undocumented peasant rebellion referred to as "the revolt of the southern provinces," an event that Mariátegui demanded to be informed about in detail on his return from Europe in 1923.[8]

For many commentators, the outstanding feature of the revolt is that its protagonists were not restricted to the free Indians of the villages who had led most of the uprisings over the last four hundred years; they also included *colonos*—Indians living in semifeudal conditions on the haciendas that marked the Peruvian highlands as late as the 1950s.[9] There is no cohesive historical account of the movement. The label *revolt* is itself misleading, since the rebellion was not a single event but a series of largely unrelated uprisings. Manuel Burga and Alberto Flores Galindo, two of its passionate cartographers, characterize the rebellion as inorganic, able to transcend "the district or the province, with an anonymous and indigenous leadership, violent, lacking in programs, without written statements—an illiterate revolt, but a revolt that sought to subvert the status quo, that sought to turn the world upside down" (1980, 40). Neither is there any agreement about the dates that bracket the movement: different historians provide different dates for the rebellion's beginning and end.[10] Finally, information allowing the reconstruction of these events is both scarce and unreliable. "All sources," Flores Galindo complains, lead back "to the landlord, the journalist, the judge, the *prefecto* or any other authority. All references come from the national press or local newspapers, from government reports or judicial cases" (1988, 262).

So only a few features of the cycle of uprisings can be pointed out based on the existing scholarship. The revolt was, if not prompted by, at least related to a governmental initiative to investigate Indian grievances. When a commission sent by President Leguía reached the highlands to report on the indigenous population, Indian groups simultaneously advanced their claims through the official representatives and used these conduits to organize a rebellion. The governmental commission, known as Roca-Rubin, lacked defined boundaries with the state-sponsored Asociación Pro-Indígena Tahuantinsuyo, formed by *indigenistas* and highlanders living in Lima. The Asociación Pro-Indígena's degree of involvement in the actual organization of the revolt remains difficult to determine, but newspapers—never a measure of objectivity in this context—singled out representatives of the Asociación as movement ideologues. In the eyes of *gamonales* and *hacendados*, it was plain that the government was using Indian agitation as a political tool in its policy of expanding state control over the highlands. Despite their relation to the commission, however, the uprisings took definitive subaltern forms. The revolt (or series of revolts) was marked by the widespread use of what James Scott calls "weapons of the weak": informal methods of political resistance. Gossip, for instance, took on enormous value. In some sense, the peasants even managed to impose this modality on the whole struggle, and the revolt soon took the form of a war of rumors between Indians and *hacendados*. Creoles spread a rumor that "Indians abandoning the hacienda will be marked with fire in the forehead." Indians replied by circulating the rumor that "all indigenous people were obligated to kill white and *misti* people on the spot, cut their throats like dogs until they are all dead" (Valencia 1980, 100). Such accounts were not completely credible, since the admonitions had been voiced in Indian meetings attended—everybody assumed—by unidentified *misti* spies. Moreover, terrible threats were uttered alongside resolutions about hiring lawyers or setting a strategy for negotiation with the authorities. The organizational features of the insurrection and the exact dates of the uprisings betray an active mythical substratum. A notorious feature of the rebellion was the use of "symbolic inversion" as an agonic weapon. For example, since the war was identified as a war against "whites," many groups proceeded to kill white dogs, cats, and domestic birds.[11] Mythic modalities, especially in relation to the time of the attacks, seem to have dictated the behavior of the indigenous groups. Flores Galindo notes: "The rebellions do not happen at any moment. Most begin in September and last until October or November. . . . September is the month of regeneration in the Andean calendar: the month when epidemics . . . are expelled from the community"(Burga 1986, 495).

As disputed as its duration, geographical extension, and nature is the movement's outcome. Although the state was still too weak to mediate in the conflict, or at least effectively intervene, the *gamonales*, who had access to relatively modern weapons, put the insurrection down in the bloodiest ways.[12] However, one aftereffect of the fight was the steady decay of *gamonal* power in the region. The *peones de hacienda* did not return to work, and the *ayllus'* numbers grew. "In some parts of Azángaro," Flores Galindo concludes, "the *mistis* never recovered their land. In the entire south, the expansion of the haciendas at the expense of communitarian land finally came to a halt" (1988, 259).

I have lingered on the great rebellion not only because its importance has been overlooked but also to point out that its very outlines figured prominently in the development of *indigenismo* and, more specifically, in the work of José María Arguedas. Issues like the ambivalence between a passionate and an objective description of the highlands, the use of symbolic inversion as a constitutive moment of indigenous strategy, and the blurred lines between political aims and ritual behavior are all features of the revolt that we find replicated many times in the literature of *indigenismo* at large. But more importantly, the great revolt gives us an alternative genealogy for the *indigenista* question. *Indigenismo* is not just an isolated development of socially mobile sectors that, in Angel Rama's words, use other groups to advance their own program. It is not exhausted by the editorial boom, the growing ranks of the middle class, or more dynamic capitalist engagement. *Indigenismo* is also a reaction—"a pressure of the referent," as Cornejo Polar would say. As a matter of fact, one of the most immediate consequences of the revolt was an enormous intellectual interest in indigenous matters. "Without rebellions, be they real or imaginary," Flores Galindo asks, "would awareness [of the indigenous question] ever have arisen?" (1988, 278).

The State and the Work of Recognition in *Yawar Fiesta*

Arguedas's uneasiness with the dominant groups' demands for positive recognition of the Indian people was present from the beginning of his narrative project. *Yawar Fiesta*, published in 1941, was a first general essay in this vast revolt that would take some thirty years to mature. By 1941, Arguedas was a well-established figure in the intellectual and progressive circles of Peru's political and cultural life. He was looked upon as an intellectual leader whose work could bridge the separate halves of Peruvian society. The promise of cultural unification was of paramount importance in a country that saw ethnic and social division as the origin of all its evils. But Arguedas was not able (or willing) to deliver on the promise that his readers expected from him.[13] *Yawar Fiesta* frustrated all those who believed that literature was responsible for revealing a "human" face of the Indian as a way of convincing every Peruvian of the need to incorporate these lost brothers as full citizens in the project of nation-building. Instead, the novel postulated an almost irreducible cultural difference between Indians and the national community. And to make things even more disconcerting, the author defended the recalcitrant elements of indigenous culture as more vital than any fight against economic and political oppression.

The action of the novel takes place in the 1930s, in the aftermath of the "revolt of the southern provinces," and traces of this event are noticeable in the text. A sense of deeply fissured rationality traverses the book, and perhaps this is why *Yawar Fiesta* has, literally, two beginnings. The first is an extensive description of Puquio, which takes up the first two chapters. Although these chapters are descriptive, they already rehearse the deep fissure that will be the novel's subject matter. The reader here finds competing descriptions of space, as Puquio is described from both an indigenous and a *misti* point of view. These points of view carry with them divergent valorizations of the world. The fissured nature of the represented world achieves an early apex with the opening chapter's description of Puquio's downtown: "On the Plaza de Armas are the main church, with its squat tower of white stone, the Subprefecture, the headquarters of the Civil Guard, the Court of First Instance, the Public School for Boys, the Town Hall, the jail, the pen for stray cattle; all the authorities who serve the leading citizens; all the houses, all the people with which they make themselves respected, with which they command" (Arguedas 1985, 4). This passage is remarkable for many reasons, but especially for the way it establishes the mutual alienation between the forms of the state and indigenous life. Ideological and repressive state apparatuses are indistinguishable. Their specificity disappears; only their instrumentality remains. Arguedas's criticism is not even ideological. Since these apparatuses do not have any pretension to legitimacy, there is nothing in them to be "denounced." They are forms deprived of even a semblance of reason, and nothing but capricious bad conscience grounds them in the highlands. In their sheer instrumentality, they remain incomprehensible for the Indians and meaningless for the *mistis*. Yet these forms are all the nation-state has to offer as a ground for transculturation, and Arguedas's outright rejection of them seems to prematurely close off every imaginable path of development in the novel. For this reason, *Yawar Fiesta* needs to start again, and it does so in the third chapter, where these rigid oppositions meet in a complex whirlpool of political and cultural determinations.

Chapter 3 witnesses the appearance of a governmental edict (the "circular"), issued in Lima, ordering that a professional bullfighter be hired to replace the Indians during the yearly celebration of Peru's independence. In this traditional festival, the *yawar punchau*, the Indians would enter, mostly drunk, to fight a ferocious bull, trying to recover some silver and gold coins that the señoritas of Puquio's upper class had embroidered on its spine, then to explode dynamite under the animal's belly. The government presents the measure as a civilizing crusade and a defense of the Indian people. To the Indians, however, the prohibition is devastating. The *yawar punchau* offers a yearly excuse for the demonstration of the Indians' might. Through the bullfight, the Indians are able to belie the many stereotypes that the *mistis* use on a daily basis to justify their scorn and domination. Hiring a professional bullfighter will rob the Indians of one of the few arenas in which they can still prove to the *mistis* the vitality of their way of inhabiting the highlands.

The *mistis*, who every year gather excitedly to see the Indians get butchered by the bulls, support the edict almost unanimously and swear to contribute to its enforcement. But their allegiance does not reflect a higher level of compromise with the policies of the expanding power of the state. The *mistis* do not care about the content of the circular; they simply intuit that it is an expression of power and that by submitting they may earn more power and legitimacy for themselves. They adhere to the circular out of political instinct, and to some extent against their will. The situation illustrates clearly the Gramscian idea of a hegemonic formation as a combination of coercion and assent. By pretending that the circular speaks to them, the *mistis* make themselves representatives of the law of the state and probable recipients of its favor. By the end of the process, the circular really *has* spoken to them.

The third important group in the novel, the half-acculturated *chalos* living in Lima, displays a more ambivalent attitude. The *chalos* are Indians or mestizos who have traveled to Lima and acquired a new perspective on the highlands. They have contact with various social discourses (socialism, anarchism, militant Catholicism) and consider the *gamonales* a backward force taking advantage of a large mass of suffering and perpetually duped Indians. They are coming to Puquio to make sure that the measure proposed in the circular will be enforced against what they imagine will be the opposition of *mistis* and *gamonales.* The *chalos* see their task as inseparable from their consciousness: "We who have already had our eyes opened out and our consciousness freed should not let them get away with skinning our brothers alive" (Arguedas 1985, 70). They thus profess wholeheartedly what the representatives of the state only mouth cynically.

The dialectic of recognition that the state proposes to the different Andean groups speaks only to the *chalos* and, to a lesser degree, the *mistis.* The *chalos,* who see the edict as a progressive step putting an end to the perverse pleasure of the *mistis,* immediately identify themselves with the measure—and even with the subprefect—and come to conceive of the state initiative as a weapon in their battle against the *gamonales.* Their identification points to the way in which they have come to perceive the state as the fundamental tool in the construction of a new hegemony. The Indians stand outside this circle. If the materiality of buildings does not suffice to make the image of the state's authority present, a piece of paper is an even more remote and problematic piece of *realia.*

Faced with the mighty Misitu, the professional bullfighter flees the ring. Despite the subprefect's decision to prevent the traditional festivity, supported by the *mistis* and the *chalos,* the Indians break into the ring as the distinguished people of Puquio ask for the intervention of the true brave men of the sierras. In the excitement, the *mistis* forget their fleeting allegiance to the subprefect and are again won over by the force of the traditional culture of the highlands. The spectacle unfolds quickly, without pause. Wallpa, Honrao Rojas, and others jump into the arena. In minutes, Wallpa leans, bleeding, against a wall. Honrao Rojas, dynamite in hand, runs toward Misitu with open arms. Overwhelmed with enthusiasm, the mayor whispers to the subprefect, "You see, Señor Subprefect? This is how our bullfights are. The real *yawar punchau!*" (Arguedas 1985, 147). One of the most influential readings of this novel, included in Cornejo Polar's *Los universos narrativos*, sees the ending as pointing to a reconstitution of the Andean world around traditional values (1974, 79). These traditional values include an ambiguous "we" through which the *mistis* assume identification with indigenous customs and even with the indigenous language. If the world of *Yawar Fiesta* seems cyclical and restitutive to many readers, it is because these readers assume that the novel stages a dialectic between Indians and *mistis* (through the possibility of a revolt) or between Indians and the state (through education or political allegiance). According to these readings, the object of the narrative action (understood as an action of *transformation*) should be the Indians. They lie outside history, untouched by progress and time, and need to be seduced into a historical existence. But against all expectations, the real dialectic of the novel is not between Indians and *mistis,* or Indians and the state, but between *chalos* and Indians—between the modernizing consciousness of the Andes and the search for an authentic way of inhabiting the world and living culture.

The *chalos* are the only group that gains the necessary critical distance to see the articulation of the Andean world for what it really is: a net of semifeudal, cynical chains of exploitation and deception. They are able to see, for example, how the *mistis* took advantage of the Indians' need for recognition in the case of the famous road to Nazca. The narrative voice seems to align itself with the perspective of the *chalos* when the narrator says: "In the month of January in 192– the news reached Puquio that in Coracora . . . all the people had come together in a town meeting. That the Priest had spoken in Quechua and afterwards in Spanish, and that they had agreed to build a road to the port of Chala, to make it possible to travel to Lima in five days, to show that they were better men than the Puquians" (Arguedas 1985, 59). The communities from Puquio had united to show the people of Coracora that Puquio was a stronger and more commanding community: they would build a road to Nazca, more than 180 miles away, in twenty-eight days. The *mistis,* the only group that could at this point take advantage of the road, thought the enterprise impossible. But the survival of the Indians depended on making possible the impossible. The road—a road for goats, as a truck driver complains—was ready at the appointed time.

The *chalos,* who now lived in a disenchanted world, bitterly criticized the construction of the road. Like Arguedas, they had found a stable order in Mariátegui and in the critical Marxist tradition Mariátegui had inaugurated in Peru. Not surprisingly, before leaving Lima to help abort the bullfight, one of the *chalos* talks to the portrait of the founder of Peruvian Marxism and almost prayerfully says: "You'd like what we're going to do, werak'ocha. You haven't just spoken to us for the pleasure of it—we're going to put into practice what you have preached. Don't worry, tayta: we're not going to die before seeing the justice you have called for" (Arguedas 1985, 73). The *chalos* are destined to collide painfully with the aims of the community that they seek to help.

The *chalos* believe the Indians were fooled by the authorities in the construction of the road, but Arguedas will show that the *chalos* in fact demonstrate a deeper naïveté. The *chalos* may regard the road as yet another ruse of the powerful in their never-ending exploitation of the Indian masses; what they miss, however, is that their own destiny is largely dictated by the objectivity of the Indians' deed. For the Indians, the road was a means of expressing their own vital agency in a gigantic and portentous project, and their work made possible the massive migration of highlanders to Lima. The *chalos,* then, are indeed a product of the work of the communities, and in their false consciousness they mistake the material possibility of their social existence for a greedy scheme of corrupt state officials and "unscrupulous" landowners. As the *chalos* approach the town, the most vocal of them admits: "Some students in Lima said, 'Stupid Indians, they work for the benefit of their exploiters.' It's a lie! Why can I speak with this consciousness that I have? I found the way to illumine my spirit to serve their cause . . . by going to Lima on the road they built. All of us did, brothers" (Arguedas 1985, 121). This consciousness, however, arrives too late. They come to Puquio to fight for the communities by the same road whose construction they condemned as a perverse manipulation of ignorant people. They come to help the Indians, only to find themselves siding with the authorities, even encouraging the authorities to use their rifles to prevent the bullfight.

Cornejo Polar, who describes the gap between the *chalos* and the communities as "tragic," explains that the attitude of the *chalos* does not symbolize "the old topic of the highlander that forgets his roots, becomes ashamed of his kind and, if the opportunity arises, exploits them" (1974, 74). As bad as this situation might be, what is at stake here is something "much deeper and much more painful." The *chalos* have retained their allegiance to the maternal land, but they are now in possession of "a new interpretation of reality"—an interpretation that condemns them to alienation from their original community (74). The *chalos*' "interpretation of reality" is, simply put, a hegemonic one, not in that the *chalos* accept the prevalent social structure of the highlands, but in that they see the possibilities afforded by republican, hegemonic politics as a frame within which to advance their goals. Here arises the tragic quality of the novel: following Mariátegui, the *chalos* have perhaps found a stable order in things, but simultaneously they must reckon with a force—the Indian force—that works against all visibility and stabilization. The novelty that *Yawar Fiesta* brings about—a novelty somewhat eclipsed by the idea that by the end of the novel the old world has reconstituted itself along traditional lines—is not just the assertion of an alternative power (Indian power, consciously celebrated by Arguedas himself), but the acknowledgment of an alternative source of valuation, anchored in an indigenous agency.

Opposed to the Indians' deep engagement with the world stands the alienating way in which the *mistis* of Puquio relate to the Andean space. Immediately after the first distanced description of the state apparatuses in the first chapter of *Yawar Fiesta*, Arguedas goes on to describe the lives of the *mistis* from an equally exterior and almost deautomatizing perspective:

> Day and night, the important people live on Girón Bolivar; there they seek one another out, stroll, look one another in the eye, fall in love, get drunk, hate each other, and fight. . . . When the young people show off their clothes, when they are happy, they ride their horses from one end of Girón Bolivar to the other, with their bodies erect, their heads held high, reining in the horses sharply and making them rear at every street corner. In the evening, the *mistis* congregate in the billiard parlor; there they play casino, dice, and seven-and-a-half; they talk until midnight and get drunk. The *mistis* ride up and down that street, raging and growing fat, from the time they're born until they die. (Arguedas 1985, 5)

After thus describing the *mistis* as people who perform rituals that are un-connected to beliefs, the narrator explains the origin of the *mistis'* "super-ficiality": "Puquio is a new town for the *mistis*" (5). It has been only three hundred years since they came to Puquio, and in these three hundred years they have not ventured much beyond the limits of Girón Bolivar. The In-dians, on the other hand, have been there for millennia, and Arguedas de-scribes their life as an exact counterpart to the repetitive and meaningless acts that seem to constitute the everyday life of the invaders. Sometimes, Arguedas writes, in the eyes of the Indians, "another hope is glowing, their real soul is shining forth. They laugh loudly; they may be furious too" (9). Arguedas's perspective here is almost vitalist: he suggests that the ground of this vital relationship with the world is unfathomable. We can access only its phenomenological surface, but in its sheer intensity, we can sense the reality that supports its existence.

If Arguedas is in search of an alternate and more fundamental ground for the establishment of an ethicopolitical relation to the world, how do we know that we have reached the *ground* and not another false layer of experience? Arguedas proposes one element as the regulative concept able to disclose whatever works as cause or ground: authenticity. Here the term *authenticity* describes a true dialectic among place, region (space), and cul-tural life. Arguedas is not so much concerned with showing what an au-thentic life may be; perhaps he didn't even believe in its possibility. He is just using the sense of the inauthentic as a critical vantage point from which to denounce the arbitrariness of developmentalist Peru. Inauthenticity (somewhat the positive, verifiable term of the equation) presents itself as pose, gesture, unproductiveness.

The Value of the World: 1965

The dialectic between alienation and authenticity, which dominated Ar-guedas's narrative works for decades, is at the center of his most ambitious and controversial novel, *Todas las sangres* (1964). A year after its publica-tion, the Instituto de Literatura Peruana organized a roundtable where the novel was discussed by a number of important historians, sociologists, and anthropologists (see Rochabrún 2000). Arguedas was severely criticized for his idealistic and voluntaristic picture of the highlands, and the pretended realism of *Todas las sangres* was contested by social scientists, who dismissed Arguedas's claim that the book represented a testimonial account of life in the Andes. Half ironic and half wounded, Arguedas commented, "If *Todas las sangres* is not a *testimonio*, then I have lived for nothing; I have lived in vain or have not lived" (qtd. in Rochabrún 2000, 38). The indictment of his work was devastating for Arguedas because it came from well-informed scholars. In some notes drafted shortly after the encounter, Arguedas wrote: "I think today my life has entirely lost its reason of existence. ... Two erudite sociologists and one economist [have] basically proven that my book *Todas las sangres* is negative for the country; I have nothing left to do in this world" (qtd. in Jacobsen 1993, 2). Although it was largely ignored at the time, the roundtable's criticism of Arguedas acquired its full meaning with the passage of time.

The disagreement between Arguedas and his critical readers reenacted the rift between Arguedas's production and the system of expectations built around a notion of national literature. It is worthwhile to consider the novel's flaws in the eyes of its critics. For Salazar Bondy, the novel fails to "illustrate" a vision of Peru, and he regrets that the sympathies of the author do not lie with the character that for him represents a "progressive step" (Rochabrún 2000, 25, 27). José Miguel Oviedo believes that the fact that in the novel's conflict between two brothers—one a traditional and reactionary landowner and the other an innovative, greedy, unscrupulous "national industrialist"—the Indians side with the first will confuse not only him but other readers as well (2000, 34). Surprisingly, both Bondy and Oviedo claim that they are not expressing a personal opinion but a "sociological standpoint" (34). Finally, Aníbal Quijano and the French sociologist Henri Favre level one further objection: for them, Arguedas's portrait of the highlands is simply ill informed. Quijano accuses Arguedas of having overlooked the transition from caste to class societies, while Favre notes, "I have lived for two years ... in Huancavélica, ... and did not find Indians, but only exploited peasants" (qtd. in Jacobsen 1993, 2).

As these examples make clear, an important point of contention focused on the definition of the popular subject in the Andes: is the subject an Indian or a peasant? Forty years after this meeting, few social scientists would uphold so vehemently the capitalist character of social interpellation in the highlands. Terms like *hybrid* and *cultural metissage* are now the currency used by the ethnographer or sociologist trading in Andean reality. But in 1965, the typical social scientist drew upon developmentalist paradigms that traversed the frontiers between description and prescription too unproblematically. Many critics rallied in Arguedas's support after the roundtable, but in defending him they relied on a self-defeating definition of literature. Even years afterward, they continued to call for a "literary reading" of the novel, as opposed to a reading informed by a "naive," referentialist ideology of the artistic work. They did not perceive that by denying that Arguedas's fiction was inextricably linked to reality, they were, in his view, condemning it to irrelevance. The truth is that the unskilled literary reader, sociologist, or anthropologist who measured Arguedas's novel according to the parameters of "reality" was not wrong, not even from a properly "theoretical" point of view: Arguedas's literature had always concerned the status of the real in a context so fissured along linguistic, ethnic, and cultural lines that it constantly ruins the claims to stability of any hegemonic discourse. Arguedas makes no pretense of objectivity in his rendering of the highlands. He links any claim of objectivity to the author's factual commitment—to use an old existentialist expression—to his world, opening a form of realism that Cornejo Polar describes as both description and interpretation of reality (1974, 66).

A year after the roundtable, Arguedas published a series of poems in a Quechua-Spanish edition under the title *Katatay: Temblar.* One poem in particular, "Llamado a algunos doctores" ("Appeal to Some Intellectuals"), can be read not only as a retort to the charges that Arguedas suffered at the roundtable but also as enacting a shift into the critical dimension that characterizes his last novel. Alberto Moreiras would later describe *The Foxes* as "powerful enough to arrest our world and any world," and already this process of arresting the world is the most noticeable feature of the poem, in which Arguedas returns to the question of an authentic way of inhabiting the world.[14] However, he is no longer concerned here with the identity of the Andean people, as in his previous work, but rather with the world as the ground for the adjudication of social and historical identity. This move incarnates the postcolonial enunciative position, insofar as its most immediate result is to reawaken the original epistemic and linguistic violence that is foundational to the colonial relationship. The poem's opening lines read:

> They say that we no longer know anything, that we are backward, that they will exchange our heads for better ones.
> They also say that our heart is not in tune with the times, that it is full of fears, of tears, like the heart of the *calandria*, like the heart of a great bull whose throat is cut, and for this we are considered impertinent. (1983, 253)

The poem thus begins by conceding a dominant position to intellectuals: that of "common sense," that of "the said." Some intellectuals, some *doctores,* the poem says, think the Indians are unfit for the times. The developmentalist ideology underpinning intellectual discourse is evoked through words that connote the movement of a historical modernizing impulse ("no longer," "backward," "not in tune with the times"). But Arguedas denies such epistemic authority. The deep collusion of moralism and developmentalism is made blatant through his use of the word *impertinent* to refer to the intellectual's reaction to an enduring indigenous worldview. Yet as the poem unfolds, the boundaries between the rational discourse of the intellectual and the traditional mythic discourse of the Indian poet, whose worldview is under siege, starts to break down. The intellectuals say (in a language that robs them of their language) that the Indians' heart "is full of fears, of tears, like the heart of the *calandria,* like the heart of a great bull whose throat is cut, and for this we are considered impertinent."

Arguedas wants to put an end to the intellectual's appropriation of the Andean world. This resistance to appropriation does not come through affirming the ethical right of the indigenous voice to define its own social being, as we might expect, but rather through confronting the pretensions of the *doctores* with the rock face of lived reality. "Let them speak then," the poet challenges the *doctores,* and he immediately asks:

> What is my brain made of? What is the flesh of my heart made of?
> The rivers run roaring in the deep. The gold and the night, the silver and the frightening night create the rocks, the walls of the canyon where the river sounds; that rock is the matter of my mind, my heart, my fingers. (253)

The power of the intellectual word comes from its intimacy with knowledge and science. Arguedas challenges intellectuals on a terrain that they call their own but that, in a remarkable lapse, they seem to have forgotten: the ontological ground of reality. This movement toward a primordial understanding of the being of the world is forcefully expressed in an otherwise nonsensical question: "What is the flesh of my heart made of?" The intellectuals' knowledge may not be false from a scientific point of view, but it is alienated. Thus the question-accusation: "What is there on the riverbank of those waters you do not know, Doctor?" The intellectuals own the word, but they are foreign to the land of which they speak. This knowledge-before-experience of the *doctores* acquires the status of a philosophical-political problem, Arguedas implies elsewhere, not because the *doctores* incarnate a developmentalist logic (Arguedas sees nothing wrong with the modernization of the Andes) but because they incarnate a nihilistic path that seeks to uproot the material, phenomenal bases of the world's diversity; because they seek the erasure of the world and its reconstitution in a hegemonized form of surplus knowledge.

"Appeal to Some Intellectuals" reminds us that there is a dimension of origin and originality fundamental to Arguedas's worldview. This element of originality has often been mistaken for a traditionalist discourse, but its force lies in fact in the ambiguous dimension of *poiesis*. In different texts, the element of force, of the forceful foundation of human space, is linked either to portentous works or to the grounding power of the poetic word. We must remember, however, that whatever is powerful enough to ground a world is also powerful enough to destroy it. For this reason, we would be grossly mistaken to end our reading of Arguedas's poem on a positive, celebratory note emphasizing the inexhaustible worldliness of the world, which opens through true habitation a space of originality. Not that Arguedas doesn't privilege these ideas in previous works, and not that this intonation is not present in the poem—but it is not the poem's final stance. And even if no subaltern or subordinate position can renounce the possibility of regrounding the world in a different set of values, the fact is that no values emerge from "Appeal to Some Intellectuals." Arguedas's brutal reduction of this antagonism to the ground of every possible antagonism implies a certain removal of the antagonistic logic itself. This movement, which implies the salutary subtraction of teleology, the fatality of history after it has obtained its presumed goal, keeps going, doing away with all (or almost all) positivity, just as a tornado wrecks the countryside, uprooting trees and tearing houses apart. The world that thus comes into being is barely a symbolic world. It is, rather, an undifferentiated world able to devour the very trace of the human. Its opening is less an opening to the Heideggerian-Derridean thinking of *Es-gibt,* the generosity of language, a gift beyond economy, than to the horror of the Levinassean *Il-y-a,* the irremissibility of existence, the impossibility of death that comes with the most radical reduction: "Let us imagine all beings, things and persons, reverting to nothingness. . . . But what of this nothingness itself? Something would happen, if only night and the silence of nothingness" (Levinas 1978, 57). The fact of existence—the brute fact that there is *there is*—imposes itself even in the absence of beings. After the most radical reduction, the reader summoned to a reconstruction of the world's preexistence is left with nothing but life, eternal life, the ceaseless world. The world of the poem, removed now from any "worldliness," conjures the frightening nights that stand guard over a ceaseless process of creation, which gives birth to everything, without end and without beginning.

This is the spirit in which Arguedas wrote *The Fox from Up Above and the Fox from Down Below.* The novel is a step back from the whirlpool of destruction and negativity that reigns at the core of his monumental poem. Still, some of the poetic rage that dominates "Appeal" is transposed into *The Foxes,* lending its unique aura to Arguedas's last novel.

The Foxes

In *The Foxes,* Arguedas abandons the sierra, the privileged site of *indigenista* fiction for almost a century. The locus of the narrative is no longer the small or developing towns of the highlands, but Chimbote, the "largest fisher town in the World." Chimbote, in Priscilla Archibald's words, emerged from the whirlpool that "in only two decades . . . transformed [Peru] from a millennially rural society to a predominantly urban one" (1998, 4). According to Julio Ortega, "Chimbote was, as late as the mid-1950s, a town on a beautiful bay on the northern coast of Peru, with some twelve thousand inhabitants.... During the sixties, a hundred thousand persons, mostly Andean immigrants, piled into the precarious shantytowns thrown up during successive invasions onto sandy, unhealthy lots. Two decades later, the city ... was engulfed by smoke from the plants and hemmed in by the stench for processing the fish" (2000, xi). This Babelesque city grew without any plan, beyond control and beyond any possibility of ordered modernization.

The subjects of Arguedas's narrative have also changed. In Arguedas, it has often been said, there are no heroes: individuality is rare in the indigenous characters of *Yawar Fiesta, Deep Rivers,* or *Todas las sangres*—works in which the hero is the community. *The Foxes,* on the other hand, comprises the recalcitrant singularity of different narrative voices that transform the novel into a monstrous Bakhtinian multi-monodialogic structure. The community, so vital in all previous Arguedas's novels, is in this context just a fiction that the reader must reconstruct, build anew, or even forgo. Finally, Arguedas's radical treatment of the characters' individual consciousnesses and his own narrative voice continues to advance the startling changes that had gone unnoticed in critical readings of *Todas las sangres*.[15]

The Foxes initially bewildered its readers and struck many of them as a failure—partly but not entirely because Arguedas had taken his own life before finishing the book. Cornejo Polar, for example, described *The Foxes* as "the most loyal reproduction of uncounted contradictions, which neither reality nor Arguedas ever managed to resolve" (1992, 301). The language of the novel was another source of frustration for many readers. This language is a protean or, as many critics described it, alluvial one, which "borders on a scarcely intelligible verbal delirium" (Lienhard 1981, 136). Further, this portrayal of a delirious world in a delirious language raised other, immediate concerns: How is a political stance possible in such language? How can a novel that refuses to communicate within the system of the language games allowed by hegemony be the vehicle of expression for a committed writer in a politicized universe?

Even when his work was judged by strictly aesthetic standards, Arguedas seemed to have traveled only halfway toward an aesthetic-political encounter with the system of cultural domination that he had so passionately confronted all his life. Martin Lienhard provides an account of what, to his mind, constitutes the limits of Arguedas's engagement with the predominant Western forms of literary imagination:

> Arguedas's literary operation takes place on enemy terrain—the dominant lettered culture—and does not succeed in inverting the hierarchies of imported literatures or in abolishing the dominance of writing over oral expression. And yet, a work like *The Foxes* ... (like Guaman Poma's *Nueva corónica* three hundred years before) weakens and exposes Western mechanisms of cultural domination over Peru and in so doing facilitates the possibility of a radical questioning of the sociopolitical structures that make that domination possible. (1992, 332)

Any discussion of the novel's failure, however, can only be asserted against an ideal not upheld by *The Foxes*. The horizon of optimal performance Lienhard notes seems to be none other than the historical project of Latin American literature in its progressive intonation, and his language of reversal remains imprisoned in a strategy of "positive" engagement with the existing forms of subjection. But such positive engagement (challenging the system of domination, fighting for the recognition of communities, etc.) is not the aim of the novel. Thus, how can it be faulted for not covering a program that it does not pursue? We would be better off following the advice of Pedro Trigo, who invites critics to reinvent "the whole critical apparatus just for the sake of [the novel's] interpretation" (1982, 211). But what might the starting point of such a project be? According to Arguedas, the answer rests with the highlander's identity. For almost a century, the question of Indian identity has represented the site where a nationalist emancipatory imagination meets the indigenous question. Arguedas's position in *The Foxes,* then, could not but shock his readers: here identity itself, not its attribution, goes on trial. The substance of the substantive is questioned in a last, desperate attempt to deliver the people from the complex bind of subjection, a bind for which Arguedas, as usual, finds a poetic yet precise formulation: "the shell that defends and oppresses" (2000, 231).

The Myth of Incarnation and Dissolution

The Foxes tries to locate the center of the migrant's being in the ever-changing and chaotic world of Chimbote and to make a decision based on this location. The reader cannot escape the implications of this decision, for the reader must also decide. Nowhere does the novel openly reveal the nature of the question to be determined, but we can deduce its existence from the responses elicited in more than twenty-five years' worth of critical readings of the novel. These responses seem to oscillate between two positions, which, for the sake of simplification, I will label "pessimism" and "life" (and if these words have a distinctly Nietzschean redolence, I hope that the reader can also find in them evidence of Arguedas's consistency over fifty years of writing).

In the pessimistic reading, the rupture between the highlanders and their ancestral environment cannot be survived. Arguedas's suicide confirms this feeling and makes it more terrifying. This is the interpretive path taken, although with some hesitation, by Cornejo Polar in *Los universos narrativos*. The only affirmative elements that Cornejo rescues from the novel are those related to the survival of indigenous-mythical elements. The main problem with this reading is the way it splits the migrant highlanders' cultural identity from their actual political agency as subjects of the narrative. We are told that these subjects deserve our attention because they bear a displaced indigenous identity but, simultaneously, that this identity now resides in an unconscious, subterranean layer whose real meaning remains an enigma to its own bearers.[16] The pessimistic reading cannot perceive the actual cultural practices of the migrant highlanders as the vital manifestation of a project, but only as the cipher of their alienation. Thus, confronted by the withering away of traditional culture, this reading simply emphasizes whatever element in the narrative may perpetuate the vanishing ontology of the traditional agent of emancipation, and the element that seems to support this reading most forcefully is, of course, the novel's multiple mythic references.

The first important readings of the novel, by Cornejo Polar and Martin Lienhard, granted mythical elements a central role. Lienhard notes that, far from having disappeared, mythic references are here so intense that they enable the reader to study "the forms that Andean thinking takes" (1981, 18). The Swiss critic sees *The Foxes* as representing the sublation of millennial forms of indigenous expression in the Andes, and of course this position has a solid base. The book, for example, opens with an epigraph in which two ancient foxes from Andean mythology chatter on a rock. Lienhard reads this as an unmistakable reference to the manuscript of the *Hua-rochirí*, a sixteenth-century Quechua tale whose Spanish translation by José María Arguedas was published in 1966.[17] However, Lienhard further reads the epigraph's placement of the Quechua text before the Spanish translation as a gesture that forces "us to acknowledge the priority and originality of the Quechua version, of which the Spanish version is but a translation" (1981, 178). In *The Foxes*, Lienhard continues, two traditions and two rationalities merge. One is Andean and popular, the other literary and novelesque. Traces of this collision pervade the whole text. But an epochal inversion also takes place. The European and the indigenous have existed side by side for centuries, and the European world has encroached more and more into the terrain and sensibility of the indigenous worldview. In *The Foxes*, on the other hand, the Andean elements are so powerful that they represent the actual driving force behind this new interpretation of a national reality.

Cornejo Polar's reading of the mythical elements in *The Foxes* also rests on the assumption that myth as a form of memory is the last guarantee of the highlanders' meaningful habitation of the modernizing world. Cornejo Polar's interpretation is best exemplified in the figure of Asto.[18] Like the disenfranchised people of Marx's *Eighteenth Brumaire*, who cannot represent themselves yet need to be represented, Asto cannot spring himself onto the page. Arguedas introduces Asto through the eyes of another character, the unionist Zabala, who depicts Asto as an Indian who, "naked, tied to the wharf day after day, . . . learned to swim so's he could get a fisherman's registration. He didn't use to talk Spanish before." Now he is a fisherman. "He's steppin' firm," Zavala says. "He's walkin' firm and whistlin' firm, that Indian is" (Arguedas 2000, 41). With the money earned in his trade, Asto pays for an expensive prostitute, the Argentine, and Arguedas endows their encounter with a transformative meaning. After leaving the prostitute's room, Asto hails a taxi, thinking, "Me criollo . . . from the coast, goddamnit. . . . Who highlander now?" (42). Cornejo Polar argues that Asto has rejected his Andean heritage and capriciously embraced a Creole identity. Asto has fooled himself, and the encounter with the Argentine results in a fall into alienation. This interpretation is reinforced by the fact that Asto's story replicates a mythic episode in the *Huarochirí*: the story of Tutaykire, a warrior from Up Above who is waylaid in a valley by a virgin prostitute who offers him *chicha* and a bed and finally puts him to sleep. Cornejo Polar stresses the similarities between the two situations. But in what sense does the Argentine stop Asto and put him to sleep? (And, concurrently, where is Asto going *before the encounter?*) At this point, Pedro Trigo's analysis respectfully corrects Cornejo Polar's reading, maintaining that Asto's story illustrates not the myth's perpetuation but its cancellation, because Asto changes. With the money he has earned as a fisherman, he rescues his sister from the brothel, and a new happiness subsequently surrounds him whenever he appears in the novel. Trigo does not, then, see Asto as Cornejo Polar describes him—as a "tragically grotesque figure with an extreme degree of alienation" (1974, 275). Asto's apparent denial of indigenous heritage ("Who highlander now?") can also be read as an intervention in the actuality of his existence. Far from losing himself, Asto gains a self by defying death in the water and by buying what he would otherwise be unable to obtain. He is not alienated from his own world. In fact, he has become the exact opposite of a figure of alienation: an active force able to shape the chaotic Chimbotan universe.[19] Trigo's interpretation of Asto is in line with the basic argument that I want to advance in this chapter: the driving motif of *The Foxes* is not so much the preservation of Andean identity as the subversion of traditional identities through a far-reaching criticism of what, for want of better terminology, we can call the social contract.

This vast upheaval of stable identities reaches the author himself. The mythical foxes discuss Arguedas and his place in the novel in one of their conversations, one saying, "There are worlds higher up and lower down." Immediately the question arises of the location of this Quechua-speaking writer and anthropologist, raised by the Indians in early childhood. "The individual who tried to take his own life and is writing this book was from up above. Where is he from, what is he made of now?" one fox asks (Arguedas 2000, 54). The question "What is he made of?" also appears in Arguedas's earlier works. In "Appeal to Some Intellectuals," for instance, the defiant poetic voice asks, "What is my brain made of?" But as we have already seen, the stuff of a person lies in its contemporaneity to the world, in its proximity to the origin—that is, in its authenticity. This authenticity is not, however, a "subjective" element that the person can carry along wherever he or she goes. The cipher of the authentic lies in a productive relationship to lived experience: "that rock is the matter of my mind, my heart, my fingers." In the novel, the foxes ask the subject Arguedas the same questions that Arguedas the writer asks the Chimbotan world: What are the highlanders made of? What are they made of, now that the physical world that sustained their identity for centuries is no longer present as their witness? True to a conception that he held all his life, Arguedas could not ground the highlanders' identity on the memory of an absent world. Trapped in the past, they would be as inauthentic and foreign in Chimbote as the edict or certain *mistis* were in Puquio. Whatever their cipher is, it must be an element firmly rooted in the present of their lives.

Writing some twenty years after Cornejo Polar and Lienhard, Sara Castro-Klarén also proposes a genealogical approach to the mythic elements in *The Foxes*, but one that is intertextual rather than existential. Castro-Klarén argues that the experience of translating the *Huarochirí* into Spanish in 1966—an event contemporary with the roundtable, the writing of *Katatay*, and the fieldwork that would lead to the composition of *The Foxes*—radically altered Arguedas's perception of the nature and task of literary mediation. According to Castro-Klarén's argument, Arguedas found in the *Huarochirí* a confirmation of the importance of a mythical Andean substratum in contemporary Peruvian life. But the lesson derived from this substratum is the unavoidable, constant mutability of life and world. Castro-Klarén's reading of *The Foxes* thus rejects any interpretation in which myths serve only to preserve identity: "Nothing could be further from the effect of the foxes in the novel, for the foxes' figuration stems from the creative-destructive powers of the Huarochirí deities. These deities are not 'mythic' beings in the sense that the structuralist hermeneutics of 'myth' has accustomed us to think, nor do they ever perform syncretic or Ovidian metamorphoses. As we shall see below, what haunts Arguedas's text is the transformations of the deities who, by way of Becoming Other, also maintain the difference" (2000, 312–13).[20]

Castro-Klarén's reading of the mythical in Arguedas in terms of a creative rather than a preserving energy is in line with Arguedas the ethnographer's view of how myths function for indigenous people. In a text he co-authored with Josafat Roel Pineda, Arguedas includes an interpretation of the myth of the Inkarri, according to which the dismembered body of the last Inca ruler, buried in different parts of the kingdom, would come back to life to avenge his people. The *comunero* from Puquio confidently waits for the resurrection of the Inkarri: "Such a resurrection has already begun. With the opening of the highways, the products of the Indian economy multiply. Different communities have built schools, renovated their homes. Their lettered sons, 'emergent cholos,' defy the lords. They no longer give way to others on the streets. Indignant . . . the old lords . . . have immigrated to Lima. . . . The new generation knows that mountains are *promontorios de tierra*, not gods. They have not received the myth of Inkarry as a legacy. They no longer have need of it" (Arguedas and Pineda 1973, 221). The completion of the myth is its dismissal. But the myths do not simply depart, leaving the field open to a process of modernization characterized by complete submission to the instrumental logic of capitalist developmentalism. The myth dissolves itself in the real traits of the world and at the same time brings into this world an enormous disruptive power. Mestizo, Indian, and peasant agency partakes of the labor of myth, but only after the process has transformed all identity, including their own and the myth's. The myth only confirms the ever-developing nature of the universe. As for its role in *The Foxes,* it bears an enigmatic power of destruction and dealignment in whose names it forges new, unheard-of, and provocative allegiances.

Clearing the status of the myth in Arguedas's novel is a precondition for reading *The Foxes,* but it is not the reading itself. Although the dichotomy between pessimism and life governs the most general understanding of this novel, it may be that this tension is not the best entry into the work. Many years ago, Roland Barthes stated that the question "Where to begin?" is the primary one of any literary analysis. Where to begin in the case of a complex novel whose criticism always leaves us with the impression that critical readings only capture a small portion of its vast architecture? Cornejo Polar and Martin Lienhard early established a lead that almost all subsequent criticism of *The Foxes* has followed, reading the discourses and activities of different characters as if they were monads, whose sum will give us a key to the text as a whole. I too have followed their lead, even though I am aware that other approaches to the reading of this epochal novel are also necessary.

Do You Understand? Perspectives

Some critics have characterized *The Foxes* as an "incomplete" or even "fragmentary" novel. This point is unimportant not because formal questions are beside the point, but because the most striking formal feature of *The Foxes* is its lack of a center. The closest thing to a center in *The Foxes* is chapter 3, which provocatively rehearses the problem of interpretation itself and is, in that sense, a mise-en-scène of the laborious task that awaits the reader. The themes of becoming and transformation in this dialogic chapter—"dense and hermetic," as Cornejo Polar calls it, with bizarre conversations and a "delirious closing"—are the chapter's "hermeneutical key" (1974, 273). Despite its hermetic and disorienting nature, this chapter is the only one that contains an attempt to map Chimbote as a whole, found in the conversation between the enigmatic Don Diego and the businessman Don Angel Rincón Jaramillo.

This conversation takes place on top of a building that overlooks the bay, the scenery reinforcing the motives of overseeing and mapping, which are one main subject of the exchange. Don Angel Rincón Jaramillo is the manager of the fishing company Nautilus, part of the vast economic empire of Mr. Braschi. Don Diego is an enigmatic character who comes to see Don Angel bearing a letter of recommendation from the same Braschi. But Don Diego will also reveal himself as a reenactment of the mythological fox from down below (Cornejo Polar 1974, 310; Lienhard 1981, 107–11) who comes to extract from Don Angel a narrative of his wrongdoings. Their conversation represents a mixture of verbal genres, from political analysis to cultural criticism and even random existential observations. Much of it seems governed by the need to understand Chimbote, a fact underlined by the obsessive repetition of the word *understand,* which appears dozens of times on a single page. This drive for understanding becomes even more relevant if we consider that Arguedas himself sees in his novel an attempt to understand Chimbote, a city for which he feels enthusiasm, but not real understanding.

The situation here is not without irony, since this chapter is by far the book's most difficult to understand. The conversation does not follow standard rules of communication. The assumptions organizing discourses shift constantly (e.g., from a corporate perspective to a carnivalized version of a Quechua- and Indian-like worldview), a fact that does not seem to annoy the characters. Surprisingly, however, this chaotic exchange, completely alien to the basic rules of literary verisimilitude, finally gives way to understanding. Toward the end of the chapter, Don Angel asks Don Diego, "Did you understand it?" and Don Diego triumphantly replies, "Yes, everything's clear" (Arguedas 2000, 128).

How can this be so if the exchange is so chaotic that the reader can hardly follow it? Key here is the fact that a different kind of understanding is at stake in Chimbote. The chapter can be read as a carnivalesque dramatization of Arguedas's position in the 1965 roundtable. As on that occasion, what is at stake here is the world itself, in terms not of its objective totality but rather of the possibility of apprehending the ideological conditions of its construction. There are realities that are easy to grasp: evident, solid quasi-universals. The Indians who make up most of Nautilus's labor force live in perpetual ignorance of these great determinations. Rincón Jaramillo complains to Don Diego, "No Indian has a *patria* does he? I know that for sure. They don't even know how to pronounce the name of their province" (Arguedas 2000, 123). Yet the Indians seem gifted with another kind of understanding. Jaramillo concedes that "when they're taught to run machinery, and what's more, when the engineers explain the workings of the most complicated key parts and tell how the machines function as a whole, these animals learn—rather slowly—but I would say they have a deeper understanding than the gringos themselves. Ya hear me, Don Diego? Better than the foreigners" (123). Their encounter with the machine allegorizes, of course, their encounter with modernity, but not all of modernity, because one specific part of this modernity is still impossible for the highlander migrants to grasp: the Indians do not understand their most basic political determination. Insofar as they are unable to grasp this abstraction, they are also resistant to its formative power. To understand means to understand oneself as belonging to a province, not to a community or *ayllu*. This understanding is primordial because, as Louis Althusser puts it, it is through this understanding that the subject comes into being. That is why Jaramillo swiftly corrects himself: the Indians understand machines, but insofar as they don't understand the abstract conceptualization of sociopolitical be-

longing, "they don't understand—insofar as what you might call really un-
derstandin' goes—they don't understand" (124).

For Rincón Jaramillo, this deficit of understanding does not result from
any recalcitrant particularity of the highlanders. It is, rather, a far-reaching
crisis of subjection that is not difficult to describe, even if, properly speaking, Rincón Jaramillo does not know what to do about it. As he admits, life
in Chimbote has reached a point where social reproduction is a chimera.
True, "there's methods for managing all the different temperaments that
come to this port, but not for molding them. . . . Molds have been made and
they've all been broken" (Arguedas 2000, 91). Lack of understanding, then,
is the other face of the impossibility of "molding" the different temperaments. The situation creates, Jaramillo half-confesses, a sort of "manage-
rial" crisis.

In his effort to make sense of Chimbote, Don Angel draws Don Diego a
diagram of Peru, representing the embattled forces with seven white eggs
and three red ones. Don Angel calls his diagram "objective," although any
reader will find it hermetic at best, utterly incomprehensible at worst. Don
Angel explains, "We—Peruvian industry, the U.S.A., the Peruvian government, the ignorance of the Peruvian people, and the ignorance of the Car-
dozos about the Peruvian people—are the white forces; Pope John XXIII,
communism and the blind or understandable rage of a small part of the Peruvian people against the U.S.A., against industry and the government, are
the red forces" (Arguedas 2000, 114). Intentionality is a category that has
always been in crisis in Arguedas's narrative, partly due to Arguedas's reluc-
tance to offer a strategic calculation of the value and allegiance of the indigenous people. The diagram seems to work pretty well—at least for Rincón
Jaramillo—when it comes to abstract entities (the Peruvian people), but
when it comes to a particular individual, the drawing is of no avail: "Cardozo's real color—I'm not puttin' that in" (114). The impossibility of *molding* and
mapping that Rincón Jaramillo sees as a pervasive deficit in Chimbote was
once a recalcitrant trait of some indigenous people and especially of their
leaders. The best example is, of course, Rendón Wilka, who is constantly
observed, discussed, and staged but is never grasped, and who is, besides,
characterized as a *fox*—unintentionally—by the engineer Cabrejos in *Todas
las sangres* (1964, 73). The highlanders bring with them a crisis in subjection

that has always been part of their history. They universalize this experience of insubordination, thus providing a ground for Lienhard's claim that this novel represents an inverted indigenism—although it is not the traditional culture of the Indians that takes over the narration, but rather their exaggerated modernity, their endless ability to adapt even when the prophets of modernity themselves claim enough stability for any calculation. Along the same line of thought, something of the old Arguedian topic of the fight for recognition through mighty deeds transpires in the fact that Don Angel Rincón Jaramillo is won over by the exuberance of life that the migrant highlanders have brought to Chimbote—which brings me to my last and fundamental point. The moment of real understanding between Don Angel and Don Diego comes toward the middle of the chapter, when Don Diego manages to imbue the whole encounter with a foxlike, Quechuaesque atmosphere. He starts dancing, and in spite of himself, Don Angel starts dancing too. Don Angel is thus transformed, touched by this other powerful discourse of Andean roots. The two understand each other because through the dance, and through the evocation of the force of becoming of a mythical element that appears only obliquely, they have established a common ground, which is not the common ground afforded by discourse or not, at least, by discourse alone. I will return to this point later.

Mad Moncada: The Uncanny Recipient of Public Discourse

Parallel to the crisis of the obstacles to mapping the chaotic world of Chimbote runs the deep crisis of expression that makes any word about Chimbote problematic. If *The Foxes* is to be read as an accusation leveled against capitalist development of the coast, there must be a subject able to utter it. But in this novel, which for so many critical readers comes closer than any other to enacting a politics of the people, the only public orator is "mad Moncada," who, as his nickname proclaims, is crazy. The text explains, however, that Moncada "is not crazy all the time" (Arguedas 2000, 62) (or, as the beautiful Spanish original reads, "no era loco continuo" [1992, 57]). He is just crazy in his function as a public orator, as if any public word in this Babelesque universe can emerge only under the guise of an alienated expression. Because Moncada is the only character who comes close to instantiating a sort of sui generis "public sphere," some critics have looked for a positive, politically engaged, and emancipatory meaning in his words. To some extent, they have found it. Martin Lienhard, for example, writes that "Moncada . . . completely subverts the dominant ideology"(1981, 184), while Cornejo Polar finds a certain consistency in Moncada's attack on foreigners in his speeches, reading this element as an indication of the novel's anti-imperialist stance. More interestingly, Cornejo Polar also advances the notion of an isomorphism between Moncada's speeches and the delirious reality of Chimbote: "His demential sermons are, paradoxically, the verbal consciousness of Chimbote. Confronted with chaos, being part of it, the only rational answer seems to be madness. . . . It is a circular process, and no doubt a tragic one, in which chaos can only be spoken through the language of madness" (1974, 165).

I wish to offer a third possibility: Moncada's speech can be read as a paradoxical performance of unaccountability. The unaccountable is also the irresponsible, not in that it is without concern for the self or the world, but in that it refuses to respond. It refuses the dissymmetry by which, through a logic of punishment and recognition, the subject is bound and emerges as subject to the law. One of Moncada's speech-sermons takes place at La Línea market, after a locomotive has destroyed some stands mounted along the rails, killing some pigeons:

> Ah, ah! life, death, the stink of fish meal, of genteel American monk, a gentleman who does not pronounce Castilian as it ought to be pronounced. The Yankee priest, clergy, hear this, hear this, is never going to pronounce Castilian—the kind of Spanish we speak—as it should be spoken. That doesn't matter! They don't come here to impose their will on us. They preach here, they put themselves in danger, gentlemen, amidst the pestilences, amidst the foul odors, like Moncada does, imitating Moncada, who would also preach with good deeds if he had the *monis*. The rooster has died, the guinea pigs have died; the locomotive engine kills innocently, friends. The Yankees of Talara Tumbes, Limited, and Cerro de Pasco Mining Corporation too. No, they're not responsible. Oh, ah Father Cardozo, Father Tadeo, good friends, come and raise this rooster from the dead . . . ! (Arguedas 2000, 62)

Arguedas does not introduce Moncada's words: Moncada's speech continues naturally from the narrator's voice, as if the narrative voice itself needed the disguise of unreason to pass judgment on Chimbote. But judgment is precisely what cannot come to pass. First, there is the question of language: what language can judge Chimbote? To his despair, the revolutionary Father Cardozo does not pronounce Spanish correctly (as if anybody in this novel cares much about linguistic standards). The dissolution of a language in which to pass judgment opens the road to a nuanced, complex notion of responsibility. Moncada synthesizes this insight in his observation-accusation: "the locomotive engine kills innocently."

If Moncada can be said to be the central character in the novel (an exorbitant pretension if only because, as I noted earlier, the novel has no center), this is only insofar as responsibility is his obsessive subject. This fleeting reference to the discourse of responsibility (or rather to its impossibility) is what retrospectively grounds Moncada's discourse, which can only be understood as a discourse of nonresponse. Faced with responsibility, Moncada, who is not *loco continuo,* chooses to remain irresponsible, chooses to not respond. Respond to whom or to what? Perhaps Moncada makes this much plain in the words that open his discourse in the market: "I am God's toreador. I am a beggar of His affection, not for the false affection of the authorities" (Arguedas 2000, 56). Moncada, the bullfighter, portrays himself as the one who no longer listens. Genealogy is against him: "General José Luis Orbegozo y Moncada, who was president of the Republic, ha, ha, haiee! My relative, ha ha, haiee!" (57). Moncada understands his unique place: "They're putting my picture on television in the foreign countries. My picture's going to come out in all the newspapers of the world, humanity will have to remember me" (57). His accomplishment is outstanding enough: "I fight bulls; I'm not gored by any of the temptations that make Braschi rich, or that storekeeper Mohana who ran for mayor. By now the bulls don't charge me anymore; they've all been fought" (57). The art of the bullfighter lies in his ability to elude the bull. The torero lets the bull pass by and remains untouched in the center of the ring. Likewise, Moncada avoids the calls of economy (Braschi) as much as the calls of politics (Moana, Orbegozo y Moncada). He avoids them by no longer listening to them. What does Moncada *torea,* then, if not the possible process of any hegemonic subjection?[21] Moncada's sermons place themselves beyond traditional forms of social engagement, beyond recognizable forms of the political, to reach a region for which we still have only tentative names, but one that is nonetheless becoming more and more densely inhabited by Latin American masses.

While Moncada might seem a figure of self-defeat, a retreat from reason and politics into a realm of senseless evaluations of the social, his stance as public orator does not represent an antidemocratic and self-defeating strategy. Rather, it enacts a radicalization of both literature and democratic politics on their common ground. Let us remember that the authorization to say everything—which is how Derrida characterizes the modern being of literature—also acknowledges "a right to absolute nonresponse." This nonresponse, Derrida continues, "is more original and more secret than the modalities of power and duty because it is fundamentally heterogeneous to them" (1992, 38). In not responding, Moncada remains faithful to a "hyperbolic condition of democracy which seems to contradict a certain determined and historically limited concept of such a democracy, a concept which links it to the concept of a subject that is calculable, accountable, imputable and responsible, one that has-to-respond, has-to-tell" (Derrida 1992, 23).

Bazalar and the New Face of Peru

Opposite the figure of Moncada stands the figure of Gregorio Bazalar. An organizer, Bazalar needs to speak and to be understood. Ironically, however, he has learned just enough Spanish to perform his role as a leader. He represents, as Pedro Trigo points out, the new face of Peru. He is not a well-defined figure but, rather, a project, and in this sense he is also the true representative of the Chimbotan universe. Bazalar first appears in the novel through intermittent glimpses of his persona that leave the reader wondering whether he is a communal leader or an upstart. The constitutive force Arguedas assigns to this character becomes apparent, however, when Bazalar is given a foundational activity: moving the poorest section of the cemetery to a new location. In this context, Bazalar offers one of his alluvial and revelatory speeches, addressing the multitude as Moncada stands nearby:

> Fellow citizens who bear the crosses of your dead. Here we've come in the name of the Father, the Son, the Monicipality, and the Subprefect. To bury the

crosses that we're bringing, funeral ones! Just anywhere. Here we are in the hollow. Here nobodies is gonna find us to carry us off to the Valley of Jehosephat. Forever'n ever we stay. It don't interest anybodies, to tell the truth, to have each person know where, the point where, for the eternal, his dead father, brother, sister remains. What's in our hearts is the field where the dead one's at peace, accompanyin' his town community. That's the way it is, Señor gravekeeper, representative of Señor Bishop, Governments. They don't want us to be in the modern American cemetery? Thanks be; the wall tumbles down . . . the flower gets burnt to a ugly crisp. The mountain doesn't come to an end, then. Here nobodies weep, so be it said. Amen. (Arguedas 2000, 72–73)

Given that for more than four decades the oppositional subject in Arguedas has been thought in terms of ethnic and cultural essentialisms, the most striking feature of Bazalar's discourse lies in its relentless antifoundationalism. Archibald points out that Bazalar embodies a dramatic turn in Arguedas's quest for the construction of a popular pole: he instantiates a new nationalist imagination that, although "no longer founded on cultural or ethnic essentialisms . . . still managed to resist metropolitan appropriation" (1998, 39). In this passage, we see Bazalar engaged in the primary foundational action: burial of the dead. However, only the crosses are being moved, not the actual bodies. And even the symbolic location of the dead seems a superficial issue, as Bazalar insists that "this hollow in the foothills suits us fine." This imprecision renders the new foundation unmappable ("each person know where, the point where, for the eternal, his dead father, brother, sister remains"). And if it is true that Bazalar here speaks before the representatives of the church, the municipal government, and the ethereal forces of popular religiosity, addressing them explicitly, it is also true that despite addressing them ("representative of Señor Bishop, Governments"), he also ignores them ("It don't interest anybodies," "Here nobodies is gonna find us").[22]

The novel's wager for a dynamic and transformative figure of the popular subject, embodied to some extent in Bazalar, becomes even more evident when one contrasts Bazalar with other characters who retain traditional Andean values and orient their actions around these values. Pedro Trigo notes that Hilario Caullama, who fuses a stern, traditional indigenous subjectivity with militant Marxism, has a hard time answering to the political challenges presented in Chimbote. Caullama's fidelity to his political convictions no doubt elicits the reader's admiration, but one also has the sense that the event that forms the core of Caullama's vision of Chimbote and Peru—the antagonism between the Inca and Capital—is not the event to which Arguedas's novel seeks to respond. Rather, this event, again, is the constant shifts in the subjectivity of the highlanders, their perpetual attunement to the lived world. The world of Chimbote is simply more complex, more fascinating than the opposition "Inca/Capital" allows us to think.

In previous novels, when Arguedas's conception was still dominated by a sort of inverted transculturation (Andean traits were active, not reactive; part of the form, not of the content), the destabilization of hegemonic subjectivity took the form of a crisis of intentionality, a clash of interpellations (e.g., modern and traditional), and finally of a pluriphonic and pluri-ideological vision of the world represented not by the novel as a whole but by the characters themselves. Don Bruno, in *Todas las sangres,* changes his mind on the most vital subjects without ever falling into contradiction. These earlier novels perform the textuality of the textual. The paradigmatic and syntagmatic dimensions of language appear in the same space, according to a logic that our hermeneutics, based on the identification of discourse and personality, can hardly analyze. The Freudian symptom that satisfies more than one agency or impulse *simultaneously* comes close to figuring how this phenomenon of a cluster of meanings represented in a single speech and character might work. But while the characters in *Yawar Fiesta, Deep Rivers,* and *Todas las sangres* exemplify the dilemma of intentionality, in *The Foxes* intentionality reigns supreme, and the content of social interpellation recedes into an almost meaningless background. The receding of the world is in an economic relationship to the emergence of self-sustained characters.

Fire in the Heart

With *The Foxes,* the historical project of Latin American literature comes to an end, because the structure of representation that granted rights in exchange for subjection has finally come to be thematized as such. As Martin Lienhard saw quite well, this dissolution of traditional literatures could not leave the building of Latin American literature untouched. Here dissolution means not only that a project has been consummated but also that its obscene side has been exposed for all to see. The revelation thus produced does not create a comfortable hermeneutic space. If anything, it produces "a wash of insecurity, anxiety, and hopelessness across a political landscape formerly kept dry by the floodgates of foundationalism and metaphysics."[23] The pessimistic tone so pervasive in some criticism of *The Foxes* is an indirect reminder of how difficult it is to embrace the opening that Arguedas leaves as his unmatched heritage. In part, the difficulty of experiencing this heritage stems from the fact that we wish to offer an optimistic reading to counter the pessimistic one; but in Arguedas, as I remarked earlier, the opposite of pessimism is not optimism, but life. The real hero of *The Foxes* is Becoming itself. Don Diego appears as a Dionysian character who dances to destroy the rigidity of identification and understands this destruction as a properly political work.[24] This is the same rigidity that is destroyed in Bazalar's stern rejection of state territorialization of the popular space or in Moncada's withdrawal from the universe of inheritance, political interests, and economic calculation. This dissolution of a fixed origin is not a dissolution of origin *in general*. Bazalar, Asto, Moncada, and even Don Angel Rincón Jaramillo are all highly original characters in that they are situated near the origin: they are originals rather than reproductions.[25] They possess what Walter Benjamin would have called "aura." But their circumstantial origin can no longer be asserted, investigated, established. Or, better yet, that origin no longer holds over them a power of determination. If this is true, what stands for origin and ground in this cosmogonic novel? If Chimbote is Babel, it is also a perfect anti-Babel. In Babel, people could not understand each other because they spoke different languages. In Chimbote, everybody speaks a private language, yet everyone understands everyone else—perhaps, indeed, too perfectly. The best place to find an answer to this question is, of course, in chapter 3, where two characters who speak mutually unintelligible social languages nonetheless seem to come to a perfect understanding. Reflecting on this issue, Don Diego claims to share with other characters what he calls "fire in the hearth."

We are at this point ready to enunciate the perplexing alchemy through which the motives of *recognition* and *work* that dominate Arguedas's previous novels are transformed in *The Foxes* into an affirmation of life. Work and the poetic are now understood as pure performance. But performance, in turn, is utterly poetic. In other words, work is a self-foundational activity.[26] The Chimbotan universe is poetic not because even the humblest character resorts to poetic language when it comes to self-presentation (a fact that should of course be granted its due import), but because each character—and the whole Chimbotan world—finds justification for existence in the mere act of existence itself. Bazalar, the political poet, models himself after this knowledge, and his life also appears to him in the light of an event of origination and dealienation. Arguedas, who frequently displays a certain irony toward his character, pays Bazalar a seemingly exorbitant compliment: "'Maybe I . . .' he thought (no longer able to think in Quechua) 'It could be, maybe, in this lifetime of mine, that I won't be any longer a stranger [*extranjero*, foreigner] in this country land we've been born. First time and first person that ever finalizes that difficult deed in his lifetime existence'" (Arguedas 2000, 227–28). This self-foundation of the present introduces a formula that, far from escaping the world, sustains a gaze, as Priscilla Archibald says, "no longer founded on cultural or ethnic essentialisms" but still able "to resist metropolitan appropriation" (1998, 11). What kind of entity might perform the feat of founding an anti-essentialist world? The answer is simple: what founds without itself having a foundation is, of course, language.

This is the structure that Gareth Williams points to in the context of a discussion of what he terms Mario Vargas Llosa's "ungenerous" reading of Arguedas's novel. The target of Vargas Llosa's assessment of the novel is, unsurprisingly, its language—unsurprisingly because this novel, whose characters speak ceaselessly, is in the final analysis a pure performance of language. Vargas Llosa's particular target is the hallucinatory discourse of mad Moncada, whose language, Vargas Llosa complains, is nothing but a display of "an assortment of syntactic, phonetic, and orthographic aberrations . . . a formalism, an impoverished version of the aestheticist formula 'art for art's sake'" (qtd. in G. Williams 2004, 57). Williams grants, of course, that Moncada's language borders on the unintelligible, but he also pays attention to the dimension of the voice as the dimension of a pure intention to signify. Or, as Williams writes, *The Foxes*, particularly Moncada's discourse, represents "a pure taking place of an instance of language" (2004, 57). The taking place of language has a strictly ontological meaning (I am deviating here from Williams, who correctly underscores the subaltern problematic that subtends the question of an unintelligible language). The taking place of language represents an awareness of the fact that language cannot be reduced to an instrument of communication; rather, language is the ungrounded ground of Chimbote. The meaning of this discovery is not restricted to the limits of its regional deployment. The taking place of language is the epochal discovery of our time. The literary experience has contributed decisively to this discovery, and it is only in virtue of its allegiance to that finding that literature occupies such a privileged place in the history of modern thinking.

Giorgio Agamben gave to this discovery the label of the "solitude of language." We are, Agamben declares, at last "alone with our words; for the first time we are truly alone with language, abandoned without any final foundation" (1999, 45).

Poetics and Poiesis

That language grounds, or is itself the ground, is of course a proposition whose roots go deep into the history of Western thinking. But the grounding role of language in Arguedas also answers to a specifically aesthetic program. Having read and reread Arguedas, I am convinced that his literature remains closed off to all those purists who refuse to dirty their hands in the metaphysical mud of aesthetic speculation.[27] Of course, *aesthetic* here does not equate to a bourgeois theory of art as ornament, or a psychoanalytic notion of art as a detour of desire, or the banalities of impressionistic criticism. I seek rather to point to the productive dimension of literature—and in this sense, aesthetics coincides partially with poiesis. The productive dimension of aesthetics seeks to prioritize not the aesthetic judgment but the aesthetic act. This shift means, among other things, that the object of the aesthetic itself (what Kant would call its ground) shifts. Despite how large the venerable Kantian tradition looms in our thinking of the aesthetic, the daemon of art is not pleasure but truth. But the truth that art delivers (the truth that an engaged literature like Arguedas's delivers) is not easy to stomach. Nobody saw this earlier and more clearly than Antonio Cornejo Polar. In a passage from *Los universos narrativos* that for me reveals better than any other the experience of reading *The Fox from Up Above and the Fox from Down Below*, Cornejo Polar writes that it is not possible to read *The Foxes* "sin estremecimiento, sin pavor, sin reverencia" (1974, 263).[28] No relevant aesthetic experience of modernity comes to pass without this dimension of terror casting upon it a long shadow. In what constitutes perhaps the last aesthetic of the twentieth century, *The Man without Content*, Giorgio Agamben reminds his readers that *fear* was once the word that named the aesthetic itself. The Greeks experienced the essence of art as *Deus phobos*, a divine terror in whose name and apprehension Plato banned poets from his Republic. The classical work of art, however, was still objective in nature: more a medium for the life of the community than a direct revelation of the spirit of its author. Only in modernity does the artist lend his or her substance to the work. Insofar as this substance is, preeminently, the possibility to negate all content, and insofar as this negation constitutes the moral imperative of modern art, the work of art becomes nothing but the unbounded site of an annihilating force. We say "the work of art," as we say "the artist," because they are indistinguishable in this arrangement. More than once, Agamben notices, this annihilating capacity of the aesthetic has pushed the artist to the brink of dissolution or death (1999).

A creative power that, at its height, can only take the form of destruction: is this not the most apt and pervasive formula of *The Foxes*? Arguedas thought this tension by saying that *The Foxes* is a novel of fire. This fire figures the ground of all possibilities in its pages. In a sense, this fire is shared by all the novel's characters, to the extent that while they are constantly in conflict with one another, they also come to recognize themselves as members of a complex world of invincible wills. In the night of political disintegration and abjection, knowledge, politics, hatred, and solidarity are granted in Chimbote by the common assent that every character feels toward the world. Faced with this novel, perhaps we too should ask: how is it that an enterprise that to an unheard-of degree says No and does No to everything to which literature, culture, and politics, progressive or otherwise, have always said Yes, can nonetheless be the opposite of a spirit of denial? In *The Foxes*, all understanding and ground are secured through an

assertion of the present as a moment liberated from the oppressive domin-
ion of the past—liberated not by forgetting the past but by understanding
its contemporaneity as its own production. Such a ground is also the source
of all optimism. It is in terms of this ground as a constant reenactment of
the will that *The Foxes* acquires an inescapable political dimension and not
just an ethical or personal dimension. The mistake many critics have made
is to look for this political dimension in the positive levels of a represented
world and staged speech. Like the dominance of literature, which is structural, schematic in nature, the deliverance Arguedas proposes is also rooted
at the doorstep of the noumenal. It is the revelation of language, more than
any half-whispered political statement, that constitutes the properly political, but of course also the nonpolitical, dimension of this work. If there is
any denunciation here, it is the denunciation of the metaphysical grounds
of bourgeois politics and subjectivity. If there is any proposition implicit in
these pages, it is not a celebration of a popular exodus à la Virno (although
this exodus is an uncontestable historical fact) but a declaration of the self-
sufficiency of life—a hard-won self-sufficiency wrested from a whole history
of metaphysical anchorings. As in his poem "Appeal to Some Intellectuals,"
the level thematized here is a primordial one that comes even before or
concurrently with the establishment of the subjectivities that an engaged
project seeks to mobilize. Arguedas leaves to us the task of figuring out
what kind of politics will be in keeping with that discovery.

But is it not senseless to propose a seemingly unlimited *Yes* to life from a
writer who killed himself? "Understanding how the author's death can also
be here the figure of a utopian space of regeneration is of course a task of
extraordinary difficulty," Alberto Moreiras wrote in an essay that advances
the question of Arguedas's suicide as a properly political one (2001, 201).
Arguedas died. If we are to believe his diaries, his work could not save him.
This failure cannot be read as a personal one. He did not survive the change
in the substance of the community that he had charted so passionately for
almost forty years.

This substance, I argued before, had become, in *The Foxes*, pure becoming itself. Its anchor to the world does not lie in the transformation of the
world (praxis) but in its creation (poiesis). And it is because of this foundational role of the poetic that the aesthetic dimension is the unavoidable

defile that any reading of *The Foxes* has to traverse. Poetry and life share roots in the poietic, creative, and productive essence of humanity. Arguedas believed in the roots of art and life in production, even if he used other names for it or refused to name it altogether. If our times are the times of consumption without production, is this anchoring of the human in the productive dimension of life merely a historical configuration whose last days are already at hand? While this difficult, crucial question lies outside the scope of this study, Arguedas did entertain it: his literature from 1964 on largely enacts a probing into forms of alienation whose center lies precisely in the foreclosure of the dimension of *traditional* production. But we are still looking at the question of Arguedas's suicide in relation to a writer's unconditional affirmation of life. In the experience of art, Agamben suggests, the poietic reveals its Janus face of foundation and destruction—the paradoxical link between negativity and genesis. This dialectic appears repeatedly in Arguedas's last works. In Arguedas's final years, when he wrote "Appeal to Some Intellectuals" and *The Foxes,* Arguedas sought desperately to transcend the realm of the merely aesthetic to contribute to the great struggle that he saw unfolding "in Peru and elsewhere." But the result of this attempt, focused as it was on the poietic ability of the highlanders, could only baffle even his admirers. In *The Foxes,* life takes an all-affirming yet enigmatic, almost incomprehensible shape. Perhaps what Arguedas discovered after the majestic failure of *Todas las sangres* were the limits of affirmation in the essential realm of art. The more he strove to ground Chimbote in what was unique to it, the more he unearthed the abyss of the event of language, whose terrifying effect his work not only fails to appease but even conjures, more profoundly than the work of any other writer in modern Latin America. Arguedas's unique lot was to uncover this frightening power of the aesthetic in the dissolution of the historical project of Latin American literature, and no doubt beyond.

Notes

Chapter 1

1 I use the word *enunciation* as a way to stress the event character of the literary word. For this use of *enunciation*, see Benveniste 1966.

2 Slavoj Žižek discusses culture as adaptation in *The Sublime Object of Ideology* (1989, 5–7). See also Gilles Deleuze and Félix Guattari's essay "Apparatus of Capture," in *A Thousand Plateaus* (1987, 424–73).

3 See Rama 1987; Cándido 1995; Ludmer 2002; Viñas 1964.

4 Exemplary cases are those of *testimonio* and women writing. See Trigo 2001; Franco 1991; G. Williams 2002.

5 Derrida's exposition of the "being" of literature comes close to the general structure that Terry Eagleton lays down for his understanding of literature as a historical form in the opening pages of "The Rise of English" (1993, 17–20).

6 Ortiz 1995; Rama 1987; Cornejo Polar 1994; García Canclini 1995; Mignolo 1995; Moreiras 1999; Pratt 1992.

7 For a passionate but ultimately mostly rhetorical attack on the use of the notion of postcoloniality in Latin American studies, see Klor de Alva 1992. The postcolonial mark of Latin American literature is affirmed, on the other hand, in two of the most important recent books on Latin Americanism: Sommer 1999; Moreiras 2001.

8 The phrase "cultural Real" may seem a contradiction in terms, but this contradiction is arguably the kernel of what is called "heterogeneity" in Latin Americanism. Angel Rama makes a similar argument about the question of singularity and translation into the universal in chapter 3 of *The Lettered City* (1996).

9 Susan Buck-Morss's essay "Hegel and Haiti" can be read as an oblique commentary on this point (2000).

10 We touch here on a question increasingly discussed under the heading of the "coloniality of power." For a discussion of the concept, see Mignolo 2000, esp. 17–18.

11 Rainer Schulte and John Biguenet have assembled an anthology on translation reaching, as its subtitle declares, "from Dryden to Derrida," collecting thoughts on translation by Valery, Goethe, Benjamin, Pound, Nabokov, Jacobson, and Paz (1992). These authors meditate about translations from German into French, Italian into English, Spanish into French—all houses fixed in the same neighborhood, where, to make things worse, everybody speaks the same language: the language of literature. On the other side of the spectrum we have texts of a subalternist and postcolonial inflection, like Gayatri Spivak's "Politics of Translation," in *Outside the Teaching Machine* (1993), or the pages Dipesh Chakrabarty devotes to translation in *Provincializing Europe* (2000, esp. chapter 3).

12 Unless otherwise noted, or unless a translator is indicated in the reference list, all translations are my own.

13 In 1920, Asturias was a politically engaged intellectual who had not only undertaken a transculturating project with his *Leyendas de Guatemala* but also embarked on an ethnographic recuperation of indigenous heritage through his cotranslation into Spanish (from the French version) of the *Popol-Vuh*, the sacred book of the Quiché people. As Martin Lienhard discerns, "Through . . . an aesthetic indigenization of literary discourse, Asturias strives to create a new literary subject, a Guatemalan subject, able to conceive the country as a totality" (1996, 572).

14 See Cornejo Polar's discussion of González Prada in *La formación de la tradición literaria en el Perú* (1989, 103); Carlos Alonso's study of *criollismo* in *The Spanish American Regional Novel* (1990); and Mabel Moraña's overview of literature in the modernizing period in *Literatura y cultura nacional en Hispanoamérica* (1984).

15 Liberalism underlies the motives of self-interest, rationality, private property, and religious tolerance and turns them into universal or—as early liberals used to say—"natural" rights. The word *liberal,* which comes from the Latin *liber* (free), is rooted in the philosophy of the Enlightenment. John Locke, who published *A Letter Concerning Tolerance* in 1689, is considered by many to be the first liberal philosopher. However, it was not until Adam Smith's *The Wealth of Nations* (1776) that liberal dogma was established on firm grounds. As for the political notion of liberalism, the authors of the Spanish constitution of 1812 (the so-called Cadiz constitution) were the first to use the word *liberal* with a political connotation.

16 Attempts have been made to disengage the subject from this process of subjection. Some authors, then, reserve *subjection* to signal the production of socially integrated subjectivities and *subjectification* to designate the process of
becoming a subject in a development that preserves the relationship between
the subject and its truth. Thus, against the Althusserian notion of the subject
as produced by ideological state apparatuses, late Lacanians such as Mladen
Dolar expressed their conviction that since the term *subject* names in Lacan
a blank, unassailable space of human experience, the process of becoming a
subject should make room for this radical inadequacy. Other authors, including
Judith Butler and Linda Zerilli, eschew or relativize the distinction between
subjection and subjectification, a position that Dolar himself came to take in
later work (2006). See Butler 1997; Zerilli 1998.

17 See Alberto Moreiras's discussion of transculturation (2004).

18 Gareth Williams captures this affinity between transculturation and state integration when he circumscribes transculturation in terms of "the fictive relation
between the state and the notion of the people that constitutes collectivities
as particular represented populations that are (supposedly) naturally inserted
into the specific mechanisms and calculation of the nation's constituted power
structures and truth regimes" (2002, 24).

19 Flores Galindo exhorts his readers to "no longer seek an Inca" (1988, 168).

20 Along with Moreiras 2001 and G. Williams 2002, see Beverley 1999, Franco
2002.

21 Markell Patchen discusses recognition from the perspective of political science
in *Bound by Recognition* (2003). As his title suggests, Patchen also sees recognition as invested in a process of binding rather than marking an inalienable
property of the subject.

Chapter 2

1 Stephen Greenblatt discusses the value of wonder in the early colonial period
in his *Marvelous Possessions* (1991). *Wonder* is an ambivalent word. As a noun, it
recognizes and cancels an element of surprise. As a verb, it points to a figure of
desire (the desire to go beyond the self) and thus connects the theme of "wondering" to the question of otherness.

2 Solis "discovered" the River Plate in 1516 and was killed by the Indians. As Gustavo Verdesio puts it, an accepted (but not proved) version has Solis eaten by
his captors (2001, 25).

3   "Since I owe them my life, it is only fair that I should repay them by each day reliving their lives" (Saer 1990, 147).

4   The humanist tone belongs to the novel, not to my interpretation: "For me the Indians were the only men on this earth, and . . . since the day they had sent me back, with the exception of Father Quesada I had met only strange, problematic beings whom only custom or convention dignified with the name 'man'" (Saer 1990, 109).

5   Gabriel Riera discusses the centrality of the ontological problematic in the novel; see Reira 1996.

6   In addition to Riera's essay, see Díaz Quiñones 1992; González 2000.

7   On this question, see Koyré 1957; Blumenberg 1987.

8   The *Meditations* reads: "But then were I perchance to look out my window and observe men crossing the square, I would ordinarily say I see the men themselves just as I say I see the wax. But what do I see aside from hats and clothes, which could conceal automata?" (Descartes 1996, 68). Even if Descartes's logic is flawless, the passage exemplifies the reduction of otherness to representation, which Vicent Descombes deems to be the definitive trait of Idealism (Descombes 1980, 22).

9   Around 1754, a pessimistic Jean-Jacques Rousseau wrote: "For the three or four hundred years since the inhabitants of Europe inundated the other parts of the world and continually published new collections of travels and stories, I am convinced that we know no other men but the Europeans alone" (1987, 99).

10 The narrator comments at large on the sense of homeliness that surrounds the Indians' life: "For them that place was the home of the world. If anything existed, it could not do so outside that place. In fact, to say that the place was the home of the world is a mistake on my part since for them that place and the world were one and the same thing" (Saer 1990, 126).

11 Simon Critchley notes that nowhere in his writings does Descartes use the word *subject* in its modern sense (1996).

12 Almost every important philosopher from the sixteenth to the eighteenth century felt the compulsion to write an Optics, and Descartes was no exception. As a matter of fact, one can argue that it is only in his *Optics* that the world of scholastic philosophy is really overcome.

13 Descartes refers to this work in the *Discourse on Method* when, in part 5, he writes, "I tried to explain my principles in a Treatise which certain considerations prevented me from publishing" (1996, 76).

14 Levinas's criticism of "light" is intended in more than one sense. Heidegger's clearing of Being, the Enlightenment, and the primacy of vision in modern ontology are just some of the sources of Levinas's suspicion of this rhetoric. In the final analysis, it is the implicit collusion between knowledge and illumination that Levinas finds troubling, any time that an illumination of the other (which is not a self-manifestation) favors its immobilization and objectification. See Levinas 1969, 350–52. See also Derrida's discussion of the violence of light in an essay devoted to Levinas: "Violence and Metaphysics" (1978).

15 For a discussion of the "metaphysics of presence," see Jacques Derrida's "Structure, Sign and Play in the Discourse of the Human Sciences" in *Writing and Difference* (1992, 278–93).

16 The narrator also mentions the adverb *negh* (Saer 1990, 130).

17 In one passage, the *entenado* mimics his story of captivity in front of a sleepy crowd. As the representation—devoid of any truth, as the narrator says—progresses, it advances in his mind a creeping sense of unreality that turns the whole world into a phantasmagoria. The theatrical representation, a representation in which nothing is accomplished or communicated, is the exact reverse of the novel: it is made of "meanings," but insofar as it is irresponsible or oblivious to the memory of those who are the excuse for the play, it plunges into meaningless gesticulation that threatens to devour the very consistency of the world.

18 This possibility of conceiving contingency and facticity not as facts open to intellection but as the act of intellection is, Levinas writes, "the great novelty of contemporary ontology" (1996, 3).

19 A methodology of reduction (which is always the methodological correlate of genuine idealism) is common to Descartes, Levinas, and Merleau-Ponty. But in every case, the reduction yields a different, even irreconcilable result. For Descartes, the reduction is a road toward absolute immanence in the assertion of a transcendental subject. For Levinas, it is a way of investigating the concrete, worldly forms of the ethical injunction. For Merleau-Ponty, it signals a path toward a plenitude of being in which the body reencounters a primary communion with the world.

20 I have in mind a book like Shoshana Felman and Doris Laub's *Testimony: Crises of Witnessing in Literature, Psychoanalysis, and History* (1992).

21 Jacques Derrida notices that witnessing also implies a problematic close to the inheritance. He calls attention to the connection between the question of witnessing and "testimonium," with the "testamentum . . . of surviving, living on before and beyond the opposition between living and dying" (2000, 181).

22 Derrida asks whether an absolutely transparent testimony "would still be a testimony" (2000, 183).

23 Merleau-Ponty's notion of reversibility arises in direct opposition to the phenomenology of Jean-Paul Sartre. In *Being and Nothingness,* Sartre elaborates a notion of "touching" that entails a radical separation between subject and world ("To touch and to be touched . . . exist on two incommunicable levels" [1992, 116]). Merleau-Ponty criticizes this disjunction severely. In *The Phenomenology of Perception,* he emphasizes the fundamental unity that should be presupposed if any experience of "touching" (my left hand touching my right hand was the phenomenologists' favorite example) were to be finally accounted for. Merleau-Ponty also denies that touching and being touched could be simultaneous. Instead he asserts the structural ambiguity in the subject's relation to the world: an alternation of perception and affection underscoring a basic continuity. Merleau-Ponty names this continuity *reversibility.* Reversibility cannot be confused with identity. In the act of using my right hand to touch my left hand, I may feel on my right hand the texture of the left, or on my left the touch of the right, but never both simultaneously. The human body itself is an exemplary instance of the principle of reversibility that characterizes the individual's essential relationship to the world. In the continuum of the world that Merleau-Ponty calls "the flesh," representation is still an event to come and the other a condition of any "presencing." See Merleau-Ponty 1968, 1993.

24 In a general reference to the phenomenological project, Slavoj Žižek discards the possibility of a reduction to a prereflective—understood by him as prelinguistic—state of being. Žižek's argument moves itself in the style of the clear-cut and antigenetic structuralist articulation. As Mladen Dolar explains, this strategy recognizes that "structure always springs up suddenly, from nothing, without any transitional stages" (1993, 77). For Žižek, the structure in question here is the symbolic register as the operation that severs the human link to nature and ruins any explanation of a genetic passage from a naturelike to a culturelike stage. "There is no subjectivity," writes Žižek, "without [a] gesture of withdrawal. . . . The withdrawal-into-self, the cutting-off of the links to the environs, is followed by the construction of a symbolic universe that the subject projects onto reality as a kind of substitute-formation" (1998, 259). This cutting-off from nature is an event, not a process, and in his text Žižek attacks the phenomenologists for defending the possibility of an ego and a world "before meaning." The same point was leveled against Merleau-Ponty in the early 1990s by Claude Lefort, the editor of Merleau-Ponty's unfinished *The Visible and the Invisible* (cf. "Flesh and Otherness" [Lefort 1990]). No argument is, in these matters, either easy or straightforward, and I cannot presume to settle the

matter in a footnote. However, it is difficult to accuse Merleau-Ponty—whom Levinas credited with demonstrating the impossibility of conceiving a thinking severed from language—of not paying attention to the constitutive role of language in the advent of a human world. It should be observed, however, that the very definition of language is in Merleau-Ponty not necessarily or primarily *linguistic* in character. If on the one hand Merleau-Ponty said that "meaning is invisible" (1968, 215), this affirmation does not lock every meaning within the ideality of language. There is also an invisible that transports itself to the realm of the visible. Merleau-Ponty's twist consists in asserting that this transposition has always already occurred, since the very act of perception draws a "meaning perceptual gestalt" (Low 1992, 71). Douglas Low points to the fact that at the time of his death, "Merleau-Ponty was just beginning to analyze the relationship between this perceptual gestalt or idea and the abstract ideas of language. For Merleau-Ponty, the transition from one to the other is to be accomplished by the body, for perception is already a gesture, is already expression" (71–72).

25 As Jean Laplanche notices, the published translation of the English title ("Foundational Investigations of the Phenomenological Origin of the Spatiality of Nature") partially misses the deep thrust of Husserl's position. The German original reads "Umsturz dek kopernikanischen Lehre: Die Erde als ur-Arche bewegt sich nicht." Commenting on the published translation, Laplanche observes that while the German word *Arche* means "ark," as in Noah's Ark, "it may also allude to the Greek *arché* meaning the cause, origin or beginning" (1999, 58).

26 Derrida makes this point in regard to Levinas in "Language and Metaphysics." Later, however, in *Specters of Marx* (1994), he concedes to the Levinassean other a paradoxical phenomenality.

Chapter 3

1 See also Adorno 1988.

2 The process exemplifies Adorno's observation that "the ritual act of naming is one of the most conflictive points in the relationship" between (indigenous) people and Europeans in the sixteenth century (1996, 102).

3 See my discussion of Fabian's notion of this denial of coevalness in chapter 1.

4 The enunciative system of the "Nueva Corónica" is complex. The letter that Waman Poma included in his correspondence with the king is addressed directly to "AL RREY PHELIPO" (8). The first plate, however, orients the same enunciative system to an authority higher than the king: *su santidad* (Guamán Poma de Ayala 1980, 1).

5   The monk Mendoza y Luna, aide of the Viceroyal of Peru, seems to have taken
    Waman Poma as a source for his own writings on the colony. See Adorno 1987,
    xxii.

6   The need to question the promotion of literature to its status as the general in-
    terpreter of colonial semiosis is enunciated by Walter Mignolo in "El metatexto
    historiográfico y la historiografía indiana" (1981).

7   León Portilla's text bears the suggestive subtitle *De la oralidad y los códices meso-
    americanos a la escritura alfabética.*

8   See also Mignolo's "Record Keeping without Letters and Writing Histories of
    People without History" (Mignolo 1995, 125-69).

9   Martin Lienhard notes that several indigenous texts collected by authors like
    León Portilla and Angel Maria Garibay represent "forerunners of a concept
    of Latin American literature built upon the appropriation of the alphabetic
    script" (1991, x).

10 Pre-Columbian texts are written in a hieroglyphic form using means of rep-
    resentation based on iconic references. Iconic elements can be purely iconic
    (depictions of gods) or have a logographic function (approaching a level of con-
    vention that removes them from their iconic referent). There are four main tra-
    ditions of record keeping in Mesoamerica: the Aztec, the Mixtec, the Zapotec,
    and the Maya (Marcus 1992, 45-93). Pre-Columbian writing relies on either a
    hieroglyphic system, which can combine phonetic and nonphonetic elements
    (like the Maya script), or a pictorial system, which shows no presence of pho-
    netic features and conveys its meaning through iconic and conventional ele-
    ments (like the Aztec and Mixtec systems). Not all texts appear in "books," but
    many have been registered from ruins and archeological sites. Although the use
    of the word *books* to refer to the codices is by now standard, critics like Walter
    Mignolo object to this assimilation of a Mesoamerican practice into a Western
    cultural vocabulary (see Mignolo 1994). For a representative selection of these
    codices, descriptions, and locations, see Aguilera 1979.

11 The *escribano* Francisco López de Xerez (to use the alternative spelling) pub-
    lished his *Verdadera Relación de la Conquista del Perú* in 1534.

12 For a history of educational institutions in New Spain, see Gómez Canedo 1982.

13 The earliest known texts written in alphabetic Nahuatl date back to the 1530s
    or 1540s. These texts compose a body of works "written by various indigenous
    persons, manipulating the script very much in their own way but betraying
    their schooling in a single orthographic canon" (Lockhart 1992, 335).

14 My use of the word *genre* to refer to indigenous productions may be perceived

as a repetition of the same mistake that I criticize in the expansion of the word *literature* to the level of a contextless interpretative apparatus. However, I believe that "genres" are what linguists call a "linguistic universal." In this sense, the famous Bakhtinian proposition—that we speak and think in genres rather than words—seems to hold for every particular cultural context. Upon close observation, the Nahuatl genres described by authors such as Miguél León Portilla, Serge Gruzinski, and James Lockhart do not duplicate or derive from a "Western" norm but are deduced from the properties of Nahuatl culture itself through a process akin to the one that Dell Hymes calls "ethnography of speech." See León Portilla 1996, chapter 6; Lockhart 1992, chapter 4; Bakhtin 1986; Hymes and Gumperz 1986.

15 On the subject of religious and secular history among indigenous groups of Mesoamerica, see Florescano 1999, 177–378.

16 I distinguish "intertextuality" from "grafting." Intertextuality presupposes not only a commensurable space (the space of the inter-) but also the category of author, with all its juridical determinations. Grafting, on the other hand, is not a virtual space but a space constructed by the materialization of a discourse that supplements or interrupts another discourse. The process of grafting is also evident in texts originally written in Spanish, like Alvaro Tezozómoc's *Crónica mexicana*. Grafting is so widespread in the Spanish text that some critics believe that Tezozómoc was actually translating from Nahuatl sources. Lockhart, for instance, observes that some rhetorical characteristics of the chronicle, like inversion ("superiors call their aides their fathers, inferiors call the king their grandchild" [1992, 390]), speak to a kind of translated Nahuatl. The same process appears in the *Título de Totonicapán*, translated into Spanish (from Quiché) by Robert Carmack. Carmack notes that the first seven folios are "grafted" from the *Theologia Indorum*, a manuscript written by the Dominican priest Domingo de Vico a year before the production of the title. A summary analysis of this procedure in the titles of Zoyatzingo appears in Gruzinski 1993, 110–14.

17 Gibson 1964; Brotherston 1995; Florescano 2002; Gruzinski 1993; Haskett 1991; Lockhart 1991, 1992; Robertson and Robertson 1975; Hill Boone and Cummins 1980. Hill Boone and Cummins's collection, *Native Traditions in the Postconquest World*, contains an interesting comparative essay on Mesoamerica and the Andes by James Lockhart (1980).

18 For a general introduction to the subject, see Florescano 2002.

19 It is also important to consider the role played not only by the titles but by the different maps in cementing a sense of communal identity. On this point, see Leibsohn 1994.

20 I am not suggesting that universalization was not possible under preconquest historical conditions, only that it cannot be derived as one of the possible effects of a formal system of communication.

21 The status of writing in Mesoamerican cultures did not remain fixed throughout its whole and convoluted history. The knowledge of the Maya script, for instance, was reserved for the sacerdotal class in the classic period (300–900 A.C.E.), but it was extended to nobles and some state functionaries in the postclassic period (900–1500 A.C.E.). Enrique Florescano remarks on the important shifts that the profession of the *tlacuilo* suffered in a relatively short period of time and the autonomy that some *tlacuilo* enjoyed in the years immediately preceding the Spanish conquest (1994, 110–23).

22 The activity of mapping, representing, and making sense of the Spanish other had already begun in the early stages of the Spanish invasion of Mesoamerica. The Florentine codex includes detailed depictions of the battle for Tenochtitlan, and many post-Cortesian annals register the fight for political and military control of Mexico after the arrival of the Europeans. For a discussion of the indigenous representation of the conquest in the cryptographic tradition, see Brotherston 1995, chapter 2.

23 In the version translated by Adrian León in 1947, the same passage reads: "Hela aquí, que aquí comienza, se verá, está asentada por escrito la bonísima, veracísima relación de su renombre" (Alvarado Tezozómoc 1975, 2).

24 Milner discusses the relationship between the modern subject of science and the modern subject of culture (1995). For a discussion of the importance of the zero in the rise of Renaissance humanism, see Rotman 1987.

25 See Germán Vázquez's introduction to Ixtlilxochitl 1995 (23–27).

Chapter 4

1 Bürger recognizes that the representational function of literature and art has an immediate ideological value. I would like to show, however, that this representational character goes beyond what terms like *mimesis* and *representation* allow us to think.

2 On the criticism of "figure" in Levinas, see Robbins 1999, 40–43.

3 A full discussion of the correspondence (and the usual lack of correspondence) of technical terms across the three critiques is beyond the scope of this chapter, but some general definitions are possible. *Spontaneity,* for instance, is presented as the function of combining the manifold offered by sensibility in the *Critique of Pure Reason.* The spontaneous is, to an important extent, what is not contam-

inated by any remnant of receptivity. It would be interesting to establish the correspondences between the ethical and cognitive uses of the word in Kant and its posterior slide into Romantic and post-Romantic aesthetics. If we take another key term of Kant's *First Critique*, such as *intuition* (which designates an immediate form of knowledge), it is plain that its implications were carried over into the realm of aesthetic expression and theory, especially around the theory of the genius, the one who follows the rules without having learned them (which, as sections 46–50 of *The Critique of Judgment* explain, would be an inadmissible contamination of his spontaneity).

4   For Lloyd and Thomas, the Kantian *sensus communis* "as the universal substrate of human reason" works as "the foundation equally of the aesthetic and the public sphere. For this reason aesthetic judgments ... constitute a kind of precursor to any possible politics, insofar as any social contract which will assume the participation of autonomous (munding) citizens demands equally their prior ethical formation" (1998, 5).

5   We find a similar statement in Tony Bennet's reading of the *Third Critique:* "Will the universality of taste, once it has been produced, turn out to be the natural and original property of the human subject? Or will the subject to which a universality of taste can appropriately be attributed turn out to be the product of a process of cultural and historical unification?" (1990, 162).

6   For a discussion of *Bildung* in Romantic theory, see Nancy and Lacoue-Labarthe 1988, 32. See also the references to Nancy and Lacoue-Labarthe later in this chapter.

7   Discussing *culture* in *Marxism and Literature*, Raymond Williams asks, "Are we to understand 'culture' as 'the arts' ... or as a 'whole' way of life?" (1977, 13).

8   For Jacques-Alain Miller's discussion of extimacy, see Miller 1984. "Extimacy" is also the title of Miller's 1985–86 seminar. For Mladen Dolar's discussion of extimacy and criticism of Althusser's subject of interpellation, see Dolar 1993.

9   *Subjection/subjectification:* the terms are unstable and ambivalent. Dolar passionately critiques Althusser's theory of interpellation from the point of view of subjectification in "Beyond Interpellation" (1993). This criticism was later approvingly picked up by Slavoj Žižek in *The Sublime Object of Ideology* (1989). Linda Zerilli problematizes Dolar's and Žižek's critique in "This Universalism Which Is Not One" (1998). In *The Psychic Life of Power* (1997), Judith Butler uses the two terms alternatively and indistinguishably. It is probable that if forced to establish the operational limits between *subjection* and *subjectification,* we will have to agree that their logical and functional meanings do not coincide.

10 The character of the extimacy of culture is widely repressed in most critical accounts. David Lloyd and Paul Thomas point to the surprising formula with which Matthew Arnold inaugurates a new thinking about the relationship between culture and state: "Culture suggests the idea of the State" (Lloyd and Thomas 1998, 1). Yet they understand this formula as implying that "only in the slow but steady emergence of state institutions did literature and fine arts become the exemplary objects of pedagogy" (2). The hurry to cast the whole problematic of expression in a pedagogical mold fails to do justice to the subtlety of Arnold's formulation. For Arnold, culture only *suggests* the idea of the state, and it does so in a transcendental way. Any overvaluation of the pedagogic instance (e.g., via its reduction to a form of state agency) dissolves the real process by which the expression of the will denotes simultaneously its capture by the state apparatus.

11 Tony Bennet forcefully articulates a neo-Foucauldian approach to cultural studies; see Bennet 1990. My observation that any critical reading of culture must relate to consciousness, affect, and practices may well stand by three approaches to cultural studies: Žižek and his work on fantasy and the symptom (1989), Grossberg and his use of a Deleuzian notion of "affect" for cultural studies (1997), and the neo-Foucauldian charting of the relationship between culture and governmentality. Tony Bennet's manifesto, although dated, exemplifies the neo-Foucauldian approach.

12 Even a book deeply informed by the notion that the modern use of literature depends on its relationship to the pedagogical, such as Ian Hunter's *Culture and Government* (1988), faces the problem of accounting for a complex ideology of the act of reading as an act of identification. In the opening pages of his book, Hunter highlights the way in which Arnold conceived of British literature as a pedagogical tool, based on its exemplary nature. However, as Hunter's quotation from Arnold reveals, this exemplary function is secondary to the primordial function that the act of reading serves: becoming the basis for an expressive act by the students.

13 Among the few works that explore this intersection is Robert Conn's book *The Politics of Philology* (2002), which explores the tension between classical and Romantic-nationalist philology in Alfonso Reyes.

14 Arnold holds a special place in the most explicit of Henríquez Ureña's essays on cultural policy: "La cultura de las humanidades" (see Henríquez Ureña 1960).

15 Section 47 of Kant's *Critique of Judgment* opens with this sentence: "On this point everyone agrees: that genius must be considered the very opposite of a spirit of imitation" (1966, 176).

16 The subsumption of literature into the school apparatus is discussed thoroughly by Juan Poblete in *Literatura chilena del siglo XIX* (2003).

17 In *Memorias de Mamá Blanca* (1991), there is an explicit opposition between two male figures: Cochocho, the illiterate peon of the ranch, whom de la Parra describes more than once as a natural-born bard; and the author's father, a patriarchal figure who at the pinnacle of the author's rejection of his authority is compared to the statue of Simon Bolivar, Venezuela's national hero.

18 It is highly suggestive that the criticism contemporaneous with the publication of Latin American regionalist novels portrays them alternatively as realist or poetic.

19 "The way to the head must be opened though the heart" / "The development of man's capacity for feeling is, therefore, the more urgent need of our age" (Schiller 1967, 107).

20 For a thorough discussion, see Beiser 1992, 95–99.

21 See Oscar Terán's description of Cané's attitude (2000, 37).

22 For Heidegger's interpretation of Kant, see Heidegger 1962. For Žižek's identification of the noumenal with the real, see Žižek 1999, 197–98.

23 Rousseau was not the first to formulate the hypothesis of the state of nature, but he was the first to ascribe to it a merely hypothetical, theoretical value in his "Discourse on the Origin of Inequality" (1987).

Chapter 5

1 In a similar vein, Aguilar Mora observes that, unlike their counterparts in Argentina and Peru, Mexican writers failed to constitute a literary-political avant-garde in the two first decades of the twentieth century (2000, 13).

2 If, following Doris Sommer, we accept that an allegorical constitution of the imagined community—normally based on the structure of the romance—is decisive in the modern forms of nation-building in Latin America, it quickly becomes obvious that no national romance occurs in the literature of the Mexican Revolution and that the revolution itself, as an event, is unsuited to allegorical motifs. In 1930, Agustín Vera published a novel entitled *La revancha,* which presents all the motifs of the family romance, although in an inverted form. Set in the small state of San Luís Potosí, this novel tells the story of a popular rebellion of local peasants who, led by General Guerrero, take over the hacienda and kill the owner in reprisal for past injustices. Many years later, Guerrero meets Lupe, the former fiancée of the deceased *hacendado,* in Mexico City. (Some the-

atrical versions of the novel make her the *hacendado*'s daughter.) Unaware of the past they share, they fall in love. They return to the hacienda, where they plan to live after getting married. There Lupe finds out that General Guerrero is the assassin of her former fiancé and kills him. At the end, the only allegorical reading that the novel allows is of the revolution as a "chance" event.

3   Revisionist historiography was not the first place these doubts were raised. Leonard Folgarait, who authored an interesting analysis of Rivera's murals, writes: "I shall continue to call it the Revolution, if not a 'true' revolution, that is, one that would transfer political power from one class to another and change the basic structure of the economy" (1998, 5).

4   Žižek writes, "Narrative as such emerges in order to resolve some fundamental antagonism by rearranging its terms into a temporal succession" (1997, 10). Kant discusses time as the condition for the connection between categories and intuitions in the "Analytic of Principles" (also known as the "Transcendental Doctrine of Judgment").

5   This point, earlier made in one of the fundamental books of Mexican historiography, *Everyday Forms of State Formation* (1994), is repeated in the conclusion that Claudio Lomnitz wrote for the ambitious collection *The Eagle and the Virgin* (Vaughan and Lewis 2006).

6   On this point, I agree with Gerald Martin's conclusion that "although scrupulously honest," Azuela "never fully understood the real political issues at stake in the Revolution" (1989, 40).

7   Among the many similarities between Vasconcelos's and Guzmán's writings on the subject of their participation in the revolution, an outstanding one is the pendular movement between revolutionary praxis and critical contemplation that each is constantly forced to take.

8   Commenting on this aspect of the sublime, Gilles Deleuze writes: "At first sight we attribute this immensity, which reduces our imagination to impotence, to the natural object, that is to sensible Nature. But in reality it is reason which forces us to unite the immensity of the sensible world into a whole. This whole is the Idea of the sensible, in so far as this has a substratum of something intelligible or suprasensible. Imagination thus learns that it is reason which pushes it to the limit of its power, forcing it to admit that all its power is nothing in comparison to an Idea" (1984, 51).

9   For an analysis of the ideological evolution of Mexican cultural and political life in turn-of-the-century Mexico, see Villegas 1993.

10   For a summary of the social tensions that determined the beginning of the

Mexican Revolution, see the opening chapter of Aguilar Camín and Meyer 1993.

11 "La juventud intelectual mexicana y el actual momento histórico." The text that appeared in *Revista de revistas* on June 25, 1911, is reproduced in Luna 1984, 135–38.

12 In his Plan de Ayala, Emiliano Zapata denounced the failure to dissolve the federal army and the retention, even promotion, of the old, reactionary military leadership formed under Díaz. Revolutionary militias, in contrast, had been ordered to disarm immediately. Land distribution was halted, and the Zapatista villages subjected to control and repression (Aguilar Camín and Meyer 1993, 26). Simultaneously, another front opened for the government in Mexico City, where nostalgic reactionary forces and an irresponsible press, which Madero himself had freed from almost immemorial censure, also contested government policies.

13 An indirect proof of this natural solidarity between education and class interest is offered by Alfonso Reyes, who wrote, "It would not be strange that after becoming a lawyer, Porfirio Diaz would make of this person a congressional representative for some *inverosimil* region of Mexico" (1960, 18).

14 This "German road" presupposed that social change could be introduced through educational reform. To some extent, the paradigm was successful in the Southern Cone (Argentina, Chile, Uruguay), never really implemented in other areas (Bolivia, Guatemala), and a notorious failure in Mexico.

15 See Legrás 2003.

16 Guzmán knew Madero personally and in 1911 shared the political tribune with him. Guzmán's father, an officer in the federal army, died during the revolution. In 1914, Guzmán himself became an officer in the Villista army. In the 1920s, his participation in a frustrated coup against Obregón forced him into exile. He returned to Mexico and joined the PRI, whose constitution he championed in the 1930s. In the 1940s and 1950s, he became a prominent journalist and editor. In 1968, Tlatelolco found him squarely in the group of intellectuals loyal to the Mexican state. A condemnatory silence then began to surround his figure. In 1976, he died a PRI senator for the Distrito Federal. For other biographical data, see Curiel 1993.

17 The dehumanizing rhetoric of counterinsurgent prose is already a classic element in subalternism's critical arsenal. In "Subaltern Studies as Postcolonial Criticism" (1990), Gyan Prakash observes that a customary trait of subalternizing description lies in the presentation of human actions (in Prakash's study,

those of India's peasants) through nouns that evoke natural phenomena such as storms, earthquakes, and wind. (One is reminded of Annita Brenner's *The Wind That Swept Mexico*.) Students of the Mexican Revolution have long noticed an inclination to depict revolutionary fighters through images or words that connote animality. Joseph Sommers calls attention to this fact in Azuela's *The Underdogs*, where, he remarks, "the dehumanization . . . characterizes not only the particular lives of Demetrio and his men, but the entire atmosphere of the Revolution" (1968, 10). (Sommers's book, ironically, is entitled *After the Storm*.) On the other hand, Ronald Paulson points out that "the imagery of the phenomenon of the Revolution itself merged the powerful natural force (Robespierre's 'tempête révolutionnaire,' Desmoulins's 'torrent révolutionnaire') with the indistinguishable, vague, indeterminate shape of the sovereign people" (1983, 21).

18 See Alberto Moreiras's analysis of this scene in terms of subalternity (2001, 123–26).

19 The extraneous vignette is reprinted in the introduction that Jorge Aguilar Mora wrote for the Ediciones Era edition of *Cartucho* (see Campobello 2000).

20 Irene Matthews has authored a modest but reliable biographical study on Campobello: *Nellie Campobello: La centaura del Norte* (1997).

21 All quotes from *Cartucho* are taken from the English translation by Doris Meyer (Campobello 1988). Aguilar Mora attacks this translation bitterly, accusing Meyer of "unforgettable omissions," but in the sections that I quote here, I find the translation accurate and acceptable.

22 Nostalgia for the frontier and ranch life was a permanent leitmotif for Villa. His ideal world, however, had already been assaulted by his modernizing imaginary, chiefly his tenacious admiration of the United States. Zapata began his revolutionary career professing a wholehearted allegiance to traditional communal indigenous life, but the experience of the revolution made him aware of the project's impractical nature.

23 For Knight's conviction about the paucity of theories of revolution, see Knight 1994, 27. In the same text, Knight concludes that the word *revolution* is "useful for general conversation but fatal to detailed analysis" (27).

24 Trotsky writes: "The symbolism of a revolution is too grandiose; it fits in badly with the creative work of individuals. For this reason artistic reproductions of the greatest mass dramas of humanity are so poor" (qtd. in Paulson 1983, vii).

25 Claudio Lomnitz offers a comprehensive view of death as a national totem in Mexico in his *Death and the Idea of Mexico* (2005).

Chapter 6

1   For a summary of Roa Bastos's views on literature, see Roa Bastos 1991a, 1991b.

2   Except for *Son of Man*, all translations of Roa Bastos's works are my own.

3   Charles Ferguson's pioneering work on bilingualism contains a reference to Paraguay as an exemplar of a bilingual society with diglossic functioning. The fact that every Paraguayan is able to speak both Spanish and Guaraní constitutes its bilingualism—although direct experience tells us that Guaraní is dominant in the countryside, where the hold of Spanish weakens notably. But these two languages are not equal in terms of prestige and function. Spanish is the language of education, state, and media; Guaraní is a subordinate language and, as standard diglossic theory goes, the language of affection, family, and play. Many things have changed since Ferguson published his essay "Diglossia" in 1959. Guaraní became an official language in 1992, gaining much recognition in the media and other forms of public representation.

4   This absence of an indigenous Guaraní speaker should not lead to the erroneous conclusion that there are no Indians in Paraguay. The bibliography on the contemporary indigenous population in Paraguay is extensive. Especially relevant to our subject is the compilation by Richard Arens, *Genocide in Paraguay* (1976), a volume that not only maps indigenous populations in contemporary Paraguay but also includes a sharp criticism of Stroessner's policy of extermination of different indigenous groups throughout the country.

5   Roa Bastos is far from upholding a naive or positivistic notion of orality defined in opposition to writing. What Roa Bastos terms *oral* and what he terms *written* are in fact both modalities of writing.

6   For an insightful study of the tension between the oral and the written in Paraguay, see Orué Pozzo 2002. One of the best general introductions to the relationship between the Guaraní language and Paraguayan society can be found in Meliá 1986.

7   On Rafael Barrett, see Corral 1994.

8   See Foster 1978.

9   Arguably, subaltern studies was inaugurated by Ranajit Guha's *Elementary Aspects of Peasant Insurgency in Colonial India* (1983). A comprehensive presentation of the Indian group can be found in *Mapping Subaltern Studies and the Postcolonial* (2000), edited by Vinayak Chaturvedi. In the field of Latin Americanism, a subaltern studies group was constituted in the early 1990s.

Its "Founding Statement" is reproduced in *The Postmodernism Debate in Latin America* (1995), edited by John Beverley, José Oviedo, and Michael Aronna.

10 Subalternity is a problem that has plagued the study of Latin America for many decades. Alberto Flores Galindo gave one of the most poignant accounts of the question of subalternity in his influential book *Buscando un Inca* (1988), in a polemic directed at the historian Jurgen Golte over the latter's explanation of the behavior of indigenous-peasant movements in Peru: "Peasants in the nineteenth century," Flores Galindo observes, "end up dissolved into structural mechanisms governed from Lima or Europe. These mechanisms condition their lives and leave only a narrow margin within which to respond instinctively by means of revolts, which end up being no more than sterile rural 'frenzies'" (1988, 104). This "spasmodic" conception of history, as Flores Galindo has dubbed it, is premised on a notion of behavioral symmetry that qualifies peasant revolt as merely reactive. The history of peasant and indigenous revolts in Peru is thus understood in a methodological and theoretical framework that, by following the general coordinates of the "historical situation," obliterates whatever distinct meaning the revolt had for its actors. A subaltern perspective on historical issues strives, on the other hand, to uncover and underline the originality and autonomy (though this latter word must be qualified) of the revolting people.

11 Besides Guha's pioneering work, see Spivak 1988; Moreiras 2001; Beverley 1999.

12 This explains the "thinness" of literary characters in *Son of Man*, an issue discussed by Bareiro Saguier (1983).

13 In 1961, the Argentine director Lucas Demare took *Son of Man* to the screen and enlisted Roa Bastos as screenwriter. Of the two dimensions in which the novel moves—the isolated life of the people of the small towns and the war—the movie is concerned only with the second. The opening image establishes the film within the aura of the nation-state as a historical transcendental form, a perspective that Roa Bastos avoided carefully in his book. The film, the director protests, is a testimony to the unfortunate event of a war between two neighboring countries. Demare's film is entertaining, but what the reader of the novel will miss most is the presence of any popular life that is not already fully incorporated into the life of the nation-state. I am not faulting Demare here, especially since Roa Bastos himself authored the screenplay. It is almost impossible to imagine how a movie could offer a filmic representation of Roa Bastos's fundamental insight about the delirious nature of Paraguayan reality, the weak hold of hegemonic formations on popular life, the dialectics of Guaraní and Spanish, and the inscription of a politicized memory of disaster in the very rhythm of the everyday life of the people.

14 Little is known of Mathias Grunewald. The circumstances of his birth are as disputed as the correct spelling of his name and the exact date of composition of his most famous piece: the Isenheim altarpiece. For information on Grunewald, see Huysmans 1958; Schmitt 1960.

15 The figure of the "Anthropos" emerges in the context of Gnostic thinking in the first centuries of the Christian era and belongs entirely to the process by which the Judeo traits of Christianity became increasingly Hellenized, hence its connection with the so-called Son of Man controversy, which hinges on the question of how to interpret the biblical reference to Jesus as "the Son of Man." One possibility is to read in this phrase the assertion that Jesus was a human being in a physical sense (this embodiment goes well with Hegel's interpretation of Jesus as the embodiment of the Spirit in the sphere of the Absolute). The second possibility is to read no Messianic significance in the designation.

16 "In the absence of the State, there is no people" (Virno 2004, 11). I discuss this passage in chapter 5.

17 For a discussion of the subaltern as lying outside the hegemonic articulation, see Moreiras 2001, 112–26.

18 See Clastres 1993.

19 See my discussion of extimacy in chapter 4.

20 For a report on the significant "Jornadas por la democracia en el Paraguay," which took place in Madrid in 1987, see Giménez Guanes 1987.

21 For a general introduction to these publications, see Amigo 2002.

22 A leaflet, *Cacique Lambaré*, was written almost entirely in Guaraní.

23 Roberto Amigo notes that the development of this satirical press "cannot be separated from the process of the opening to and imposition of European models undertaken by López" (2002, 19). The interest of these representations lies, in fact, in the way they expose "the inherent contradiction between the European model, more in tune with *porteño* liberalism, and the popular base that supported the López regimes" (19).

Chapter 7

1 According to José Deustua and José Luis Rénique, who authored the first extensive study on this topic in Peru, there was a substantial increase in publications between 1918 and 1930 (around 265 percent). See Deustua and Rénique 1984.

2 The expansion of the capitalist market and the state's influence marked Leguía's government. In 1915, the Peruvian state collected $15 million in taxes. Toward

1927, the amount climbed to $275 million (Deustua and Rénique 1984, 13). For a brief history of the period, see also Klarén 2000, 236–50.

3   Alberto Escobar offers a narratological approach to the question in "La hacienda y la realidad en la obra de J. M. Arguedas," included in *Arguedas o la utopía de la lengua* (1984). The hacienda as a privileged locus of *indigenista* fiction also appears in the novels of Ciro Alegría, Jorge Icaza, and Rosario Castellanos.

4   González Prada famously pointed (perhaps with some exaggeration) to regions where "judges and *gubernators* belong to the serfdom of the hacienda" (1976, 42).

5   The most important figures in this field are Manuel González Prada, Dora Mayer, Hildebrando Castro Pozo (author of *Del ayllu al cooperativismo socialista*), José Carlos Mariátegui, and Luis Valcárcel. For an overview of their work, see Marzal 1993. Deustua and Rénique point to the period 1900–1930 as a golden age of intellectual creation in Peru and as the true laboratory of social ideas that would guide the intellectual life of the country for most of the twentieth century (1984, 12–13). The growth in the circulation and availability of publications offers a meaningful background for the vibrant *indigenismo* of the 1920s and 1930s in cities like Cusco and Puno. Cusco, where such key figures of modern *indigenismo* as Luis Valcárcel, Uriel García, and José Angel Escalante were active, was an *indigenista* stronghold at least from the beginning of the twentieth century, home to important journals like *Kosko* and *Kuntur*. Puno, another radical center for *indigenista* agitation, also has a long history of activism that reaches back to the nineteenth century. In the 1920s, the group Ork'opata emerged there. One of its members—Gamaliel Churata, the enigmatic author of the enigmatic novel *El pez de oro*—published *Boletin Titikaka*, which formed important connections with Mariátegui's *Amauta* and other avant-garde journals of South America.

6   An overview of these publications can be found in Tord 1978, 153–59. See also Tamayo Herrera 1980; Vich 2000.

7   González Prada published his essay "Nuestros indios" in 1904—a lucid analysis, but laden with contradictions. As for Valcárcel, Mariátegui explained the limits of his approach to the indigenous question in his foreword to *Tempestad en los Andes* (1927). Finally, Uriel García published the insightful essay "El nuevo indio" in 1930, but its political valence remained questionable.

8   "Mariátegui returned to Peru when the rebellion is almost over. However, other intellectuals like Valcárcel, Romero, and Churata informed him to a great extent about the rebellion" (Flores Galindo 1988, 268).

9   Manuel Burga and Flores Galindo explain that different attempts at introducing wage labor in the haciendas were a failure. Up to 1930, on some haciendas in southern Peru, Indians worked half a year for the owner of the hacienda and the other half for themselves (Burga and Flores Galindo 1980, 24). A 1946 study by Maxime Kuczynksi established that the total monetary equivalent of the feudal indigenous production on a given hacienda was well below the would-be cost of Indian labor, if Indians were paid the miserable minimum salary established by law (Burga and Flores Galindo 1980, 27). The semifeudal organization of the hacienda also had a great cultural and social impact on the relationship between the Indians and the *gamonales*. Burga and Flores Galindo observe that the *gamonales'* worldview incorporated not only European traits but also Andean elements. As a rule, "*gamonales* observed all traditional Andean authorities that originated in indigenous groups residing in their properties" (Burga and Flores Galindo 1980, 112).

10 For Peter Klarén, the cycle of uprisings covers the years 1915–24 (2000, 248). For Flores Galindo, it is restricted to the years 1919–26 (1988, 259–68), although Flores Galindo also gives the years 1920–23 in a text he coauthored with Manuel Burga (1980, 39). Abraham Valencia, one of the first to document the movement, suggests the clearest manifestation of the movement as coming during the years 1921–23 (1980, 87–128), the same ones stressed by Wilfredo Kapsoli (1984, 19–29) and Nils Jacobsen (1993, 337–53).

11 As noted by Ranajit Guha in his *Elementary Aspects of Peasant Insurgency* (1983), the symbolization of ethnic and class antagonism through cultural proxies is an extended form of resistance/confrontation in societies where the exercise of power takes definite ritualistic forms.

12 Abraham Valencia comments on the fate of Domingo Huarca, a rebellion leader who paid with his life for the audacity of traveling to Lima to state the Indians' point of view. After he was tortured and killed, his body was exhibited for days in the tallest tower of the church (1980, 47).

13 To some extent, *Deep Rivers,* the most literary of Arguedas's works, is an exception to this rule.

14 The quote is from the back cover of the English edition of *The Fox from Up Above and the Fox from Down Below* (2000).

15 The characters in *Todas las sangres* put the concept of literary character itself into crisis. Given these characters' different ideologies and beliefs, the ultimate reasons for their behavior more often than not strike the reader as inscrutable. Meanwhile, the narrator almost disappears in this novel, which is perhaps best

described as a filmic rendering of a theatrical play. Unlike *Todas las sangres*, where characters seem possessed by ideologies, *The Foxes* presents recalcitrantly singular characters who are, however, more heroic than their counterparts in the earlier novel. Orphans of the ideologies grounding their world, they become the site of a new grounding: the complexity of the world now rests on their shoulders. As for the narrative voice, which Arguedas subsumes in *Todas las sangres* in favor of a more or less direct presentation of different characters' speeches and worldviews, *The Foxes* is even more radical: Arguedas here separates the narrator's voice from its function in the narration.

16 Cornejo Polar changes his perspective on the subject in his last essay, "Condición migrante e intertextualidad cultural" (1995). However, although this essay's title evokes Arguedas, it reconsiders the question of the Indians' identity not from the perspective offered in the novel in 1971, but from the perspective, inescapable now, of the vast crisis of governmentality that afflicted Peru through the last quarter of the twentieth century.

17 The version widely used in academic studies is the English translation by Frank Salomon and George L. Urioste (1991).

18 See Cornejo Polar's analysis of the figure of Asto in *Los universos narrativos* (1981). For Pedro Trigo, see 1982, 215–16. Lienhard furthers Cornejo Polar's analysis in 1981, 80–82.

19 A similar predicament emerges in reference to other characters, like the Aymara *patron de lancha* Hilario Caullama. Pedro Trigo contests those readings that see the incorruptible Caullama as the "man of the future." Caullama is, Trigo agrees, "a respectable man, full of inner power, unmovable. But he belongs to the past. He will remain incólumne, but will leave behind no descendents." Trigo concludes, "To see him as the man of the future means overlooking the extension of the caesura that *The Foxes* represents in Arguedas's work" (1982, 222).

20 Among those who have commented on the mythical elements in Arguedas, Roland Forgues is perhaps the one who reads the reactive character of the myth most intensely. For Forgues, *The Foxes* brings about a closure of Arguedas's negotiation of the modern and the traditional by producing a sense of mythical eternity (1990, 312–13). Julio Ortega, on the other hand, thinks that "the mythic promise (to resolve opposites and fuse subject to object, language to the world) is fulfilled dramatically in Arguedas's final project" (2000, xiv).

21 In the same way that Moncada rejects individualization, he is unable to individualize anybody in his audience while he is speaking: "In such circumstances,

Moncada did not recognize individuals precisely; he could perceive subtle variations in figures, colors and sounds" (Arguedas 2000, 138).

22 One can contrast the stance of the migrant community regarding their dead with Juan Rulfo's depiction of Luvina. Rulfo—one of the writers most admired by Arguedas—portrays a community enchained to its roots, whose inhabitants remain although Luvina has become barren and inhospitable. "If we go away," one of Rulfo's characters reasons, "who will take our deads? They live here, and we can't leave them alone" (1971, 95).

23 I am borrowing these words from Wendy Brown's description of the political present in *Politics Out of History* (2001, 5).

24 Father Cardozo maintains that Chimbote is where humanity can find its greatest hope. As usual in Arguedas, the vocabulary is strongly redolent of Nietzschean imaginary: "Here I find more needs and more hope, strong, every day more desire, more potency for perfection" (Arguedas 2000, 211). For the Peace Corps, meanwhile, Maxwell sees the Indians as "if they were dancing inside of a wall or on the edge of an abyss" (232).

25 On origin and originality, see Agamben 1999, 61–62.

26 We touch at this point on the complex kernel that makes of *The Foxes* both a dazzling and an inscrutable text. To begin with, following Arguedas on how language and world are knotted in poiesis, we must abandon the critical illusion that our commentary can be isomorphic with the text on which we are commenting. The order of the aesthetic word and the order of the language of academic presentation are at this point separated by a gulf that cannot be bridged. The reason for this incommensurability is that the poetic word holds together elements (language, subject, ideological intentions, represented world) that can only appear in the language of analysis as discrete and separate entities.

27 In the foreword to the 2004 reprint of her book on Arguedas (originally published in 1973), Sara Castro-Klarén writes: "The feature that I would underline today in Arguedas's work . . . is the limitless creative power that wells up in each of his texts" (9).

28 It is difficult to translate this phrase—and I in fact prefer to leave it untranslated—because each word overdetermines the others, the words together blending, in a single movement, the messianic reassurance of a religious experience and the ungroundable terror that comes only when we are able to think the end of all things.

References

Abrams, M. H. 1953. *The Mirror and the Lamp: Romantic Theory and the Critical Tradition.* New York: W. W. Norton.

Aching, Gerard. 1997. *The Politics of Spanish American "Modernismo."* Cambridge: Cambridge University Press.

Adorno, Rolena. 1987. Guamán Poma: El autor y su obra. In *Guamán Poma de Ayala, Felipe: Nueva corónica y buen gobierno,* ed. J. Murra, R. Adorno, and J. L. Urioste. Madrid: Historia 16.

———. 1988. Nuevas perspectivas en los estudios literarios coloniales hispanoamericanos. *Revista de Crítica Literaria Latinoamericana* 28: 11–28.

———. 1996. Bautizar al Inca: El acto de poner nombre en el Perú de la postconquista. In *Asedios a la heterogeneidad cultural,* ed. J. A. Mazzotti and U. J. Z. Aguilar. Philadelphia: Asociación Internacional de Peruanistas.

Agamben, Giorgio. 1999. *The Man without Content.* Trans. G. Albert. Stanford: Stanford University Press.

———. 1999. *Potentialities: Collected Essays in Philosophy.* Trans. D. Heller-Roazen. Stanford: Stanford University Press.

———. 2005. *State of Exception.* Trans. K. Attell. Chicago: University of Chicago Press.

Aguilar Camín, Héctor, and Lorenzo Meyer. 1993. *In the Shadow of the Mexican Revolution: Contemporary Mexican History, 1910–1989.* Austin: University of Texas Press.

Aguilar Mora, Jorge. 2000. El silencio de Nellie Campobello. In Campobello 2000.

Aguilera, Carmen. 1979. *Códices del México Antiguo.* Mexico D.F.: SEP-INAR.

Alonso, Carlos. 1990. *The Spanish American Regional Novel: Modernity and Autochtony.* New York: Cambridge University Press.

Althusser, Louis. 1993. Ideology and Ideological State Apparatuses (Notes towards an Investigation). In *Essays on Ideology.* London: Verso.

Alvarado Tezozomoc, Fernando. 1949. *Crónica Mexicayotl*. Trans. A. León. Mexico: Imprenta Universitaria.

———. 1975. *Crónica Mexicayotl*. Trans. A. León. Mexico D.F.: UNAM.

Amigo, Roberto. 2002. *Guerra, anarquía y goce: Tres episodios de la relación entre la cultura popular y el arte moderno en el Paraguay*. Asuncion: Museo del Barro.

Andreu, Jean L. 1976. Hijo de hombre, fragmentación y unidad. *Revista Iberoamericana* 42, nos. 96–97: 473–83.

Anglería, Pedro Mártir de. 1964. *Décadas del Nuevo Mundo*. Mexico: Porrúa.

Archibald, Priscilla. 1998. Andean Anthropology in the Era of Development Theory: The Work of José María Arguedas. In *Reconsiderations for Latin American Cultural Studies*, ed. J. M. Arguedas. Athens: Ohio University Press.

Arendt, Hannah. 1992. *Lectures on Kant's Political Philosophy*. Ed. R. Beiner. Chicago: University of Chicago Press.

Arens, Richard, ed. 1976. *Genocide in Paraguay*. Philadelphia: Temple University Press.

Arguedas, José María. 1964. *Todas las sangres*. Buenos Aires: Losada.

———. 1966. *Perú vivo*. Lima: Juan Mejía Baca.

———. 1975. *Formación de una cultura nacional indoamericana*. Mexico: Siglo XXI.

———. 1983. Llamado a algunos doctores. In *Obras completas*, vol. 2. Limda: Editorial Horizonte.

———. 1985. *Yawar Fiesta*. Trans. F. H. Barraclough. Austin: University of Texas Press.

———. 1992. *El zorro de arriba y el zorro de abajo*. Ed. E.-M. Fell. Mexico: Colección Archivos.

———. 2000. *The Fox from Up Above and the Fox from Down Below*. Trans. F. H. Barraclough. Ed. J. Ortega. Pittsburgh: University of Pittsburgh Press.

———. 2002. *Deep Rivers*. Trans. F. H. Barraclough. Long Grove: Waveland Press.

Arguedas, José María, and Josafat Roel Pineda. 1973. Tres versiones del mito del Inkarri. In *Ideología mesiánica del mundo andino*, ed. J. M. Ossio. Lima: Ignacio del Prado Pastor.

Azuela, Mariano. 1945. *Andrés Perez, maderista*. Mexico: Botas.

———. 2002. *The Underdogs: A Novel of the Mexican Revolution*. Trans. B. E. Jorgensen. New York: Random House.

Badiou, Alain. 2003. The Fifteen Theses on Contemporary Art. Oral presentation, Drawing Center, New York City, December 4, 2003. *Lacanian Ink*, no. 23, http://www.lacan.com/issue22.htm.

———. 2005. *Le siècle*. Paris: Seuil.

Bakhtin, Mikhail. 1986. *Speech Genres and Other Late Essays.* Trans V. W. McGee. Ed. C. Emerson and M. Holquist. Austin: University of Texas Press.

——. 1998. *Rabelais and His World.* Trans. H. Ilswolsky. Bloomington: Indiana University Press.

Bareiro Sagueir, Rubén. 1974. La noción de personaje en *Hijo de hombre. Nueva narrativa hispanamericana* 4: 69–74.

——. 1983. La noción de personaje en las novelas de Augusto Roa Bastos. In *En torno a Hijo de hombre de Augusto Roa Bastos,* ed. A. Sicard and F. Moreno. Nanterre: CRLA.

Barker, Francis. 1984. *The Private Trembling Body.* London: Methuen.

Barrett, Rafael. 1987. *El dolor paraguayo.* Caracas: Biblioteca Ayacucho.

——. 1988. *Obras completas.* Ed. F. Corral. Asuncion: ICI.

Beiser, Fredrick. 1992. *Enlightenment, Revolution, and Romanticism: The Genesis of Modern German Political Thought, 1790–1800.* Cambridge: Harvard University Press.

——. 2002. *German Idealism: The Struggle against Subjectivism, 1781–1801.* Cambridge: Harvard University Press.

Bennet, Tony. 1990. Putting Policy into Cultural Studies. In Bennet, Martin, Mercer, and Wollacott 1990.

Bennet, Tony, Graham Martin, Colin Mercer, and Janet Woollacott, eds. 1990. *Outside Literature.* London and New York: Routledge.

Bensaid, Daniel. 2002. *Marx for our Times: Adventures and Misadventures of a Critique.* Trans. G. Elliott. London: Verso.

Benveniste, Emile. 1966. *Problèmes de linguistíque génèrale.* Paris: Gallimard.

Beverley, John. 1999. *Subalternity and Representation: Arguments in Cultural Theory.* Durham: Duke University Press.

Beverley, John, José Oviedo, and Michael Arona, eds. 1995. *The Postmodernism Debate in Latin America.* Durham: Duke University Press.

Bhabha, Homi. 1994. *The Location of Culture.* London and New York: Routledge.

——. 2000. On Cultural Choice. In *The Turn to Ethics,* ed. M. Garber, B. Hansson, and Rebecca L. Walkowitz. New York and London: Routledge.

Bierhorst, John. 1985. *Cantares Mexicanos: Songs of the Aztecs.* Stanford: Stanford University Press.

Biguenet, John, and Schulte Rainer, eds. 1992. *Theories of Translation: An Anthology of Essays from Dryden to Derrida.* Chicago: University of Chicago Press.

Blanchot, Maurice. 1986. *The Writing of the Disaster.* Trans. A. Smock. Lincoln: University of Nebraska Press.

———. 1995. Literature and the Right to Death. In *The Work of Fire*. Stanford: Stanford University Press.

Blumenberg, Hans. 1987. *The Genesis of the Copernican World*. Cambridge: MIT Press.

———. 1993. Light as a Metaphor for Truth: At the Preliminary Stage of Philosophical Concept Formation. In *Modernity and the Hegemony of Vision*, ed. D. M. Levin. Berkeley: University of California Press.

Brotherston, Gordon. 1979. *Image of the New World: The American Continent Portrayed in Native Texts*. London: Thames and Hudson.

———. 1992. *Book of the Fourth World: Reading the Native Americas through their Literature*. Cambridge: Cambridge University Press.

———. 1993. La visión americana de la conquista. In Pizarro 1993.

———. 1995. *Painted Books from México: Codices in UK Collections and the World They Represent*. London: British Museum.

Brown, Wendy. 2001. *Politics out of History*. Princeton: Princeton University Press.

Bryson, Norman. 1984. *Tradition and Desire: From David to Delacroix*. Cambridge: Cambridge University Press.

Buck-Morss, Susan. 2000. Hegel and Haiti. *Critical Inquiry* 26: 821–76.

Burga, Manuel. 1986. Los profetas de la rebelión (1919–1923). In *Estados y naciones en los Andes: Hacia una historia comparativa: Bolivia/Colombia/Ecuador/Perú*, ed. J. P. Deler and Y. Saint-Geours. Lima: Instituto de Estudios Peruanos/Instituto Francés de Estudios Andinos.

Burga, Manuel, and Alberto Flores Galindo. 1980. Feudalismo andino y movimientos sociales. In *Historia del Perú republicano: Procesos e instituciones*, ed. M. Baca. Lima: JMB.

Bürger, Peter. 1992. *The Decline of Modernism*. Trans. N. Walker. University Park: Pennsylvania State University Press.

Butler, Judith. 1997. *The Psychic Life of Power*. Stanford: Stanford University Press.

Butler, Judith, Ernesto Laclau, and Slavoj Žižek. 1997. *The Psychic Life of Power: Theories in Subjection*. Stanford: Stanford University Press.

Cadogan, León. 2002. *Ayvu Rapyta: Textos Míticos de los Mbyá-Guaraní del Guairá*. Asuncion: Del Lector.

Campobello, Nellie. 1988. *Cartucho* and *My Mother's Hands*. Trans. D. Meyer. Austin: University of Texas Press.

———. 2000. *Cartucho: Relatos de la lucha en el norte de México*. Mexico: Era.

Candido, Antonio. 1995. Literature and Underdevelopment. In *On Literature and Society*, ed. H. Becker. Princeton: Princeton University Press.

Caravedo Molinari, Baltazar. 1978. Economía, producción y trabajo. In *Historia del Perú republicano*. Lima: Mejia Baca.

Carpentier, Alejo. 1970. *The Kingdom of This World*. Trans. H. de Onis. New York: Collier Books.

Caso, Antonio. 1934. *Nuevos discursos a la nación mexicana*. Mexico: P. Robredo.

Castro-Klarén, Sara. 2000. Like a Pig When He's Thinkin': Arguedas on Affect and on Becoming an Animal. In Arguedas 2000.

———. 2004. Prefacio. In *El mundo mágico de José María Arguedas*. Paris: Indigo.

Chakrabarty, Dipesh. 2000. *Provincializing Europe: Postcolonial Thought and Historical Difference*. Princeton: Princeton University Press.

Chatterjee, Partha. 2000. The Nation and Its Peasants. In *Mapping Subaltern Studies and the Postcolonial*, ed. V. Chaturvedi. London: Verso.

Chaturvedi, Vinayak. 2000. *Mapping Subaltern Studies and the Postcolonial*. London: Verso.

Cheyfitz, Eric. 1997. *The Poetics of Imperialism: Translation and Colonization from The Tempest to Tarzan*. Philadelphia: University of Pennsylvania Press.

Chimalpahin Cuauhtlehuanitzin, Domingo Francisco de San Antón Muñoz. 1965. *Relaciones originales de Chalco Amaquemecan*. Mexico: Fondo de Cultura Económica.

Chytry, Joseph. 1989. *The Aesthetic State: A Quest in Modern German Thought*. Berkeley: University of California Press.

Clastres, Hélene. 1993. *La tierra sin mal: El profetismo Tupí-Guaraní*. Trans. V. Ackerman. Buenos Aires: Ediciones del Sol.

Clastres, Pierres. 1989. *Societies against the State: Essays in Political Anthropology*. New York: Zone Books.

Clifford, James. 1988. On Ethnographic Surrealism. In *The Predicament of Culture: Twentieth-Century Ethnography, Literature and Art*. Cambridge: Harvard University Press.

Conn, Robert. 2002. *The Politics of Philology: Alfonso Reyes and the Invention of the Latin American Literary Tradition*. Lewisburg: Bucknell University Press.

Cornejo Polar, Antonio. 1980. *Literatura y sociedad en el Perú*. Lima: Losantay.

———. 1981. *Los universos narrativos de José María Arguedas*. Buenos Aires: Losada.

———. 1989. *La formación de la tradición literaria en el Perú*. Lima: CEP.

———. 1992. Un ensayo sobre "Los zorros" de Arguedas. In Arguedas 1992.

———. 1994. El indigenismo andino. In Pizarro 1993.

———. 1995. Condición migrante e intertextualidad cultural: El caso de José María Arguedas. *Revista de Crítica Literaria Latinoamericana* 42: 101–9.

———. 2004. Indigenismo and Heterogeneous Literatures. In *The Latin American Cultural Studies Reader,* ed. A. del Sarto, A. Rios, and A. Trigo. Durham: Duke University Press.

Corral, Francisco. 1994. *El pensamiento cautivo de Rafael Barrett: Crisis de fin de siglo, juventud del 98 y anarquismo.* Madrid: Siglo Veintiuno.

Critchley, Simon. 1996. Prolegomena to Any Post-Deconstructive Subjectivity. In Critchley and Dews 1996.

Critchley, Simon, and Peter Dews, eds. 1996. *Deconstructive Subjectivities.* Albany: State University of New York Press.

Curiel, Fernando. 1993. *La querella de Martín Luis Guzmán.* Mexico D.F.: Diálogo Abierto.

Curtius, Ernst. 1953. *European Literature and the Latin Middle Ages.* New York: Harper.

Dawson, Alexander. 1998. From Models for the Nation to Model Citizen: Indigenismo and the Revindication of the Mexican Indian, 1920–1940. *Journal of Latin American Studies* 30: 279–308.

de la Parra, Teresa. 1991. *Memorias de Mamá Blanca.* Mexico: Editores Mexicanos Unidos.

de Man, Paul. 1983. Aesthetic Formalization: Kleist's *Uber das Marionettentheater.* In *The Rhetoric of Romanticism.* New York: Columbia University Press.

———. 1996. *Aesthetic Ideology.* Minneapolis: University of Minnesota Press.

Deleuze, Gilles. 1984. *Kant's Critical Philosophy: The Doctrine of the Faculties.* London: Athlone.

Deleuze, Gilles, and Félix Guattari. 1987. *A Thousand Plateaus: Capitalism and Schizophrenia.* Minneapolis and London: University of Minnesota Press.

Derrida, Jacques. 1976. *Of Grammatology.* Trans. G. C. Spivak. Baltimore: Johns Hopkins University Press.

———. 1978. *Writing and Difference.* Trans. A. Bass. Chicago: University of Chicago Press.

———. 1992a. Force of Law: The Mystical Foundation of Authority. In *Deconstruction and the Possibility of Justice,* ed. M. R. D. Cornell and D. G. Carlson. New York: Routledge.

———. 1992b. Passions: "An Oblique Offering." In *Derrida: A Critical Reader,* ed. D. Wood. Oxford and Cambridge: Blackwell.

———. 1992c. "This Strange Institution Called Literature": An Interview with Jacques Derrida. Trans. R. Bowlby. In *Acts of Literature,* ed. D. Attridge. New York and London: Routledge.

———. 1994. *Specters of Marx: The State of the Debt, the Work of Mourning and the New International.* Trans. P. Kamuf. London and New York: Routledge.

———. 2000. A Self-Unsealing Poetic Text: Poetics and Politics of Witnessing. In *Revenge of the Aesthetics: The Place of Literature in Theory Today,* ed. M. P. Clark. Berkeley: University of California Press.

Descartes, René. 1996. Discourse on the Method *and* Meditations on First Philosophy. Ed. D. Weissman. New Haven: Yale University Press.

———. 1998. *The World and Other Writings.* Ed. S. Gaukroger. Cambridge: Cambridge University Press.

Descombes, Vincent. 1980. *Contemporary French Philosophy.* Trans. L. Scott-Fox and J. M. Hardy. Cambridge: Cambridge University Press.

Deustua, José, and José Luis Rénique. 1984. *Intelectuales, indigenismo y descentralismo en el Perú: 1879–1931.* Cuzco: Centro Bartolomé de las Casas.

Díaz Quiñones, Arcadio. 1992. *El Entenado:* Las palabras de la tribu. *Hispamérica* 63: 3–14.

Dolar, Mladen. 1993. Beyond Interpellation. *Qui Parle* 2: 75–96.

———. 2006. *A Voice and Nothing More.* Cambridge: MIT Press.

Eagleton, Terry. 1990. *The Ideology of the Aesthetic.* Cambridge: Basil Blackwell.

———. 1993. *Literary Theory: An Introduction.* Minneapolis: University of Minnesota Press.

Escobar, Alberto. 1984. *Arguedas o la utopía de la lengua.* Lima: Instituto de Estudios Peruanos.

Escobar, Ticio. 1999. *La cicatriz: Obra de Osvaldo Salerno.* Madrid: Casa de América.

Fabian, Johannes. 1983. *Time and the Other: How Anthropology Makes Its Objects.* New York: Columbia University Press.

Felman, Shoshana, and Doris Laub. 1992. *Testimony: Crises of Witnessing in Literature, Psychoanalysis and History.* New York: Routledge.

Ferguson, Charles. 1959. Diglossia. *Word* 15, no. 2: 325–40.

Florescano, Enrique. 1994. *Memoria mexicana.* Mexico: Fondo de Cultura Económica.

———. 1999. *Memoria indígena.* Mexico: Taurus.

———. 2002. El canon memorioso forjado por los Títulos primordiales. *Colonial Latin American Review* 11, no. 2: 183–230.

Flores Galindo, Alberto. 1979. Los intelectuales y el problema nacional. In *7 ensayos: 50 años en la historia,* ed. T. Escajadillo. Lima: Amauta.

———. 1988. *Buscando un Inca: Identidad y utopia en los Andes.* Lima: Horizonte.

Folgarait, Leonard. 1998. *Mural Painting and Social Revolution in Mexico, 1920–1940: Art of the New Order.* Cambridge: Cambridge University Press.

Forgues, Roland. 1990. Por qué bailan los zorros. In Arguedas 1992.

Foster, David William. 1978. *Augusto Roa Bastos.* Boston: Twayne.

Foucault, Michel. 1971. *The Order of Things: An Archaeology of the Human Sciences.* New York: Vintage Books.

———. 1972. *The Archaeology of Knowledge* and *The Discourse on Language.* Trans. A. M. S. Smith. New York: Pantheon Books.

———. 2003. "Society Must Be Defended." In *Lectures at the Collége de France, 1975–1976,* trans. A. I. Davidson. New York: Picador.

Franco, Jean. 1988. Afterword. In *Son of Man,* trans. R. Caffyn. New York: Monthly Review Press.

———. 1991. *Plotting Women: Gender and Representation in Mexico.* New York: Columbia University Press.

———. 2002. *Decline and Fall of the Lettered City: Latin America in the Cold War.* Cambridge: Harvard University Press.

Freud, Sigmund. 1961. *Beyond the Pleasure Principle.* Trans. J. Strachey. New York and London: W. W. Norton.

Gamio, Manuel. 1916. *Forjando patria: Pro-nacionalismo.* Mexico: Porrúa.

García, Uriel. 1937. *El nuevo indio.* Cuzco: H. Y. Rozas.

García Canclini, Néstor. 1995. *Hybrid Cultures: Strategies for Entering and Leaving Modernity.* Trans. C. L. Chiappari and S. L. López. Minneapolis: University of Minnesota Press.

———. 2001. *Consumers and Citizens: Globalization and Cultural Conflict.* Trans. G. Yúdice. Minneapolis: University of Minnesota Press.

Gardner, Sebastian. 1999. *Kant and the Critique of Pure Reason.* London: Routledge.

Garibay, Angel María. 1971. *Historia de la literatura Náhuatl.* Mexico: Porrúa.

Gibson, Charles. 1964. *The Aztecs under Spanish Rule: A History of the Indians of the Valley of Mexico, 1519–1810.* Stanford: Stanford University Press.

Giménez Guanes, Gloria. 1987. *Los duendes de la rebeldía: Crónica de las jornadas por la democracia en el Paraguay.* Madrid: Editorial Don Bosco.

Glantz, Margo. 1989. Apuntes sobre la obsesión helénica de Alfonso Reyes. *NRFH* 37: 425–32.

Gómez Canedo, Lino. 1982. *La educación de los marginados durante la época colonial: Escuelas y colegios para indios y mestizos en la Nueva España.* Mexico: Porrúa.

Gómez Martínez, José Luis. 1989. Reyes y el pensamiento mexicano. *NRFH* 37: 453–63.

Gonzalez, Eduardo. 2000. Caliban; or, Flesh-Eating and Ghost Text in Saer's *El entenado*. *Dispositio/n* 50: 1–18.

González Echevarría, Roberto. 1985. The Case of the Speaking Statue: Ariel and the Magisterial Rhetoric of the Latin American Essay. In *The Voice of the Masters: Writing and Authority in Modern Latin American Literature*. Austin: University of Texas Press.

———. 1990. *Myth and Archive: A Theory of Latin American Narrative*. Cambridge: Cambridge University Press.

González Prada, Manuel. 1976. Nuestros indios. In *Páginas libres: Horas de lucha*. Caracas: Biblioteca Ayacucho.

Gramsci, Antonio. 1971. *Selections from the Prison Notebooks*. Trans. Q. Hoare and G. N. Smith. New York: International Publishers.

———. 2000. *The Antonio Gramsci Reader: Selected Writings, 1916–1935*. Ed. D. Forgacs. New York: New York University Press.

Greenblatt, Stephen. 1991. *Marvelous Possessions: The Wonder of the New World*. Chicago: University of Chicago Press.

Grossberg, Lawrence. 1997. *Dancing in Spite of Myself.* Durham: Duke University Press.

Gruzinski, Serge. 1993. *The Conquest of Mexico: The Incorporation of Indian Societies into the Western World, 16th–18th Centuries*. Trans. E. Corrigan. Cambridge: Polity Press.

Guamán Poma de Ayala, Felipe. 1980. *Primer nueva corónica i buen gobierno*. Caracas: Biblioteca Ayacuho.

———. 1987. *Nueva cróncia y buen gobierno*. Ed. J. V. Murra, R. Adorno, and J. L. Urioste. Madrid: Historia 16.

Guha, Ranajit. 1983. *Elementary Aspects of Peasant Insurgency in Colonial India*. Delhi: Oxford University Press.

Guzmán, Martín Luis. 1965. *The Eagle and the Serpent*. Trans. H. de Onis. New York: Dolphin Books.

———. 1970. *La querella de México*. Mexico: Compania General de Ediciones.

———. 1991. *Memorias de Pancho Villa*. Mexico D.F.: Editorial Porrúa.

Habermas, Jürgen. 1993. *The Philosophical Discourse of Modernity*. Trans. F. Lawrence. Cambridge: MIT Press.

———. 1993. *The Structural Transformation of the Public Sphere: An Inquiry into a Category of Bourgeois Society*. Trans. T. Burger and F. Lawrence. Cambridge: MIT Press.

Hall, Stuart. 1981. Notes on Deconstructing the Popular. In *People's History and Socialist Theory*, ed. R. Samuel. London: Routledge.

———. 1989. Cultural Identity and Cinematic Representation. *Framework* 36: 68–81.

Haskett, Robert. 1991. *Indigenous Rulers: An Ethnohistory of Town Government in Colonial Cuernavaca*. Alburquerque: University of New Mexico Press.

Hegel, Georg Wilhelm Friedrich. 1956. *The Philosophy of History*. Trans. H. B. Nibbet. New York: Dover Publications.

Heidegger, Martin. 1962. *Kant and the Problem of Metaphysics*. Trans. J. S. Churchill. Bloomington: Indiana University Press.

———. 1992. *Parmenides*. Trans. A. Schuwer and R. Rojcewicz. Bloomington: Indiana University Press.

Henríquez Ureña, Pedro. 1960. *Obra crítica*. Mexico D.F.: Fondo de Cultura Económica.

———. 1984. La obra de José Enrique Rodó. In *Conferencias del Ateneo de la Juventud*, ed. J. Hernández Luna. Mexico D.F.: Universidad Nacional Autónoma de México.

Hernández Luna, José, ed. 1984. *Conferencias del Ateneo de la Juventud*. Mexico D.F.: Universidad Nacional Autónoma de México.

Hill Boone, Elizabeth. 1994. Introduction: Writing and Recording Knowledge. In Hill Boone and Mignolo 1994.

Hill Boone, Elizabeth, and Tom Cummins, eds. 1980. *Native Traditions in the Postconquest World*. Washington D.C.: Dumbarton Oaks Research Library and Collection.

Hill Boone, Elizabeth, and Walter Mignolo, eds. 1994. *Writing without Words: Alternative Literacies in Mesoamerica and the Andes*. Durham: Duke University Press.

Hunter, Ian. 1988. *Culture and Government: The Emergence of Literary Education*. Houndmills: MacMillan Press.

Husserl, Edmund. 1964. *The Idea of Phenomenology*. Trans. W. P. Alston and G. Nakhnikian. The Hague: Nijhoff.

———. 1967. *Cartesian Meditations*. Trans. D. Cairns. The Hague: Nijhoff.

Huysmans, J. K. 1958. *Grunewald, the Paintings*. London: Phaidon Press.

Hymes, Dell, and John Gumperz. 1986. *Directions in Sociolinguistics: The Ethnography of Communication*. New York: Oxford University Press.

Ixtlilxochitl, Fernando de Alva. 1985. *Historia de la nación chichimeca*. Madrid: Historia 16.

Jacobsen, Nils. 1993. *Mirages of Transition: The Peruvian Altiplano, 1780–1930.* Berkeley: University of California Press.

Jameson, Fredric. 1999. Marx's Purloined Letter. In *Ghostly Demarcations: A Symposium on Jacques Derrida's* Specters of Marx, ed. M. Sprinker. London and New York: Verso.

Jay, Martin. 2003. Drifting into Dangerous Waters: The Separation of Aesthetic Experience from the Work of Art. In *Aesthetic Subjects,* ed. P. Matthews and D. McWhirter. Minneapolis: University of Minnesota Press.

Johnson, Galen A., ed. 1993. *The Merleau-Ponty Aesthetic Reader: Philosophy and Painting.* Evanston: Northwestern University Press.

Joseph, Gilbert, and Daniel Nugent, eds. 1994. *Everyday Forms of State Formation: Revolution and the Negotiation of Rule in Modern Mexico.* Durham: Duke University Press.

Kant, Immanuel. 1966. *Critique of Pure Reason.* Trans. M. Muller. New York: Anchor Books.

———. 1987. *Critique of Judgment.* Trans. W. S. Pluhar. Indianapolis: Hacket.

Kantorowicz, Ernst. 1997. *The King's Two Bodies.* Princeton: Princeton University Press.

Kapsoli, Wilfredo. 1980. *El pensamiento de La Asociación Pro-Indígena.* Cuzco: Debates Rurales.

———. *Los ayllus del sol: Anarquismo y utopía andina.* Lima: Asociación de Publicaciones Educativas.

Klahn, Norma, and Wilfrido H. Corral, eds. 1991. *Los novelistas como críticos.* Mexico: Fundo de Cultura Económica/Ediciones del Norte.

Klarén, Peter. 2000. *Perú: Society and Nationhood in the Andes.* New York: Oxford University Press.

Klor de Alva, Jorge. 1992. Colonialism and Post Colonialism as (Latin) American Mirages. *Colonial Latin American Review* 1–2: 3–24.

Knight, Alan. 1990. *The Mexican Revolution.* Lincoln: University of Nebraska Press.

———. 1994. Weapons and Arches in the Mexican Revolutionary Landscape. In Joseph and Nugent 1994.

Kouvelakis, Stathes. 2003. *Philosophy and Revolution: From Kant to Marx.* Trans. G. M. Goshgarian. London: Verso.

Koyré, Alexander. 1957. *From the Closed World to the Infinite Universe.* Baltimore: Johns Hopkins University Press.

Kraniauskas, John. 1998. Cronos and the Political Economy of Vampirism: Notes on a Historical Constellation. In *Cannibalism and the Colonial World,* ed. F. Barker, P. Hulme, and Margaret Iversen. Cambridge: Cambridge University Press.

———. 2000. Hybridity in a Transnational Frame: Latin-Americanist and Postcolonial Perspectives on Cultural Studies. *Nepantla: Views from South* 1, no. 1: 111–37.

Krauze, Enrique. 1976. *Caudillos culturales en la Revolución mexicana.* Mexico D.F: Siglo XXI.

Krieger, Murray. 1994. The Anthropological Persistence of the Aesthetic: Real Shadows and Shadow Texts. *New Literary History* 25, no. 1: 21–33.

Laclau, Ernesto. 1996. *Emancipation(s).* New York: Verso.

Lamming, George. 1991. *In the Castle of My Skin.* Ann Arbor: University of Michigan Press.

Laplanche, Jean. 1999. *Essays on Otherness.* London: Routledge.

Larsen, Neil. 1995. *Reading North by South: On Latin American Literature, Culture and Politics.* Minneapolis: University of Minnesota Press.

Latin American Subaltern Studies Group. 1993. Founding Statement. *Boundary 2,* no. 20: 110–21.

Leal, Antonio Castro. 1960. Introduction. In *La novela de la Revolución Mexicana,* ed. A. C. Leal. Mexico: SEP-Aguilar.

Lefort, Claude. 1990. Flesh and Otherness. In *Ontology and Alterity in Merleau-Ponty,* ed. G. A. Johnson and M. B. Smith. Evanston: Northwestern University Press.

Legrás, Horacio. 2003. El Ateneo y el nacimiento del Estado ético en México. *Latin American Research Review* 38, no. 2: 34–60.

León Portilla, Miguel. 1966. *La filosofía Nahuatl estudiada en sus fuentes.* Mexico: UNAM.

———. 1969. *Pre-Columbian Literatures of Mexico.* Trans. G. Lobanov and M. León Portilla. Oklahoma City: University of Oklahoma Press.

———. 1990. *Endangered Cultures.* Trans. J. Goodson-Lawes. Dallas: Southern Methodist University Press.

———. 1992. *The Aztec Image of Self and Society: An Introduction to Nahua Culture.* Salt Lake City: University of Utah Press.

———. 1996. *El destino de la palabra: De la oralidad y los códices mesoamericanos a la escritura alfabética.* Mexico: El Colegio de México.

Levinas, Emmanuel. 1969. *Totality and Infinity.* Trans. A. Lingis. Pittsburgh: Duquesne University Press.

———. 1978. *Existence and Existents.* Trans. A. Lingis. The Hague: Nijhoff.

———. 1981. *Otherwise than Being; or, Beyond Essence*. Trans. A. Lingis. The Hague: Nijhoff.

———. 1996. *Emmanuel Levinas: Basic Philosophical Writings*. Ed. A. Peperzak, S. Critchley, and R. Bernasconi. Bloomington: Indiana University Press.

Leibsohn, Dana. 1994. Primers for Memory: Cartographic Histories and Nahua Identity. In Hill Boone and Mignolo 1994.

Lienhard, Martin. 1980. La última novela de Arguedas: Imagen de un lector futuro. *Revista de Crítica Literaria Latinoamericana* 12, no. 2: 177–96.

———. 1981. *Cultura popular andina y forma novelesca: Zorros y danzantes en la última novela de Arguedas*. Lima: Latinoamericana Editores.

———. 1991. *La voz y su huella: Escritura y conflicto étnico social en América Latina*. Hanover: Ediciones del Norte.

———. 1992. La "andinización" del vanguardismo urbano. In Arguedas 1992.

———. 1993. Los comienzos de la literatura "latinoamericana": Monólogos y diálogos de conquistadores y conquistados. In Pizarro 1993.

Lloyd, David, and Paul Thomas. 1998. *Culture and the State*. New York: Routledge.

Lockhart, James. 1980. Three Experiences of Culture Contact. In Hill Boone and Cummins 1980.

———. 1991. *Nahuas and Spaniards: Postconquest Central Mexican History and Philology*. Nahuatl Studies Series. Stanford: Stanford University Press.

———. 1992. *The Nahuas after the Conquest: A Social and Cultural History of the Indians of Central Mexico, Sixteenth through Eighteenth Centuries*. Stanford: Stanford University Press.

Lomnitz, Claudio. 2005. *Death and the Idea of Mexico*. Cambridge: MIT Press.

López Caballero, Paula. 2003. *Los títulos primordiales del centro de México*. Mexico: Conaculta.

Low, Douglas. 1992. *Merleau-Ponty's Last Vision: A Proposal for the Completion of* The Visible and the Invisible. Evanston: Northwestern University Press.

Ludmer, Josefina. 2002. *The Gaucho Genre: A Treatise on the Motherland*. Durham: Duke University Press.

Luna, J. Hernández, ed. 1984. *Conferencias del Ateneo de la Juventud*. Mexico D.F.: Universidad Nacional Autónoma de México.

Marcus, Joyce. 1992. *Mesoamerican Writing Systems: Propaganda, Myth, and History in Four Ancient Civilizations*. Princeton: Princeton University Press.

Mariátegui, José Carlos. 1871. *Seven Interpretive Essays on Peruvian Reality*. Trans. M. Urquidi. Austin: University of Texas Press.

————. 1927. Prólogo a *Tempestad en Los Andes.* In *Tempestad en Los Andes,* by Luis E. Valcárcel. Lima: La Sierra.

Martí, José. 1977. *Our America: Writings on Latin America and the Struggle for Cuban Independence.* Trans. E. Randall. New York: Monthly Review Press.

Martin, Gerald. 1979. *Yo el Supremo:* The Dictator and His Script. *Forum for Modern Language Studies* 15, no. 2: 169–83.

————. 1989. *Journeys through the Labyrinth: Latin American Fiction in the Twentieth Century.* London: Verso.

————, ed. 1992. *Hombres de maíz.* Madrid-Paris: Archivos.

————. 1996. Génesis y trayectoria del texto. In *Hombres de Maíz,* ed. G. Martín. Madrid: Unesco.

Marzal, Manuel. 1993. *Historia de la antropología indigenista: México y Perú.* Barcelona: Universidad Autónoma Metropolitana.

Matthews, Irene. 1997. *Nellie Campobello: La centaura del Norte.* Mexico: Aguilar, León y Cal Editores.

Mazzotti, José Antonio. 1988. Nuevas perspectivas en los estudios literarios coloniales hispanoamericanos. *Revista de Crítica Literaria Latinoamericana* 14, no. 28: 11–27.

Meliá, Bartomeu. 1986. *La lengua Guaraní del Paraguay: Historia, sociedad y literatura.* Madrid: Mapfre.

————. 1991. Una metafora de la lengua en el Paraguay. *Cuadernos Hispanoamericanos,* nos. 493–94: 65–73.

————. 1996. *El guaraní conquistado y reducido.* Asuncion: Del Lector.

————. 2002. Notes to the Present Edition. In *Ayvu Rapyta: Textos Míticos de los Mbyá-Guaraní del Guairá,* ed. L. Cadogan. Asuncion: Del Lector.

Merleau-Ponty, Maurice. 1962. *Phenomenology of Perception.* Trans. C. Smith. London: Routledge and Kegan Paul.

————. 1968. *The Visible and the Invisible.* Trans. A. Lingis. Evanston: Northwestern University Press.

————. 1993. Eye and Mind. In *The Merleau-Ponty Aesthetic Reader: Philosophy and Painting,* ed. G. Johnson. Evanston: Northwestern University Press.

Mignolo, Walter. 1994. Afterword: Writing and Recorded Knowledge in Colonial and Postcolonial Situations. In Hill Boone and Mignolo 1994.

————. 1981. El metatexto historiografico y la historiografia indiana. *MLN* 96, no. 2: 358–402.

————. 1992. On the Colonization of Amerindian Languages and Memories: Renaissance Theories of Writing and the Discontinuity of the Classical Tradition. *Comparative Studies in Society and History* 34, no. 2: 301–30.

——. 1995. *The Darker Side of the Renaissance: Literacy, Territoriality and Colonization.* Ann Arbor: University of Michigan Press.

——. 2000. *Local Histories/Global Designs: Coloniality, Subaltern Knowledges, and Border Thinking.* Princeton: Princeton University Press.

Miller, Jacques Alain. 1994. Extimité. In *Lacanian Theory of Discourse: Subject, Structure, and Society,* ed. M. Bracher. New York: New York University Press.

Milner, Jean-Claude. 1995. *L'ouevre claire: Lacan, la science, la philosophie.* Paris: Seuil.

Mondloch, James L., and Robert Carmack. 1983. *Título de Totonicapán.* Mexico: UNAM.

Monsiváis, Carlos. 1976. Continuidad de las imágenes. (Notas a partir del archivo Casasola). *Artes Visuales* 12: 13–15.

——. 1989. La toma de partido de Alfonso Reyes. *NRFH* 27: 505–19.

——. 1997. Notas sobre la cultura mexicana en el siglo XX. In *Historia General de México.* Mexico D.F.: El Colegio de México.

Moran, Dermot. 2001. *Introduction to Phenomenology.* London: Routledge.

Moraña, Mabel. 1984. *Literatura y cultura nacional en Hispanoamérica (1910–1940).* Minneapolis: University of Minnesota Press.

Moreiras, Alberto. 1999. *El tercer espacio.* Santiago: LOM Ediciones/Universidad Arcis.

——. 2001. *The Exhaustion of Difference: The Politics of Latin America Cultural Studies.* Durham: Duke University Press.

——. 2004. Introduction: The Conflict in Transculturation, In *Literary Cultures of Latin America: A Contemporary History,* Vol. 3, ed. M. Valdés and D. Kadir. New York: Oxford University Press.

Muñoz, Rafael. 1960. *¡Vámonos con Pancho Villa!* In Leal 1960.

Nancy, Jean-Luc, and Phillipe Lacoue-Labarthe. 1988. *The Literary Absolute: The Theory of Literature in German Romanticism.* Trans. P. Barnard and C. Lester. Albany: State University of New York Press.

Nietzsche, Friedrich. 1974. *The Gay Science.* Trans. W. Kaufmann. New York: Vintage.

O'Malley, Ilene V. 1986. *The Myth of the Revolution: Hero Cults and the Institutionalization of the Mexican State, 1920–1940.* New York: Greenwood Press.

Orozco, José Clemente. 1962. *José Clemente Orozco.* Trans. R. C. Stephenson. Austin: University of Texas Press.

Ortega, Julio. 2000. Introduction. In Arguedas 2000.

Ortiz, Fernando. 1973. *Hampa afro-cubana: Los negros brujos. Apuntes para un estudio de etnología criminal.* Miami: Universal.

———. 1995. *Cuban Counterpoint: Tobacco and Sugar.* Trans. H. de Onis. Durham: Duke University Press.

Orué Pozzo, Aníbal. 2002. *Oralidad y escritura en Paraguay.* Asuncion: Arandurá Editores.

Parra, Max. 2005. *Writing Pancho Villa's Revolution: Rebels in the Literary Imagination of Mexico.* Austin: University of Texas Press.

Patchen, Markell. 2003. *Bound by Recognition.* Princeton: Princeton University Press.

Paulson, Ronald. 1983. *Representations of Revolution (1789–1820).* New Haven and London: Yale University Press.

Peperzak, Adriaan. *To the Other: An Introduction to the Philosophy of Emmanuel Levinas.* Purdue: Purdue University Press, 1993.

Pizarro, A., ed. 1993. *América Latina: Palavra, literature e cultura.* Sao Paulo: Memorial.

Poblete, Juan. 2003. *Literatura chilena del siglo XIX: Entre públicos, lectores y figuras.* Santiago: Cuarto Propio.

Poniatowska, Elena. 1971. *La noche de Tlatelolco.* Mexico: Era.

———. 1988. Introduction. In Campobello 1988.

Poulet, Georges. 1969. Phenomenology of Reading. *New Literary History* 1, no. 1: 53–68.

Prakash, Gyan. 1990. Subaltern Studies and Postcolonial Criticism. *American Historical Review* 99: 383–408.

Pratt, Mary Louise. 1992. *Imperial Eyes: Studies in Travel Writing and Transculturation.* New York and London: Routledge.

Prieto, René. 1993. *Miguel Angel Asturias's Archaeology of Return.* Cambridge: Cambridge University Press.

Rama, Angel. 1987. *Transculturación narrativa en América Latina.* Mexico: Siglo Veintiuno Editores.

———. 1996. *The Lettered City.* Trans. J. Chasteen. Durham: Duke University Press.

Ramos, Julio. 2001. *Divergent Modernities: Culture and Politics in Nineteenth-Century Latin America.* Trans. J. D. Blanco. Durham: Duke University Press.

Rappaport, Joanne. 1994. Object and Alphabet: Andean Indians and Documents in the Colonial Period. In Hill Boone and Mignolo 1994.

Readings, Bill. 1994. *The University in Ruins.* Cambridge: Harvard University Press.

Renan, Ernest. 1990. What Is a Nation? In *Nation and Narration*, ed. H. K. Bhabha. New York. Routledge.

Reyes, Alfonso. 1960. Pasado inmediato. In *Obras completas de Alfonso Reyes*, vol. 7. Mexico: Fondo de Cultura Económica.

Reyes, Alfonso, and Pedro Henríquez Ureña. 1986. *Correspondencia: Alfonso Reyes/ Pedro Henríquez Ureña*. Mexico D.F.: Fondo de Cultura Económica.

Ricoeur, Paul. 2005. *The Course of Recognition*. Cambridge: Harvard University Press.

Riera, Gabriel. 1996. La ficción de Saer: ¿Una "antropología espculativa"? (Una lectura de El entenado). *Modern Language Notes* 111: 368–90.

Roa Bastos, Augusto. 1983. Reportaje y autocrítica: Interview with David Maldavsky. In *En torno a Hijo de Hombre*, ed. A. Sicard and F. Moreno. Potiers: Centre de Recherche Latino-Américaines.

———. 1985. *Hijo de hombre*. Madrid: Anaya and Mario Muchnik.

———. 1987. Una cultura oral. *Río de la Plata* 16: 4–6.

———. 1988. *Son of Man*. Trans. R. Caffyn. New York: Monthly Review Press.

———. 1991a. El texto cautivo. (Apuntes de un narrador sobre la produccion y la lectura de textos bajo el signo del poder cultural). In Klahn and Corral 1991.

———. 1991b. Notas sobre la narrativa hispanoamericana actual. In Klahn and Corral 1991.

———. 1993. *El fiscal*. Mexico: Santillana.

———. 1995. *Contravida*. Buenos Aires: Norma.

———. 2000. Moriencia. In *Cuentos completos*. Asuncion: El Lector.

Robbins, Jill. 1999. *Levinas and Literature: Altered Readings*. Chicago: University of Chicago Press.

Robertson, Donald, and Martha Barton Robertson. 1975. Catalog of Techialoyan Manuscripts and Paintings. *Handbook of Middle American Indians* 14: 265–80.

Rochabrún, Guillermo, ed. 2000. *La mesa redonda sobre "Todas las Sangres."* Lima: Pontificia Universidad Católica del Perú.

Romano Thuesen, Evelia. 1995. El entenado: Relación contemporánea de las memorias de Francisco del Puerto. *Latin American Literary Review* 23, no. 45: 43–63.

Rotman, Brian. 1987. *Signifying Nothing: The Semiotics of Zero*. Stanford: Stanford University Press.

Rousseau, Jean Jacques. 1987. Discourse on the Origin of Inequality. In *Basic Political Writings*, ed. D. A. Cress. Indianapolis: Hackett Publishing Co.

Rubione, Alfredo. 1983. Estudio preliminar. In *En torno al criollismo: Textos y polémicas*. Buenos Aires: Cedal.

Rulfo, Juan. 1971. Luvina. In *The Burning Plain and Other Stories*, trans. G. D. Schade. Austin: University of Texas Press.

———.1987. Luvina. In *Obras*. Mexico: Fondo de Cultural Económica.

———. 1995. *Pedro Páramo*. Trans. M. S. Peden. New York: Grove Press.

Rutherford, John. 1971. *Mexican Society during the Revolution: A Literary Approach*. Oxford: Clarendon Press.

Saer, Juan Jose. 1990. *The Witness*. Trans. M. J. Costa. London: Serpent's Tail.

Salerno, Osvaldo. 1998. Presentación. In *El Centinela: Periódico de la guerra de la triple alianza*, ed. Ana Sofía Piñeiro. Asuncion: CDI/Museo del Barro.

Sartre, Jean Paul. 1988. *What Is Literature?* Cambridge: Harvard University Press.

———. 1992. *Being and Nothingness: A Phenomenological Essay on Ontology*. Trans. H. E. Barnes. New York: Washington Square Press.

Schiller, Friedrich. 1967. *On the Aesthetic Education of Man*. Trans. E. M. Wilkinson and L. A. Willoughby. Oxford: Clarendon Press.

Schlegel, Friedrich. 1991. *Philosophical Fragments*. Trans. P. Firchow. Minneapolis: University of Minnesota Press.

Schmitt, Pierre. 1960. *The Isenheim Altar*. Berne: Hallweg Ltd.

Scott, James. 1994. Foreword. In Joseph and Nugent 1994.

Sicard, Alain, and F. Moreno. 1994. *En torno a Hijo de Hombre*. Potiers: Centre de Recherche Latino-Américaines.

Solomon, Frank, and George L. Urioste. 1991. *The Huarochiri Manuscript*. Austin: University of Texas Press.

Sommer, Doris. 1992. *Foundational Fictions*. Cambridge: Harvard University Press.

———. 1999. *Proceed with Caution when Engaged by Minority Writing in the Americas*. Cambridge: Harvard University Press.

Sommers, Joseph. 1968. *After the Storm: Landmarks of the Modern Mexican Novel*. Albuquerque: University of New Mexico Press.

Spivak, Gayatri Chakravorty. 1985. Subaltern Studies: Deconstructing Historiography. In *Subaltern Studies*, ed. R. Guha. London: Oxford University Press.

———. 1988. Can the Subaltern Speak? In *Marxism and the Interpretation of Culture*, ed. C. Nelson and L. Grossberg. Urbana and Chicago: University of Illinois Press.

———. 1993. *Outside of the Teaching Machine*. New York and London: Routledge.

———. 1999. *A Critique of Postcolonial Reason: Toward a History of the Vanishing Present*. Cambridge: Harvard University Press.

Tamayo Herrera, José. 1980. *Historia del indigenismo cuzqueño*. Lima: Instituto Nacional de Cultura.

Taylor, Charles. 1992. *Sources of the Self: The Making of Modern Identity*. Cambridge: Harvard University Press.

———. 1994. The Politics of Recognition. In *Multiculturalism: Examining the Politics of Recognition*, ed. A. Gutmann. Princeton: Princeton University Press.

———. 1998. *Hegel*. Cambridge: Cambridge University Press.

Taylor, Mark. 1987. *Altarity*. Chicago: University of Chicago Press.

Terán, Oscar. 2000. *Vida intelectual en el Buenos Aires fin-de-siglo (1880–1910): Derivas de la "cultura científica."* Buenos Aires: Fondo de Cultura Económica.

Thurner, Mark. 2001. *From Two Republics to One Divided: Contradictions of Postcolonial Nationmaking in Andean Peru*. Durham: Duke University Press.

Tord, Luis Enrique. 1978. *El indio en los ensayistas peruanos, 1848–1948*. Lima: Editoriales Unidas.

Trigo, Benigno. 2001. *Foucault and Latin America: Appropriations and Deployments of Discursive Analysis*. London: Routledge.

Trigo, Pedro. 1982. *Arguedas: Mito, historia y religión*. Lima: Centro de Estudios y Publicaciones.

Valencia Espinoza, Abraham. 1980. Las batallas de Rumitaqe: Movimientos campesino de 1921 en Canas. In *Rebeliones indígenas quechuas y aymaras*, ed. J. F. Ochoa and A. V. Espinosa. Lima: CEAC.

Vargas Llosa, Mario. 2001. *The Storyteller*. New York: Picador.

Vaughan, Mary Kay. 1997. *Cultural Politics in Revolution: Teachers, Peasants, and Schools in Mexico, 1930–1940*. Tucson: University of Arizona Press.

Vasconcelos, José. 1964. *Ulises criollo*. Mexico: Jus.

———. 2000. *La tormenta*. Mexico: Trillas.

Vaughan, Mary Kay, and Stephen E. Lewis. 2006. *The Eagle and the Virgin: Nation and Cultural Revolution in Mexico, 1920–1940*. Durham: Duke University Press.

Vega, Garcilaso de la. 1966. *Royal Commentaries of the Incas, and General History of Peru*. Trans. H. V. Livermore. Austin: University of Texas Press.

Vera, Agustín. 1960. *La revancha*. In Leal 1960.

Verdesio, Gustavo. 2001. *Forgotten Conquests: Rereading New World History from the Margins*. Philadelphia: Temple University Press.

Vich, Cynthia. 2000. *Indigenismo de vanguardia en el Perú: Un estudio sobre el "Boletín Titikaka."* Lima: Pontificia Universidad Católica.

Vienrich, Adolfo. 1905. *Azucenas quechuas*. Huancayo.

Villegas, Abelardo. 1993. *El pensamiento mexicano en el siglo xx*. Mexico: Fondo de Cultura Económica.

Viñas, David. 1964. *Literatura argentina y realidad política*. Buenos Aires: Jorge Alvarez.

Virno, Paolo. 2004. *A Grammar of the Multitude*. Trans. I. Bertoletti, J, Cascaito, and A. Casson. Los Angeles: Semiotext(e).

Watt, Ian. 1957. *The Rise of the Novel: Studies in Defoe, Richardson, and Fielding*. Berkeley: University of California Press.

West, Cornell. 1999. The New Cultural Politics of Difference. In *The Cornell West Reader*. New York: Basic Civitas Books.

Williams, Gareth. 2002. *The Other Side of the Popular: Neoliberalism and Subalternity in Latin America*. Durham: Duke University Press.

———. 2004. Chimbote and the Shores of Indigenismo: Biopolitics and Bare Life in *El zorro de arriba y el zorro de abajo*. *Revista de Estudios Hispánicos* 38, no. 1: 43–68.

Williams, Raymond. 1977. *Marxism and Literature*. Oxford: Oxford University Press.

Zerilli, Linda. 1998. *This Universalism Which Is Not One*. Diacritics 28, no. 2: 3–20.

Žižek, Slavoj. 1989. *The Sublime Object of Ideology*. London: Verso.

———. 1991. *Looking Away: An Introduction to Jacques Lacan through Popular Culture*. Cambridge: MIT Press.

———. 1997. *The Plague of Fantasies*. London: Verso.

———. 1998. Cartesian Subjects versus Cartesian Theater. In *Cogito and the Unconscious*, ed. S. Žižek. Durham: Duke University Press.

———. 1999. *The Ticklish Subject: The Absent Centre of Political Ontology*. London: Verso.

Index